Ethics and the CPA

Ethics and the CPA

Building Trust and
Value-Added Services

Charles H. Calhoun, CPA
Mary Ellen Oliverio, CPA
Philip Wolitzer, CPA

JOHN WILEY & SONS, INC.
New York • Chichester • Weinheim • Brisbane • Singapore • Toronto

This publication is designed to provide accurate and authoritative
information in regard to the subject matter covered. It is sold with
the understanding that the publisher is not engaged in rendering
legal, accounting, or other professional services. If legal advice or
other expert assistance is required, the services of a competent
professional person should be sought.

Library of Congress Cataloging-in-Publication Data:

Calhoun, Charles H.
    Ethics and the CPA: building trust and value-added services /
Charles H. Calhoun, Mary Ellen Oliverio, Philip Wolitzer.
        p.   cm.
    Includes index.
    ISBN 0-471-18488-8 (cloth : alk. paper)
    1. Business ethics.   2. Accounting—Moral and ethical aspects.
3. Finance—Moral and ethical aspects.   I, Wolitzer, Philip.
II. Oliverio, Mary Ellen.   III. Title.
HF5387.C33 1998
174'.4—dc21   98-17658

Printed in the United States of America.

10 9 8 7 6 5 4 3 2 1

To our families.

Contents

Preface

Has tolerance for corruption and fraudulent behavior in the workplace reached a point of serious concern? There is some evidence that the answer may be "yes." A million dollar takeover of a securities firm was halted because of uncertainty about potential legal and regulatory inquiries about the practices of the targeted firm. The acquirer was stung by the financial collapse of Orange County (California), for which a penalty of $30 million was paid in 1997 and of $400 million in 1998. Yet, the securities firm was still not completely free of the legal consequences of Orange County's bankruptcy. A major insurance company announced plans for a new organizational structure. Some policy holders expressed skepticism as to the promises being made in the light of the company's sales practices, which led to a class action suit. Analysts estimated that the unethical practices may cost the company as much as $1.5 billion.

Attention to ethics in U.S. society reflects a far more sophisticated expectation on the part of the public than was the case in earlier decades. Not only are pressures for ethical behavior mounting, but there is a desire for verification of what is proclaimed to be true—to know the reality. Therefore, a new role for independent public accountants has developed.

CLAIMS ABOUT ETHICAL BEHAVIOR

Leaders of all types of organizations make claims about the quality of ethical behavior that they maintain in their organizations. They often point to well-written codes of conduct and to company policies and procedures to support their efforts. In fact, some businesses acknowledge their attention to ethics in management statements that appear in annual reports. The following is illustrative of such a statement:

> Management . . . recognizes its responsibility for fostering a strong ethical climate so that the company's affairs are conducted according to the highest standards of personal and corporate conduct. This responsibility is communicated to all employees in a variety of ways, including training sessions. The Ethics Program is based upon a document called "The Standards of Ethical Business Practices." The standards address, among other things, the necessity of ensuring open communication within the company; potential conflicts of interest; compliance with all domestic and foreign

laws, including those relating to financial disclosures; and the confidentiality of proprietary information. The company maintains a systematic program to assess compliance with these standards.

However, this statement had no independent appraisal to support it. The credibility of such a statement is undermined by the increasing skepticism of thoughtful citizens as they read accounts of misrepresentations in financial statements and of violations of regulations in the popular press.

EXTENSION OF THE TRADITIONAL ROLE OF THE PUBLIC ACCOUNTANT

The need for an independent appraisal for the effectiveness of ethical programs in business is somewhat parallel to the need for an independent appraisal for financial information that became evident at the end of the 1800s as companies began to seek outside funding for their expansion.

A century ago, public accounting was in its infancy. Those who emerged as the early successful leaders were those who believed that public accounting should be a profession. They saw that the most critical contribution that could be offered related to two factors: expertise knowledge of accounting and auditing and unassailable integrity in performing their services to businesses. The former without the latter was of limited value; the former totally integrated with the latter had powerful value.

Long before the establishment of the Securities and Exchange Commission (SEC) and the requirement for audited financial statements for publicly owned companies, the accounting profession had accepted its responsibility. The profession adhered to the requirements of professional status. Practitioners developed rules to govern their own behavior. They developed accounting rules and principles. They developed a code of conduct. They provided for continuing education.

Thus, the first group of commissioners of the newly formed SEC in 1934 determined that the profession could continue to have responsibility to set rules and monitor behavior of its members. Of course, oversight responsibility resided with the SEC.

At the close of the twentieth century, the disenchantment with mere words of achievement and promise, especially in the realm of human behavior, is widespread. Even the long-respected public accounting profession has faced severe criticism and challenges to its public responsibilities. When Alvin Toffler, the observer of emerging trends, was asked about changes he saw on the horizon, he answered: "Virtual reality points to a boundless capacity for deception . . . we are increasing the sophistication of deception faster than the technology of verification . . . the consequence of that is the end of truth. The dark side of the information explosion is that it will breed a population that believes nothing."[1]

---

[1]Claudia Dreifus, "Present Shock," *The New York Times Magazine* (June 11, 1995), 48.

Toffler acknowledges that some of his earlier predictions had been wrong; this one, too, may not be realized in the American society. We believe he must be wrong. A society without truth—and the related quality of trust—will not long endure. There must be a redressing of the cynicism present in contemporary society.

The skepticism of the thoughtful contemporary American who reads the business press undermines the credibility of pronouncements of "high ethical standards." The news items in daily and business newspapers, feature stories in popular business periodicals, and detailed accounts of scandals in full-length books support an uneasiness about the quality of our ethical conduct, especially in the business world.

We believe there is a valuable range of services public accountants can provide to business, government, and nonprofit entities that want assistance related to their ethical programs. That range is from providing guidance in establishing a relevant ethical program to performing an audit of a total program. This is to some extent unchartered territory for the public accountant. However, there are relevant precedents to guide the professional public accountant. We must remember that there was little guidance for the first public accountants a century ago who determined to perform professional services. Public accountants understand the need for objective guidance; they understand the significance of independent judgment; they understand the need for relevant evidence. In brief, public accountants have internalized a process, based on independent, analytical problem solving, that is the foundation upon which to build strategies and procedures for meeting a specific ethical engagement's objectives.

WHAT IS PRESENTED

There are three parts to this book. These are as follows:

- Part 1: Consideration of Ethical Services CPAs Can Provide, which discusses in general what public accountants can provide and the relevant competencies public accountants have developed.
- Part 2: The Contemporary Environment: The Need for Services, which presents some ethical failures in well-known organizations, the regulatory demands on organizations, and the results of a survey we undertook.
- Part 3: Value-Added Services: Leading and Promoting Ethics, which discusses public accountants' commitment to ethical behavior in their own professional work, the nature of ethical services needed, and what public accountants face that is related to ethical policies and standards.

OUR OVERRIDING POSITION

We believe the ethical environment of an organization determines long-term economic stability and profitability. We believe that the ethical environment determines the implementation of policies and procedures that assure fair, just, and humane relationships at all levels of an enterprise. We believe that improvement is possible and needed in the quality of ethical behavior in the American society. Enhanced attention to candid assessment—including the contribution of an independent public accountant—is justified.

One consultant to companies noted "that clients aren't interested in doing what is right; they are interested in avoiding wrong doing." Such a position may appear to be clearly within the propensity to be pragmatic in the American society. However, a careful dissecting of what is stated will reveal a serious flaw. In an environment where the leaders care only about "avoiding wrong doing," the cost of avoiding wrongdoing without concern for doing what is right is prohibitive. The environment in such an organization would require a level of monitoring that would be both costly and oppressive. It is our position that doing right has rich rewards over the long run. The stability of an organization is clearly dependent on an ethical foundation.

We wish we could identify and acknowledge specifically all our colleagues who have contributed to our interest in ethics and the public accounting profession. Because we cannot draw up a complete list, we merely say thank you for your insight, your thoughtfulness, your willingness to explore and to speculate about what an ethical world would be.

We have encountered these colleagues in discussions at professional meetings, organized and by chance. Meetings of the Internal Auditors Committee of the New York State Society of CPAs were especially influential for us. Two general questions were raised initially after reading the Report of the Special Committee on Fraudulent Financial Reporting (Treadway Report). These were: "Have such long-honored qualities as integrity, honesty, objectivity, and concern for the public interest become outmoded in the United States?" and "What is the responsibility of auditors?" We are grateful for shared ideas in striving to find some answers.

Charles H. Calhoun, CPA
Mary Ellen Oliverio, CPA
Philip Wolitzer, CPA

PART 1

Ethics Services CPAs Can Provide

Chapter 1

Ethics Services Needed

"While the CPAs are licensed to provide certain services to the public, the CPA designation also connotes a level of education and training that enables us to provide a whole range of services for which we are not licensed."[1]

In this age of accountability, there is a new task for the public accountant. The ethical behavior of organizations has become a sensitive topic. American companies are poignantly realizing that violations of rules and regulations imposed by government as well as of their own codes of conduct can be communicated speedily throughout the world. Violations have severe economic consequences, in addition to impact on reputations. Such repercussions concern the leaders of organizations.

Flagrant ethical flaws in the functioning of companies have been considered factors in the fall of such major firms as E. F. Hutton, Drexel, Kidder, Peabody, and Barings. Reviewers of the behavior in such firms have concluded that unethical behavior appears to have been tolerated far too long in such companies.

Leaders of all types of organizations who want to maintain a culture where integrity is prized need some type of assurance that such a goal is being achieved. The public accountant, an independent outsider, is qualified to provide such assurance. The pronouncements of chief executive officers (CEOs) far too frequently are inspired and developed in isolation from the reality of behavior in the organization. In too many instances, the operational implementation of what is proclaimed has been left undeveloped.

Of course, in some cases, such pronouncements do reflect the reality of the entity. However, there persists a question about the extent to which reality matches pronouncements without some type of independent review or assessment. There have been too many instances in the business press of variance between the words of key officials and the behavior that was tolerated within the organization. Words about integrity and honesty have rung hollow. Such words continue to be unimpressive to many who must listen to carefully worded presentations of what happens in "our environment." With extensive reporting about business behavior in the public media, skepticism has intensified.

Astute leaders in American companies have begun to realize that descriptions of ethics codes and policies are not sufficient to be confident about what actually is happening in their organizations. Good intentions have no power if there are

---

[1]Philip Chenok, "Professional or Trade Organization," *The CPA Journal* (October 1997), 30.

not operational policies and procedures that assure valid feedback about what is declared to be company expectations.

Observations of the contemporary ethical environment are relevant to the question of what contribution the public accountant can provide related to ethics.

1.1 PERCEIVED NEED FOR CREDIBILITY

Failures of companies, including those that reflect an unethical environment, increasingly are reported in the extensive business press that have developed in the United States. The responses of representatives in the organization where the unethical practice was alleged have met with varying levels of credibility. In many instances, the initial response has been that of overwhelming surprise. Company officials have been stunned at negative reactions of stakeholders and the challenges to company credibility.

One illustration of the extent of the current concern about credibility is evident in the topic chosen for the 1997 Corporate Communications Conference sponsored by the Conference Board. The lack of credibility of information provided to the public was a key theme, although somewhat muted. The participants' attention was directed to communications-related crisis management. The need for such communications reflects the speed with which stories of wrongdoing by companies are widely disseminated. Communications media have the stories before officials of the highlighted company have gathered all the details. Among key points from presentations were the following:

> The keynote speaker Frank Vogl (President of Vogl Communications) noted that corporate communicators need to strive to be on the forefront in trying to influence their corporation's vision, mission, and values—to position the company globally.[2]

Facts plus truth equals credibility, so stated the Director of Communications at Coca-Cola Company, Linda Peek. Furthermore, she noted that "putting an early spin on the news [akin to a quick soundbite in broadcasting] has become an operational tactic for many public relations people instead of having a complete story of all the facts; it is one reason why public relations people are viewed with such cynicism by the press."[3]

Morri Berman, senior vice president and partner of Fleishman-Hillard, Inc., discussed what she believed are the four "Rs" of crisis management:

1. *Regret.* The first comment made should be that the company is sorry a problem has developed, even if that problem is not the fault of the company.

2. *Reform.* The press and public need to know what steps the company will take to ensure the problem will not recur.

---

[2]Margaret Hart, *Communicating for Global Competitive Advantage* (New York: The Conference Board, Corporate Communications Conference, 1997), 5.
[3]Id., 14.

3. *Restitution.* When appropriate, companies need to detail how they will compensate those affected by the problem.
4. *Responsibility.* Companies need to be prepared to take responsibility for solving the problem, regardless of whether the company is at fault.

It was Berman's judgment that actions must reinforce words and provide a credible demonstration of the organization's commitment.[4]

Will Flowers, Vice President, Communications and Community Relations, Waste Management, suggested that his colleagues write down some of the positive human values which their organization truly embraces that have earned the public's trust. He noted that how a company deals with a difficult situation determines, to a considerable extent, how the company will be perceived by the public and whether trust in that company will be saved or lost.[5]

It is interesting to note that in early 1998, the Waste Management company, under the leadership of a temporary chairman, was in the process of undoing years of aggressive and questionable accounting. For the last quarter of 1997, a charge of $1.5 billion against earnings was made to reflect corrections that are intended to reduce skepticism about the reliability of its financial statements. Equity on December 31, 1997, was $1.3 billion from a reported $4.88 billion a year earlier.[6]

The speakers at the 1997 conference seemed to be implying that putting the appropriate public relations spin on a company's position must not only be grounded in the reality of a company's vision, mission, and values, but also implemented. Increasingly, image building and astute public relations do not seem to be sufficient to provide a sustaining reputation with the many stakeholders organizations face. There is need for independent review and verification. The CPA can bring this additional step to an organization's efforts.

1.2 REPRESENTATIONS ABOUT INTEGRITY

The annual reports of many publicly owned companies, for example, provide statements about the significance of integrity in their operations. Note the following statements excerpted from two recent annual reports:

> Our management philosophy begins with two key beliefs—respect for the dignity of the individual and uncompromising integrity in everything we do. This helps to create an environment of empowerment for all in a culture of participation. . . .

> Highest Standards of Integrity: We are honest and ethical in all our business dealings, starting with how we treat each other. We keep our promises and admit our mistakes. Our personal conduct ensures that _____'s name is always worthy of trust.

---

[4]Id., 12.
[5]Id., 11.
[6]*The Wall Street Journal* (February 25, 1998).

In addition to statements in annual reports, some corporations issue special bulletins highlighting their social responsibilities. Because such reports, for the most part, are internally developed, their credibility is often suspect. Many who read them classify them as "public relations information."

Company officials make speeches, participate in interviews for the public, and lecture to future employees in colleges and universities. They also meet with new employees during orientation and training sessions, with attention to ethical concerns reflected in such encounters. The company's position regarding ethical behavior is often noted and discussed.

The hollowness of pronouncements made to new employees during orientation can be the basis of serious discontent with the actual environment at work. As three young managers—all from the same former company—discussed that company, one said:

> We joined the company right after our college graduation—and we met during our three weeks of initial orientation and training for our new jobs. What an impressive company we were joining.
>
> Even the CEO talked to us and told us of the ethical standards that were upheld in the company. Human Resources staff talked about the code of conduct that guided all behavior of the total company's staff. *We believed what we heard during those first three weeks.*
>
> With the build-up of how the company functioned, I was expecting the type of environment that I find comfortable. Well, within weeks, I guess all of us realized that we had been sold a litany of words—words that were not at all representative of behavior. I personally could not tolerate the coverup for the senior executive to whom I was to report. He was always available, so he said. But, he was never there. Apparently, no one wanted to face how he was using his time. As long as I or his assistant said he was temporarily away from his desk, all seemed fine. I thought possibly my initial observations were not typical of what would happen in the company. So, I was willing to continue for a year. Yet, as I witnessed the misrepresentations in travel reports, the unwillingness to share information with others with whom our office should be communicating, etc., I realized that a year was just too long a trial period when no day was free of unethical decisions. After ten months I left, even though I didn't have another job. It was a traumatic experience.

The two friends agreed with the assessment. All three had left the company where they had originally met. While they questioned their expectations, especially when others told them they were being idealistic to even think that business behavior was guided by ethical standards, they concluded that the entire business environment could not be the same. They held on to the belief that some organizations did strive, in good faith, to encourage high ethical standards. By the time of the conversation, all were employed in businesses where they felt there was good faith effort to maintain high ethical standards.

What do such representations mean in a society that has grown cynical by the disclosures of violations of the society's ethical expectations? What is the value of rules and codes of conduct that business leaders have proclaimed to guide behavior in their organizations? What assurance is there that significant departures from expectations will be discovered in a timely fashion, with corrective actions taken?

Many stakeholders have an interest in knowing what the reality is. Is there not value in providing some level of assurance about an organization's success in meeting the substance of its claims?

Representations of integrity are obviously perceived to be of value since they are made to stockholders, employees, potential employees, customers, and even to the general public. What is the value of such representations if they are not in some way verified? Stockholders, for example, whose only interaction with the company is via the written words in reports, may have a positive response to the declared level of ethical standards that guide decisions in the company. Some employees, though, in the same company, may have first-hand experiences that again and again contradict the pronouncements. Some customers, too, may have had experiences that challenge the quality of ethical behavior in the company.

If pronouncements are to reflect reality, company officials need to identify operationally what each aspect of their declarations about ethics means. A deliberate strategy must be devised for determining the extent to which the company is meeting its goals. Good faith effort needs to match actions with words.

The task of measuring ethical achievements in a company is not an easy task. However, critical factors, from the company's point of view, can be identified. Then operational specification of objective evidence to provide a measure of how each factor is actually reflected in the behavior of the people in the organization can be developed. Objective verification—of varying levels of assurance—can be provided by public accountants.

1.3 CONTINUING CHALLENGES TO ETHICAL BEHAVIOR IN BUSINESS

At the same time that pronouncements and special bulletins are proclaiming the honorable behavior of American business, beginning in the mid-80s there has been increased voicing of disenchantment with the level of ethical behavior in the American society. It appears that appropriate ethical behavior was assumed in an earlier period. For example, there were only seven articles identified with business ethics indexed in the July 1960–June 1961 edition of *Guide to Business Periodicals*. Yet, in the August 1990–July 1991 edition, there were 132 articles.

Since 1976, the Gallup Organization has conducted a poll of the U.S. public to determine perceptions of honesty and ethical standards among 26 occupations. When the figures from polls of 1981 through 1997 are considered, there appears to have been variability in perceptions for some occupations. For example, druggists/pharmacists top the ratings list, with 69 percent of the respondents responding "very high" or "high" as regards adhering to ethical standards. This percentage is 10 percent higher than the ranking in 1981, when the first position was gained by the clergy. (In 1997, clergy were in second place, with 59 percent of the public giving them one of the two top ratings.) Among the categories that included occupations closely associated with business, the following were the percentages in the four top categories for three years (accountants were not among the occupations included in the poll):

	Bankers	Business Executives	Stockbrokers	Advertising Practitioners
1981	39%	19%	21%	9%
1991	30%	21%	14%	12%
1997	34%	20%	18%	12%

Except for the advertising practitioners' ratings, the 1997 percentages for the four occupational groups are approximately the average of the preceding percentages. In general, the respondents indicated the largest percentage for the average ranking for all four of these occupational groups (Bankers, 51%; Business Executives, 55%; Stockbrokers, 54%; and Advertising Practitioners, 49%). These poll results over a period of 16 years do not show a significant difference in perception of ethical behavior for business-related occupations.

The cover story of *Time* magazine, for example, was "What Ever Happened to Ethics?" The cover stated "Assaulted by sleaze, scandals, and hypocrisy, America searches for its moral bearings." Included was the reporting of a poll for *Time* conducted by Yankelowich Clancy Shulman in January 1987 in which 76 percent saw lack of ethics in businessmen as contributing to tumbling moral standards.[7]

The mood of the *Time* article seems not unreasonable. At about the same time, the accounting profession faced the persistent problem of ethical behavior as reflected in fraudulent financial reporting. Two significant efforts to deal with the problem followed. These were (1) the establishment of a commission to study the problem and make recommendations, and (2) a new statement from the Auditing Standards Board related to the consideration of fraud in a financial statement audit.

(a)   The National Commission on Fraudulent Financial Reporting

The extent of fraudulent financial reporting was perceived to be serious. A national commission was established by five private sector accounting associations in 1985. The Commission presented its report in October 1987. The Commission had recommendations for four groups, including independent public accountants, the Securities and Exchange Commission (SEC) and others, educa-

---

[7]"What Ever Happened to Ethics?" *Time* (May 25, 1987), 26.

tors, and public companies. All four groups were considered to have some degree of responsibility for reliable financial reporting. For public companies, the Commission believed that:

> The responsibility for reliable financial reporting resides first and foremost at the corporate level. Top management—starting with the chief executive officer—sets the tone and establishes the financial reporting environment. Therefore, reducing the risk of fraudulent financial reporting must start with the reporting company.

Among the studies that were completed to support the findings of the Commission was one by Merchant dealing with fraudulent and questionable financial reporting. The conclusions of the study were based on a review of relevant literature, an analysis of recent cases of fraudulent financial reporting, and interviews and discussions with a hundred business officials.

Merchant's study identified a broad range of deceptive financial reporting practices. While some of these practices clearly are fraudulent, many, although deceptive, are considered acceptable by some proportion of interested parties. This acceptability–judgment problem creates difficulty in dealing with deceptive financial reporting. Nevertheless, the study cautions that allowing even slightly deceptive reporting practices creates an environment that is conducive to more serious deceptions. The study concludes that in the vast majority of fraudulent financial reporting cases, the people involved were good people who got involved in small, nonmaterial manipulations, perhaps even with good intentions. Then, over time, the magnitude of the manipulations grew, and eventually laws were broken.

The author of the study concluded that:

> Over time, an individual's judgment of right and wrong can be greatly affected by the atmosphere in the workplace. For example, individuals are frequently motivated to participate in deceptive financial reporting practices because they believe or rationalize that they are acting in the organization's best interests or they have developed a corporate "team spirit" of deception.[8]

(b) The Report on Internal Control

To follow up the Report of the National Commission on Fraudulent Financial Reporting, the Committee on Sponsoring Organizations undertook further study which culminated in a 1992 report on internal control. The report presented a comprehensive view of internal control. The critical need for a positive control environment was highlighted. The role of the CEO was described in these words:

> The chief executive sets the "tone at the top" that affects control environment factors. . . . A CEO with high ethical standards can go a long way in ensuring that the

---

[8]Kenneth Merchant, "Fraudulent and Questionable Financial Reporting: A Corporate Prospective" (Abstract, Report of the National Commission on Fraudulent Financial Reporting, 1987), 97.

board [of directors] reflects those values. On the other hand a CEO who lacks
integrity may not be able, or want, to obtain board members who possess it. One
individual who serves on a number of boards of directors and audit committees
said unequivocally that if he has any reservations about the integrity of a CEO, he
will flatly turn down an invitation to serve. Effective boards and audit committees
also will look closely at top management's integrity and ethical values to determine whether the internal controls system has the necessary critical underpinnings.[9]

In the presentation of Evaluation Tools, the Report provides guidance for
assessing integrity and ethical values. Points of focus to be used as a basis of
assessing integrity and ethical values are included. Among the points are: the
existence of a code of conduct that is implemented, establishment of the "tone at
the top," and the potential pressure to meet unrealistic goals.[10]

(c) The Issuance of a New Auditing Statement

In mid 1997, the Auditing Standards Board issued a new statement to supersede
one promulgated as of January 1, 1989. This new statement (SAS 82) dealt more
directly than was the case with the superseded statement with the auditor's
responsibility to consider fraud in a financial statement audit. The statement on
Auditing Standards No. 82 was issued a decade after the issuance of the Commission on Fraudulent Financial Reporting and five years after the publication of the
extensive report on internal control sponsored by the organizations that provided
the resources for the 1985 Commission. The perception that problems related to
fraud appears to be continuing.

With SAS 82, the profession concluded that a more clearly specified strategy needed to be stated. A concern has persisted that fraudulent financial
reporting was a matter to which auditors must give enhanced attention in their
audits of financial statements. Notwithstanding the requirements included as
an amendment to the Securities Exchange Act of 1934 that impose on management the need for adequate internal control (Foreign Corrupt Practices Act
of 1977), the recommendations of the Commission on Fraudulent Financial
Reporting, and the Committee of Sponsoring Organizations of the Treadway
Commission (COSO) Report on Internal Control, it was determined that there
must be more explicit attention to the possibility of fraud in publicly owned
companies. The new statement, which was effective as of December 15, 1997,
provides a listing of risk factors. Behind each illustration of audit risk factors
is a variety of potentially unethical behavior—for example, a practice by

---

[9]Committee on Sponsoring Organizations of the Treadway Commission (COSO), Integrated Control–Integrated Framework (1992), 88.
[10]Id., 5–7.

management of committing to analysts, creditors, and other third parties to achieve what appear to be an unduly aggressive or clearly unrealistic forecast.[11]

While an ethical executive would face the reality of the company's earnings, pressure to meet a goal—and an acceptance of misrepresentation—leads to manipulation of figures so they do meet the forecast on paper!

> Significant portion of management's compensation is represented by bonuses, stock options, and other incentives, the value of which is contingent upon the entity achieving unduly aggressive targets for operating results, financial position, or cash flow.[12]

Management in the face of pressure to meet aggressive targets will engage in fraudulent reporting to provide the basis for the promised high compensation.

The rationale for SAS 82 is that the auditors cannot trust that management will adhere to unassailable ethical standards in reporting what has been achieved during the fiscal period. Skepticism continues about management's accountability for maintaining an ethical environment, which is one of the central prerequisites for an effective internal control system.

It would appear that to date there are still problems related to the ethical behavior of those who manage American organizations. Notwithstanding the requirements for maintaining adequate internal control (Foreign Corrupt Practices Act, December 1977, which amended the 1934 Securities Exchange Act); the recommendations of the Commission on Fraudulent Financial Reporting,[13] and the report on Integrated Internal Control,[14] dissatisfaction continues.

1.4   CONFERENCE BOARD: SURVEYS AND PROCEEDINGS

During the same period that the accounting profession was providing leadership in designing strategies to encourage ethical behavior in businesses and in enhancing guidance for auditors, an organization sensitive to issues in business, the Conference Board, was giving attention to the same topic. As stated in their publications, they see their role as:

> . . . to improve the business enterprise system and to enhance the contribution of business to society. To accomplish this, the Conference Board strives to be the

---

[11]American Institute of Certified Public Accountants (AICPA) Professional Standards, 289.
[12]Id., 289.
[13]Reprint of National Commission on Fraudulent Financial Reporting (October 1987).
[14]COSO (1992).

leading global business membership organization that enables senior executives from all industries to explore and exchange ideas of impact on business policy and practices.[15]

This international group, too, gave attention to ethics in the recent past, beginning in the mid-80s. Their first study was reported in 1987; others followed in 1991, 1992, 1994, and 1997. These reports illustrate the awareness of the increasingly more complex nature of issues related to ethical behavior in business. Highlights of these reports are briefly discussed here.

(a)   Corporate Ethics: International Survey and Interviews

The 1987 study report included an insert with the heading: "Is there an ethics crisis in business?" The excerpt included references to magazine cover stories and newspaper headlines that suggested that business institutions were facing a crisis of public confidence related to their ethical performance. It was noted that recent polls were inconclusive. However, a *New York Times* survey suggested far more suspicion of business as a whole and of executives in particular—53 percent said white collar crime in business is committed "very often."[16] The insert included the following:

> CEOs and top managers are concerned about potential public mistrust of business and they allude to four general perceptions that contribute to this climate: (a) the equation of size with power, along with the fear that "power corrupts;" (2) concern over the potential social impact of actions taken by large institutions; (3) the belief that the activities of major companies are so complex that, despite top management's best intentions, they are impossible to control; and (4) the apparent disparity of power between big corporations and their critics, which makes a dispute look like a "David and Goliath" struggle.[17]

The results of this study indicated that U.S. and European CEOs and senior managers viewed corporate ethics as a subject to be dealt with at three levels: the corporate mission, constituency relations, and policies and practices. There were 27 ethical issues identified. At least 76 percent of the respondents checked 11 as critical ethical issues for business. These 11 were as follows:

1. Employee conflicts of interest (91 percent)
2. Inappropriate gifts to corporate personnel (91 percent)
3. Sexual harassment (91 percent)

---

[15]Conference Board, 2.
[16]"Public Opinion," *The New York Times Magazine* (June 8, 1986), 69.
[17]Ronald E. Berenbeim, *Corporate Ethics,* A Research Report (New York: The Conference Board, 1987).

4. Unauthorized payments (85 percent)
5. Affirmative action (84 percent)
6. Employee privacy (84 percent)
7. Environmental issues (82 percent)
8. Employee health screening (79 percent)
9. Conflicts between company's ethics and foreign business practices (77 percent)
10. Security of company records (76 percent)
11. Workplace safety (76 percent)[18]

The respondents, to a considerable extent, reported that a code of ethics was a major vehicle for stating ethical principles. Three quarters of the respondents said that they had a code of ethics. Slightly half of these reporting a code of ethics also viewed an ethics training program as a useful supplement to their codes. A few companies reported ethical programs which had no official code of ethics.

Through interviews and a study of codes of ethics, six principal reasons why companies have adopted codes of ethics were noted:

1. Commitment of the CEO
2. Maintenance of public trust and credibility
3. Greater managerial professionalism
4. Protection against improper employee conduct
5. Need to define ethical behavior in light of new laws or social standards
6. Change in corporate culture or structure, such as decentralized operations or acquisitions

This report contained virtually nothing on regular monitoring of ethical efforts. The only statement referring to follow-up was: "To monitor code distribution and to promote employee understanding, some companies require a periodic written acknowledgement that employees have received a copy of the code and are complying with it. Other certification forms are more complex and ask the employees to respond to specific questions about their activities. . . ."[19]

In a discussion of compliance oversight, it was noted that companies realize that introducing an ethical program is a dynamic process. There must be attention to compliance and code amendments as time goes by and experience is reviewed. Therefore, there must be an organizational structure to oversee the distribution of the code and compliance.[20]

---

[18]Id., 3.
[19]Conference Board, 17.
[20]Id.

(b) Corporate Ethics: Developing New Standards of Accountability

In 1991, the Conference Board turned attention to dealing with ethical challenges in a variety of industries. The note of the President of the Conference Board included the following:

> When the Conference Board first published a study on corporate ethics in 1987, there were some who believed that this issue would prove to be yet another fad and simply fade away. . . . However, the public has not lowered its expectations regarding proper conduct and accountability, especially at the corporate level. . . .
>
> A comparison of the insight in the 1991 report with that presented in 1987 reveals that there had been developed more awareness of the complexity of ethical behavior. Among the points made by invited speakers, who represented a variety of positions in business—from CEOs to ombudsmen—were: Training for ethical behavior is needed since companies cannot just merely assume a consensus on ethics among their employees.
>
> Involving top executives is essential for success. And top executives must "play by the same rules as everyone else is asked to play by."
>
> The public backlash against poor corporate behavior, has forced industries to reevaluate their business practices, including the way in which they handle crises and how they inform the public of problems. There are clearly economic rewards of ethical behavior. Insider trading problems are costly, for example.[21]

The presentations, for the most part, described in detail the operational efforts as developed by various units of organizations, the methods used for training and communicating ethical behavior, the external pressure for higher ethical standards, and building credibility in the community. One participant made a unique point: "We need to be clearer at this point in our history about what 'doing the right thing' really means."[22]

Another speaker noted: "You must establish an internal control system and infrastructure that will help you find your own problems. Once you find them fix them. Don't just let them fester in the organization."[23]

Another speaker described his company's decision to have face-to-face compliance reviews on a regular basis. These small group sessions allowed for dialogue.[24]

A discussion of the responsible care initiative of the chemical industry highlighted the self-evaluations required yearly. As noted: This self-evaluation is a critical element of Responsible Care and is somewhat like a report card. At the end of each year, each company looks at each management practice and ranks itself one through six—with six as the top score—about how they think they are doing.[25]

---

[21]Conference Board, "Corporate Ethics: Developing New Standards of Accountability" (1991), 9–12.
[22]Id., 14.
[23]Id., 26.
[24]Id., 31.
[25]Id., 53.

The reporting in 1991 reflects that company programs developed to define the organization's basic ethical principles and to increase employee sensitivity to ethical issues appear to have become more sophisticated and ambitious since the first examination in 1987. However, what seems to be lacking is the independent appraisal of effectiveness. For example, while the Chemical Manufacturers Association reported that it had launched its Responsible Care initiative, its dependence on a "report card" prepared through self evaluation does raise serious questions about credibility of assessment. Except for the one participant who raised the question about whether the company was doing the right thing, speakers seem to reflect a willingness to accept the assumption that their efforts would indeed achieve the goals established. There was no discussion of objective feedback from employees throughout the organization.

(c)   Corporate Ethics Practices

In 1992, the Conference Board reported an international survey that was to supplement the 1987 report. The participants in the 1987 report had been CEOs only; in that of 1992, the views of senior human resources and finance executives, general counsels, and auditors were sought.

Overall, the 1992 report indicated that "corporate efforts to establish ethical accountability and to improve sensitivity to ethical issues have advanced considerably in sophistication."[26] Half of the companies responded that they had adopted codes of ethics since 1987. A fourth of the respondents stated that their companies had sponsored new training programs. Ten percent of the companies reported that their board of directors had ethics committees. In the Conclusion is the comment:

> None of this documentation of company effort and commitment suggests that business institutions have become more or less ethical. *What these data do affirm is that senior managers now recognize that dealing with ethical issues is part of nearly every employee's job.*[27]

(d)   Business Ethics: Generating Trust in the 1990s and Beyond

This attention to generating trust through an ethics program was the focus of the Annual Business Ethics Conference reported in 1994. The report discussed business responsibility to society and how companies are addressing the ethics issue. Presentations by key executives, from CEOs to managing partners to a co-chairman

---

[26]Ronald E. Berenbeim, *Corporate Ethics Practices* (Conference Board, 1992).
[27]Id., 21.

of a public accounting firm, noted what they were undertaking to meet their responsibilities. The Executive Summary concludes:

> As business' morality continues to be subjected to intense scrutiny by the media and the public, companies are demanding the highest ethical conduct of all [their] executives and employees. The current sentiment that business owes something to society cannot be ignored; involvement in communities and preservation of the environment are integral. Once companies stray from what the pubic expects of them, they may find it impossible to regain the trust of the consumers who control their future.

(e) An Overview of the Reports of Conference Board Conference

The reports of the ethics conferences sponsored by the Conference Board provided a view of the subject from the top of the organization. Presentations of key executives stated what they believed and what they planned for their organizations. Descriptions of programs were not supported by empirical studies following the tenets of independent research. The view provided what may indeed be the vision for an organization. Yet, it is a partial view. The actual ethical behavior of individuals interacting with each other and making decisions that are influenced by ethical beliefs and values received little more than descriptive attention. Objectively developed evidence that supported or refuted what was "on the book" was missing.

1.5 POTENTIAL FOR IMPROVEMENT NOT ASSURED

The challenge of improving ethical behavior cannot be dismissed as requiring a relatively simple strategy. Both contemporary observations of human behavior and the historical record of ethical conduct point to the need for caution in making predictions about what can be achieved. Yet, effort in this direction is justified. Indifference to the quality of ethical conduct in an organization or in a society leads to a serious undermining of stability within the entity. There is some point, yet not empirically identified, where unethical behavior is a damaging factor for the continuation of the entity. Of course, organizations and societies can be sustained with some level of unethical behavior. While not knowing what that level is—or how to measure relevant components—the leadership in organizations and societies must assume responsibility for enhancing the quality of ethical behavior.

In the workplace, there is deep cynicism about the payback of being a person of integrity. For example, persons indicted for fraudulent practices and sent to prison are released to spend the fruits of their earlier fraudulent actions. Stories of whistleblowers who lose their jobs and have difficulty finding new ones point to the cost of being honest. Students in some of the best business schools note that to be honest is to be stupid. Simple rules were learned by an earlier generation of schoolchildren, such as "Honesty is the best policy," "One should never tell a lie," or "Give attention to improving your character and doing good to others." Such statements seem old-fashioned and lack credibility for contemporary life. Aware of the complexity of every aspect of modern life, individuals of all ages are not naturally responsive to any effort to engage them in enhancing their ethical behavior.

Efforts to determine if people are more or less moral at particular times in the history of civilization have not led to clear conclusions. Crane Brinton, who wrote an impressive history of Western morals, concluded: "If there be an improvement in men's conduct in relation to their ethical standards, or even an improvement in those standards themselves, over the last three thousand years, such improvement can hardly be measured quantitatively, can hardly be given numerical indexes of any sort."[28]

1.6   FOCUS ON ETHICAL CONDUCT OR PENALTY AVOIDANCE

There are those who consider themselves both realistic and pragmatic who have observed that leaders in organizations are not interested in doing what is right; they are interested in avoiding being caught doing something wrong. Some attention to what is actually implied in such a point of view is warranted. Consider the following real-life observations.

A bank was required to disclose transactions of cash of more than a specified amount. Without communicating this ruling to all members of the staff who would ordinarily need to know this ruling, a small group of officials informed favored customers who had had large cash deposits in the past that from this point on their deposits would have to be less than the amount that triggers a disclosure to banking regulators. The bank officials felt confident that they would indeed meet the requirements of the rule—they would no longer have such large deposits. An official not in the small group of decision makers learned from a friend in another bank about the new disclosure ruling. When he returned to his bank and asked a question about the ruling, he was told that the ruling was irrelevant since the bank would not accept large cash deposits. This aroused the suspicion of the official, who was aware of earlier large cash deposits. He began to access the bank's database in relation to some customers; he soon had a suspicion of the strategy in his company. He said nothing about what he thought might be happening. However, the official to whom he addressed his question had not forgotten the question. The inquiring official was on a silent "watch-list" and it was not surprising that before a year had ended, the inquiring official's job was termed *excess* and he was dismissed. A tip to the authorities led to an investigation. The bank's clever strategy to avoid wrongdoing backfired.

In another case, the true attitude of the key executives in a large company was that they could hire whom they wanted. They were not going to really buy into the notion of equal opportunity. They read the law; they understood the good faith

---

[28]Crane Brinton, *A History of Western Morals* (New York: Harcourt, Brace and Company, 1959), 416.

effort that needed to be documented. They focused on documentation, including widespread advertisements of openings, carefully designed interviews with persons who would truly represent the wide diversity of the society, and well-written assessments of interviewees. Yet, in the end they hired from a very small pool of applicants. As long as reviews were related to effort as presented in documentation, they were fine. However, there came a point when implementation as represented as actual hires had to be documented. At this point, the company was found to be in violation of the law.

The adherence to codes of conduct established within an organization and to rules and regulations is essentially voluntary. It is difficult to monitor every action related to such guidance. Individuals who understand the probability of being caught in an environment where avoidance is the overriding attitude are likely to take the risk of not adhering to the rules. Such an environment becomes increasingly more unstable as the level of trust—of what is said, of what is interpreted as the "rule" of decisions made—drops at varying rates. The rate of loss of trust seems to accelerate as the organization begins to unravel. As the corruption grows more difficult to cover up, the entity is likely to be moving to the brink of bankruptcy or to actual bankruptcy. The power of unethical behavior drives to a powerless position those who, even in the face of a hostile ethical environment, strive to maintain their personal integrity.

Preoccupation with avoidance often leads to weakening of controls in other spheres of the organization. Attention to the earnings to be reaped from their own check kiting, as alleged at E. F. Hutton, seemed to have left the firm vulnerable to check kiting by some of their largest customers.

In one company, the treasurer's assistant took a mere $1,000 to use at the casino with every intention of returning the $1,000, since he felt confident he would be a winner at the gambling table. He was not a winner—there was not a cent left from the $1,000. While deeply distressed at his predicament, he soon realized that nothing happened back in his office. No one seemed to know or care. The officials were too involved in their own strategies to cover up large cash deposits received from favored customers. The assistant became more aggressive; only after extracting more than $500,000 was his activity discovered!

A hypothesis is implicit in what is discussed in this book. There is no empirical evidence, scientifically obtained and statistically evaluated, to establish the validity of the idea that an environment where high-level ethical conduct is valued and supported is a far more effective strategy *for the long run* than designing astute and dependable monitoring devices to be sure that rules and laws are *not* violated. Observations bear out the ability of individuals to design new strategies of unethical behavior in an accepting environment.

1.7   AN AREA FOR DEVELOPMENT

The theme of this book is that the public accountant can make a notable contribution to efforts of all types of organizations to enhance the ethical values and principles that guide the behavior of their people—from board members to support staff. The societal benefit would be significant. For example:

- Trust encourages greater interaction and participation.
- Monitoring costs can be reduced.
- Misappropriation of assets will decline.
- Victims of unsavory behavior are fewer in number.
- Morale of employees who respect ethical standards is enhanced.
- Stress related to coverup of irregularities and pressures to participate in unethical actions will subside.
- A sense of fairness and justice among all who participate in the work of the entity can enhance productivity.
- An openness—when the rules of behavior are respected—in communications will add to the effectiveness of all activities.

Public accountants are accustomed to professional guidance. Audits, reviews, compilations, agreed-upon procedures, and attestation engagements are based on carefully developed, reasonable standards and statements. To date, there are no such standards and statements for services related to ethical matters. The task is not impossible, even though it is, to a considerable extent, unchartered.

Although this is new territory, the accounting profession has a history of relevant experience. In the early part of 1900s, a few U.S. companies began to issue financial statements and affix thereto a certificate of a public accountant. There were no established standards. Auditors, gaining some knowledge from the limited publications available from the United Kingdom and from their own experience, determined relevant audit procedures, and wrote their "certificates" in a straightforward, descriptive fashion. There were no generally accepted accounting principles that had been promulgated for practitioners. A practitioner, well grounded in the need for financial information to represent the economic reality of the entity, had to resort to professional judgment in determining the adequacy of the presentation of the entity. Over time, practitioners committed to the professional nature of their occupation voluntarily established committees to deal with technical and professional issues. Over time, a responsible body of guidance for practitioners has developed.

Now, as a new century is approaching, the needs of our society have shifted. There is much support for good faith effort to build a more ethical environment if the workplace is to be perceived as fair and just for participants of all types—employees, customers, investors, and the public, in general.

1.8   AN OVERVIEW OF THIS BOOK

The content of this book focuses on what public accountants can contribute to enhancing ethical practices throughout all types of organizations. In the remaining chapter of Part One, there is attention to the professional qualifications of public accountants to provide ethics-related services and to the the critical need for such service in the workplace.

In Part Two, attention turns to the contemporary environment and identification of the need for attention to ethical behavior. Part Three focuses on the value-added services that public accountants can provide.

The public accounting profession, through the leadership of the American Institute of Certified Public Accountants, has responded to the changing world of business and the implications for this profession. A committee charged with studying assurance services provided a report that enlarges significantly the types of services public accountants are qualified to handle. The challenges that face practitioners are to venture into relatively new areas and add value to the words and practices of clients. This book supports the position that CPAs have a significant opportunity to provide value-added services related to ethics.

Chapter 2

Knowledge, Competencies, and Attitudes Relevant for New Ethics Services

"My most dependable adviser—who seems to know everything I need to know—is my public accountant." Comment made by a successful mid-size company president.

Public accountants have credibility in the United States. This statement must be realistically qualified since there have been challenges to that credibility, especially in the last 15 years. The extent of litigation is cited, by critics, as evidence that public accountants may, at times, serve as advocates of their clients' position, and, therefore, fail to maintain public interest responsibility. Public accounting firms have accepted settlement of disputes about the quality of their work by making payment without acknowledging the extent to which they were in violation of their own professional standards. The challenge to credibility persists; however, there continues to be confidence in public accountants as considerable emphasis is placed on meeting the requirements of the code of professional ethics.

Notwithstanding current challenges, the overriding responsibility to the public is strong. Public accountants have internalized that responsibility. The behavior expected is clearly understood. The alleged failures that are reported in the business media are difficult to assess in relation to what they represent. A reasonable conclusion is that inevitably there will be lapses in adherence to professional rules. The professional group has designed procedures to deal with members who are in violation.

In general, there is support for the public accountant's credibility. Several reasons exist for the perception of a public accountant's credibility. Public accountants have extensive knowledge about business, a wide range of problem-solving competencies useful in any environment, and a standard that imposes unassailable attitudes of objectivity and public responsibility in their assurance engagements. The long history of adding credibility to publicly owned companies' financial reports provides a heritage that is invaluable for accepting new types of assignments for clients.

Notwithstanding the capabilities of public accountants, there are among this professional group some who fail to see the relevance of their education and experience in providing new ethics services. One story of a practitioner reveals this failure to accept an opportunity.

"We can certainly audit your financial statements as we have done in the past. However, your asking us to make judgments about whether you are meeting your social goal is beyond our competencies."

This was the response of a partner in a public accounting firm to the head of a local social agency who had asked: "Can you give me your judgment about whether we are indeed honestly meeting our social obligation in providing counseling to the poor elderly whom we serve?" The agency head wanted assurance that her agency was meeting the societal goal that elderly citizens with limited incomes who needed counseling services did indeed receive the services. The agency head had a mission statement, operational specifications for services to be provided, and criteria from the governmental unit that provided the funding. The agency head was committed to operating the agency with high ethical standards. She had read stories of fraudulent behavior in similar programs in other communities. Although her office was at the same location as one of the centers, there are a number of centers throughout this large metropolitan area. She visited local centers from time to time. However, because she wanted *assurance* from an independent outsider, she turned to her independent accountant with her question.

Is it true that such a task is beyond the competencies of the partner's firm? A high probability is that the public accounting firm could provide such a service. There might have been at the time of the inquiry constraints on accepting new engagements. Possibly, all staff were fully engaged, with no foreseeable unbilled hours. Furthermore, the partner who talked with the agency head believed that his firm had clearly established the types of engagements that they would accept and, at the present time, there was no interest in expanding into new types of engagements.

Further exploration of this situation, however, revealed that the ordinary constraints of no free time or no interest in expansion were not viable bases for the practitioner's reluctance. Rather, the practitioner believed that there was no way to undertake a review of something so nebulous as "ethical behavior." The social agency head had to turn to another firm to undertake the engagement that she wanted completed.

Public accountants do indeed have the professional knowledge, competencies, and attitudes that qualify them to provide the type of services the agency head sought.

2.1 CRITICAL KNOWLEDGE THAT INDEPENDENT PUBLIC ACCOUNTANTS HAVE

The dictionary defines *knowledge* as "the condition of practical understanding of something with a considerable degree of familiarity gained through education and/or experience." The "something" of the definition is *business,* which includes not only profit-motivated enterprises, but also nonprofit entities and governmental units that strive to meet goals with economical use of resources. The knowledge possessed by public accountants has high transfer value to new types of services related to the ethical dimension of behavior in organizations.

(a) Knowledge of Business Functions

Accountants know how businesses operate. They know industries in depth. They know who has responsibility for what functions. They understand where decisions are made and the methods of implementation. They are intimately acquainted with the interrelationships of units in the companies where they provide accounting and auditing services.

Public accountants have a comprehensive grasp of control environments of organizations. Every audit team must determine the tone at the top; every partner considering a new audit engagement gains sufficient evidence to make a judgment about the integrity of management. As auditing guidance states:

> The auditor should obtain sufficient knowledge of the control environment to understand management's and the board of directors' attitude, awareness, and actions concerning the control environment, considering both the substance of controls and their collective effect.[1]

The knowledge accrued from many engagements includes understanding how contemporary organizations:

- Establish and communicate ethical values
- Manifest a commitment to competency among all employees
- Carry through in day-to-day actions, management's mission, and operating style
- Organize themselves
- Implement human resource policies and practices

Public accountants have empirical evidence of factors that make a difference in organization culture. The accumulation of such evidence is critical for wise diagnosis as judgments must be made for the design of efficient and effective audits. This same knowledge is valuable for a range of ethics services.

Much of a business's motivation is related to meeting goals which ultimately are shown in financial statements, whether the entity is a business or not.

---

[1]AICPA Professional Standards, Vol. 1, as of June 1, 1997, 327.

(b)   Knowledge of Rules and Regulations for Industries

Decisions related to the fairness of financial statements—whether audited, reviewed, or compiled—involve understanding the relevant rules and regulations of the industry in which a particular entity operates.

Those same rules and regulations imply an ethical dimension. Adherence to such rules and regulations impose on the entity a high-level moral responsibility. That responsibility is, as a matter of actual assessment, considered in an engagement related to accounting.

The heightened attention to contingent liabilities has led public accountants far beyond what had been perceived to be accounting considerations. For example, misrepresentation of a product's ingredients can have serious repercussions that ultimately will be reflected in the financial statements.

(c)   Knowledge of Professional Responsibilities

Accountants must abide by a code of professional conduct in their work. They know the demands of that code. (See Appendix A.)

The knowledge of appropriate professional behavior includes:

- *What the public interest is.* Public accountants have an understanding as stated in their professional code that "A distinguishing mark of a profession is acceptance of its responsibilities to the public. The accounting profession's public consists of clients, credit grantors, governments, employers, investors in the business and financial community, and others who rely on the objectivity and integrity of certified public accountants. . . ."[2]
- *What integrity means.* As stated in the Professional Code, . . . it [integrity] is the quality from which the public trust derives and the benchmark against which a member must ultimately test all decisions. . . . Integrity is measured in terms of what is right and just. In the absence of specific rules, standards, or guidance, or in the face of conflicting opinions, a member should test decisions and deeds by asking: "Am I doing what a person of integrity would do?"[3] The knowledge that provides an answer to that question is a part of the permanent memory of a competent accountant and is readily and frequently accessed as decisions are faced in professional practice situations.

(i) Objectivity.   The code states that "Objectivity is a state of mind, a quality that lends value to a member's services. . . . The principle imposes the obligation to be impartial, intellectually honest, and free of conflicts of interest."[4]

---

[2]AICPA Professional Standards, Vol. 2, as of June 1, 1997, 4301.
[3]Id., 4311.
[4]Id., 4321.

Through education and extensive experience in all types of environments, public accountants have well-honed strategies for assuring that they are responding to all aspects of an engagement with unrelenting objectivity. Public accountants are often in environments where there are vested interests, focused opinion, and partial analysis. The public accountant sees as a critical contribution that which derives from identifying what represents the factors that are central to the issue, and then guiding thought to evaluate relevant information. The skill of the public accountant in maintaining such objectivity is at the heart of the deep-seated respect for assurances provided at the conclusion of engagements.

(ii) **Independence.** "Independence precludes relationships that may appear to impair a member's objectivity in rendering attestation services."[5] While this factor is identified as a separate factor, it is indeed at the foundation of a public accountant's adherence to objectivity. Over the years, many observers of the public accounting profession have noted that independence is the cornerstone of the public accountant's contribution. In fact, independence is deemed so critical that even though what is desired is independence in mental attitude, the profession has further required that there also be present independence in appearance. However, independence in appearance is not sufficient. Independence in appearance provides the public a measure of good faith about the overriding value of independence in mental attitude.

Throughout the accounting profession, there has been emphasis on independence. For example, internal auditors have their professional organization, which issues standards and related statements. The importance of independence in performing their tasks is a component of the guidance provided. Even though they are employees of the organization where they serve as internal auditors, performing their work is to be done with full awareness of independence.

(iii) **Due Care.** The Code declares that "the quest for excellence is the essence" of due care.[6] Due care requires a public accountant to discharge professional responsibilities with competence and diligence. It imposes the obligation to perform professional services to the best of a member's ability with concern for the best interest of those for whom the services are performed and consistent with the profession's responsibility to the public.

Public accountants face a highly varied range of situations and events in their daily work. They are self-motivated to maintain an awareness of the quality of their performance. While there are strategies in public accounting firms to monitor the work of colleagues, there is a tradition of expecting each person to be able to assess the quality of what is being done.

---

[5]Id.
[6]Id., 4331.

2.2   CRITICAL COMPETENCIES PUBLIC ACCOUNTANTS POSSESS

Accountants have developed a number of general competencies to a high degree in their educational background and through experience. These competencies have high transfer value for undertaking assurance services related to ethical matters.

(a)   Insightfully Analyze a Situation

Public accountants have had much experience in entering an environment that is seemingly different from any experienced earlier. Such a situation does not unnerve the public accountant. The public accountant does not function with mental recipes for what is to be done. Instead, the public accountant has much skill in getting to the heart of the matter.

Making professional judgments is well understood by the public accountant. In a new situation in which a specified engagement is to be performed, the public accountant is an astute diagnostician. Experience and reflection of human behavior in organizations have prepared public accountants to provide extended assurance in many areas.

A large financial services company was stunned at the revelation that a massive fraud had occurred in their organization. How could this have happened? As the executive committee talked among themselves, they could not believe the revelation was true. However, they knew that it was. They reflected on what their organization stood for: high values, integrity, respect for individuals. How often these terms had appeared in annual reports and in speeches given by key executives in all types of forums. They realized that they had a professional internal audit staff, well-educated supervisors and managers.

Their communications director was attempting to contain the damage to their fine reputation in the business community. However, they knew that their response had to be more directly related to the situation as it was. They were uncomfortable with what might be the answer to the question: "Why did this happen in *our* organization?"

They turned to their public accountant. They knew they had to face reality; they had to be candid; they had to acknowledge failures, omissions, inattention, and whatever other conclusions an unassailable accountant would bring to the task.

When the chief executive officer (CEO) was asked why the executive committee had called in the public accountant, his response was, "We are ready to get to the essence of what happened. We know our public accountant will identify the problems objectively and will provide a candid report. The accountant will not spare us the stark reality. We are ready to face the truth."

(b)   Observe Astutely

Public accountants have a long tradition of looking beyond the books and records in their process of verification in financial statement audits and other financial statement engagements.

Being alert and attentive to observational evidence which will corroborate or contradict tentatively drawn impressions or generalizations is common behavior for public accountants. No aspect of an organization's behavior is summarily considered irrelevant when a public accountant is involved in a professional engagement.

Public accountants operate in complex and subtle environments. They have long experience in using insight, sensitivity, and continuing judgment as they see what is taking place or note the interaction of employees and employers in organizations.

The quality of an assurance engagement depends to a considerable extent on observational skills. Indeed, such skills are needed at the time of considering an engagement.

A public accountant was called by a CEO of a large publicly traded consumer products company. The CEO had recently become a convert to the importance of core ethical values and their need to be manifested in all aspects of the organization. The CEO was interested in having, in effect, a stamp of approval for their fine program. He explained to the accountant that they had carefully documented the program from its initial planning to the implementation. They were preparing a report. They felt it would be impressive to include a brief report from a public accountant.

The accountant who had been called about this prospective engagement had had no prior interaction with the company or the CEO.

The accountant spent a morning in the company meeting not only with the CEO but with other officials. The morning's agenda was carefully orchestrated, the public accountant observed. At the end of the morning, in a concluding session with the CEO only, the public accountant said that to support the conclusion the CEO had reached would require extensive observations, among other means of gathering evidence.

The CEO was not happy with the public accountant. The earlier graciousness gave way to subtle hostility. The CEO was stunned that his words and those of his key officials were not sufficient to permit the public accountant to say "yes" to the task of reading the documents and writing a brief assurance report. In a clearly low-key style, the public accountant noted the professional responsibility a public accountant assumes in any assurance engagement. The accountant quietly noted that there was a need to obtain corroborating evidence for the company's representations about their program. The CEO concluded the discussion with a vague comment that they would have to think about their next steps. The public accountant merely stated that his firm would be willing to talk further about the matter.

When the public accountant returned to his office and discussed his experience with colleagues, he stated: "You really have to be a careful observer. The CEO's program does sound impressive. His key officials were also able to articulate what they planned and what they had implemented. But, quickly, I observed they believed that what they had done was absolutely great and anyone who heard them would believe their claims. Yet, they obviously wanted something more; they wanted us to support their words. The CEO had quite a different personality at the end of the morning. His graciousness disappeared as he attempted to respond to what he perceived as my unreasonableness."

The accountant discussed with colleagues the critical need to maintain objectivity when considering potential engagements. He noted that companies are seemingly more concerned than formerly about their ethical environments, but somewhat reluctant to verify their pronouncements.

He concluded that their firm would not be contributing a genuine value-added service if they were essentially "rubber stamping" the words of an ethical standard. In this situation, the public accountant did get a telephone call six months later; the CEO wanted to pursue the matter further. The CEO ultimately accepted that he did not realize what his company should have assessed. The public accountant's position, in the end, was sustained.

In another situation, a public accountant was engaged to provide an audit of a client's recently instituted ethical training program. The CEO had informed the public accountant that the vice president heading the program had been carefully selected. In fact, the successful candidate for the position had met with the board of directors. The board was wholeheartedly in support of this candidate. The vice president was personable; he spoke with eloquence; he stated in clear language what ethical behavior in an organization required; he articulated what the critical factors were in a successful program. During the conversation with the CEO, the public accountant noted that the CEO was expressing no misgivings about the performance of the vice president. The accountant was listening for the "why" for providing so much information about the head of the program. The public accountant began to think that the CEO was not providing this information to influence the listener; in fact, the CEO may have been—between his words—raising questions about how effective the head actually was. As the public accountant listened, he sensed that the CEO seemed to be communicating something different from what the words alone might convey. The public accountant mentally began to speculate about what was actually the reality of the situation. The public accountant, at this point, raised two questions: "Are you wanting verification of the quality of performance of your new vice president? Have there been circumstances that have developed that challenge your enthusiasm for this individual?" The CEO seemed relieved by the questions and quickly responded: "You have read my mind! That is it exactly. We are new in this formal ethics business. We took this fellow at his word. Now we are wondering if he is the right one for the job. We began to realize that you can't assume that someone who professes to be an ethics expert manifests the quality of ethical behavior that you expect."

After further exploration of observations, tentatively offered, the CEO and the public accountant designed, in general, what needed to be done, which was an independent job evaluation of the office of the vice president. The public accountant appreciated the candidness of the CEO, after the initial ambiguity of what was being discussed. An appropriate strategy was designed and a successful engagement was completed. The new vice president's performance was significantly flawed in critical ways. A review of his past record, which had earlier been done in sketchy fashion, revealed that he had a history of failures. In the meantime, he had learned the language of ethics sufficiently to impress company officials who felt inadequate to the task of evaluating persons with such expertise. The public accounting firm was engaged again and again in relation to the ethical program of this client.

(c) Solve Problems

Services related to ethical matters are likely to be uncharted in many instances. Company officials may not be able to explain what they seek and what they want the outcome to be. Public accountants are problem solvers. Their experience with audits, for example, has enhanced basic investigative skills. The audit is a problem-solving task, similar to scientific research methodology. The identification of "the problem" specifies the risks the auditor faces. There are implied hypotheses in the evidence-gathering strategies selected.

The public accountant, therefore, brings to an engagement related to ethics a strategy for determining what the problem is. The public accountant knows how to identify difficulties in solving the problem.

A thoroughly developed case study of the implementation of the ethical program in a major company failed to consider that one critical component was behavior of scientists developing new products.

The experienced investigator—not a public accountant—concluded that the company's ethical behavior was exemplary. Yet, there had been misrepresentation of experimental results. That aspect of the program had not been identified by the investigator. A review of the investigator's strategy revealed that he had confined his attention to the areas identified by the company officials in the initial planning for the engagement.

A public accountant in such an environment would have begun initially with an analysis of every component of the company and identified the potentially key ethical concerns.

(d) Identify Relevant and Valid Evidence

Understanding relevant and valid evidence is a powerful competence of public accountants. Public accountants recognize objective evidence, know how to assess persuasiveness of evidence, and know how to measure sufficiency of evidence to support a conclusion. The task of gathering evidence is tied operationally to specifying the problem to be solved.

A company undertook an ethical training program for all levels of workers throughout the corporation. At the end of the training session, the instructor asked each participant to fill out a brief questionnaire which included the question: "What is your assessment of the extent to which you will adhere to the code as described in this session?" The instructor monitored the filling in of the questionnaires. The participants were to check a point from 1 to 5 (with 5 representing 100 percent adherence). Fewer than 5 percent of the employees did not check 5.

When a majority of the company's employees had completed the training program, the officials were quite happy with its success. In session after session, approximately 95 percent of participants checked 5! The officials felt confident that adherence to the new code of ethical conduct was being implemented.

However, in a little more than a year, several serious ethical lapses raised questions about the quality of behavior in the company. The executive committee was perplexed since they had received the glowing report of the success of the training program.

The company's public accountant was called in. The first discussion disclosed the evidence that had been provided. The inadequacy of self reports made immediately after the completion of a training program was briefly explained. The public accountant explained the timing and nature of the type of evidence that would provide a reasonably good answer to the question: "Is there implementation of our code of ethics in our company?"

The public accountant began with the problems that alerted the executive committee to a possible problem in implementation. The public accountant began with those problems and was free to obtain evidence believed relevant. There was a comprehensive engagement designed that included determining the extent to which employees had at all levels understood the code of conduct to a systematic audit of the actual performance of the procedures that had been established. The public accountant and a team of colleagues spent a considerable amount of time providing the client with an objective series of reports that provided clear recommendations for deficiencies discovered throughout their engagement.

(e) Ability to Learn Independently

Public accountants are accustomed to learning on their own. Like other professional individuals, they deal with fields of knowledge that change significantly and at a relatively rapid pace. The rate of obsolescence of knowledge has accelerated in the final quarter of the twentieth century. Realization of the need for maintaining up-to-date knowledge has led to formal programs of continuing professional education in many states. In most states, practitioners must meet mandated continuing education requirements to maintain active status as certified public accountants (CPAs).

A manager in a small public accounting firm was called in by a partner who told her that a client wanted to consider doing something about ethics. Now that the company had grown in less than three years from five employees to 200 employees, the owner believed some formal statement about ethics was needed. The partner said to the public accountant: "I realize your interest in this area and I know the experience you have had in reviewing the control environment. Would you join me in meeting with this client next week? If what I think the client wants turns out to be true, I'd see you handling the engagement." The relatively young manager was interested; the possibility of extending the nature of her assignments was appealing. She assured the partner of her willingness to attend the preliminary meeting. By the time of the meeting, the manager had spent considerable time in local libraries learning as much as possible about ethical programs of all types. She found the effort worthwhile; she was willing to make a commitment to becoming fully competent about ethics.

2.3 ATTITUDES NEEDED TO PROVIDE ETHICALLY RELATED SERVICES

Increasingly, public accounting firms are specialized. The complexity and variety of services that can be provided by public accountants encourage specialization. The survey results of the Special Committee on Assurance Services identified hundreds of services that public accountants do or could provide to companies. Public accountants function in an environment where choices can be made.

Offering assurances services related to ethical matters imposes a unique responsibility on the leadership of the firm. There is a complex interplay among knowledge, competencies, and individual and firm moral values and beliefs. In fact, knowledge and competencies are not sufficient. There has to be an unwavering commitment to moral values and beliefs.

Providing accounting services, such as writing up financial statements at the end of a month, can be performed according to established rules and regulations. Such activity can be completed within a framework of well understood principles and practices. The guidance, plus the traditions for the long-established, accounting-related tasks public accountants perform, is sufficient to assure that the work is done professionally. While there are inevitably problems that may be new and require additional study and judgment for satisfactory resolution, the frame of reference for such matters is understood from prior experience.

As soon as public accountants consider engagements related to ethics, the situation is changed. There is no established frame of reference; there is no tradition specific to such engagements. There is no codified guidance. Therefore, to determine whether a sole practitioner or a firm should extend services to ethics-related matters, there must be a candid review of critical attitudes. The quality of a firm's services in this area is likely to determine, to a degree far greater than might be predicted, the presence of influential attitudes.

(a) Belief That Commitment to Ethical Behavior Is Honorable

The individuals in a firm who are thinking about this area for providing services need to take a measure of the strength of their own commitment to ethical behavior. Is it a matter that has gotten attention individually or as a group? Or, does a candid reflection of past attention reveal indifference to ethical considerations? Has commitment been to technical know-how and only tangentially to ethics, which is perceived to be a "soft" topic, undefined and not amenable to quantification?

The individual public accountant or the firm that wants to expand services will have met a key prerequisite if there is a good faith commitment to ethical behavior that will provide an outlet for an area that is intellectually engaging for those who will participate.

Such a commitment is communicated in many ways, some of which are not explicitly spoken. Such a commitment translates into a style of credibility that earnest clients will appreciate.

Long before the recent interest in extending assurance services, public accountants had aided their clients in regard to ethical matters. One public accountant in a small firm told this tale:

> The CEO of this agricultural products company called me one morning and asked: "What would you say to coming over here and helping me with a problem we have in our warehouse? Theft has been suspected. Aren't our people honest? And, if not, why not?" I said to the CEO, "Why are you calling me?" His response: "Remember we have talked about morality in the workplace a number of times. You're the only outside person I know who understands what ethics really is—and you are authentic!"
>
> I couldn't say no. That's how we entered the area of providing assistance in this area far removed from accounting . . . but it really isn't . . . doesn't dishonesty often end up reflected in the financials?

A sole practitioner or a firm needs to ask a candid question about its own reputation in the community it serves. Firms have a variety of sources for feedback about their own ethical quality. It should be possible to get answers to questions such as: "What do we hear about our own ethical conduct that matches the truth, as we know it? Is the firm proud of how its public perceives its ethical behavior?"

(b)   Sturdy Belief That Organizations Can Improve Their Ethical Culture

There is much cynicism in the world at large about human nature. Some believe that the notion that people can change—and become more ethical, for example—is an unachievable idealistic proposition. Others hold the belief that people can change their ethical nature. Some, of course, are not sure about human nature's propensity to change.

Without a genuine belief that individuals and organizations can change, there is not likely to be the intensity of interest in analyzing a situation, in pursing relevant evidence with attention, or in providing innovative recommendations. At the same time, the complexity of changing ethical behavior, and the probability of limited, if any, measurable success in doing so must be realistically approached.

This attitude is necessary to give vitality to undertaking an engagement related to ethics. However, this attitude does not undermine the objectivity that the public accountant brings to the actual performance of any and all engagements. The understanding of human ethical behavior in the workplace is primitive, at best. The attitude that improvement can be realized, combined with a public accountant's propensity to be objective, is an invaluable combination for successfully completing an engagement. Careful observation and astute description of what transpires in the work environment can produce knowledge to be shared with others. A public accountant who has provided such services commented in this way:

> It is my belief that the ethical culture of an organization can change in either direction—becoming better or worse. Leadership can set the tone. However, I maintain professional skepticism at all times on such an engagement. Without that unrelenting awareness of objectivity—which is really the manifestation of skepticism—I really cannot feel I have completed the job responsibly. What we are trying to do on practically every engagement related to ethics is consider it as some type of research investigation—the exploratory model is frequently the only one that is viable since our understanding to date is so limited.

(c) The Belief That Ethical Issues Are Engaging and Challenging

As noted earlier, ethical engagements are likely to be unchartered. There are not simple observations, clearly recorded data, and quantifiable experiences. The complexity and subtlety of ethical phenomena that will be encountered in the real environment requires a highly interested investigator. Initial impressions merely trigger possibilities for what ought to be pursued. Often, it is not clear, without some exploration, what is the most feasible direction for reasonable conclusions.

(d) An Attitude of Being Nonjudgmental

There are often no absolute "answers" in dealing with ethical problems and issues. The ethical dilemma is uncomfortably too common. Often, the kind of analysis required, unfortunately, leads to the need to carefully weigh alternatives. Ultimately, there needs to be a prioritizing of what values are being considered. Often, in the end there must be judgments that are to some degree subjective.

It is possible that a technically competent accountant could do a commendable task of auditing financial statements with no more than a shallow interest in the value of financial statements. Such an indifference to the subject of an ethics-related engagement would be dangerous.

2.4 SIGNIFICANCE OF A PUBLIC ACCOUNTING FIRM'S CULTURE

Beyond the knowledge, skills, and attitudes considered critical in building a successful specialization in providing ethics-related services, there is an overriding consideration: the accounting firm's own culture. A public accounting firm can use its skills for a self-evaluation of its own culture. A demanding, objective self-assessment can be a highly instructive activity. Unfortunately, the actual culture is not derived from the words spoken in motivational conferences with key persons in the firm. The actual culture is the unadorned reality that employees experience day after day. Comments made by practitioners in moments of brutal candidness included:

> Yes, the memorandum states that we are not to sign off on procedures we don't perform. That is *fiction*. We know better, don't we—we are constantly showing we did work we didn't do. That is the only way to come in within the budget.
>
> Sure, the client is king. We give the client what is wanted. It is easy enough to say . . . "that's not material." Thank heavens for the flexibility of materiality.
>
> Another fiction—how can those top fellows talk like that? Don't they realize we are in the audience? Don't they realize that they have asked us to do any number of unethical steps to hold on to a client? Would you trust a partner in this firm?
>
> Our firm supports community contributions to the extent that employees are given "time off" to participate. Yet, the same employees are given quotas for the amount of new business each is to generate in the forthcoming fiscal year. Little is said about the framework in which this marketing activity is to be accomplished. Is it worth a few thousand dollars to an employee to meet the quota? A salary increase is provided if the quota is met. The reality of this quota system makes all the in-house training about integrity and objectivity pure hypocrisy.
>
> Are mistakes tolerated? "You bet they are not!" Goals are to be met . . . at any cost? What is the reward system? Is it in conflict with what is represented as our public responsibility?

As noted earlier, individual practitioners as well as firms have choices as to the types of engagements they find appealing and are willing to accept. The philosophical position relative to the value of ethics must be articulated and only if there is a high level of comfort about providing such services should effort be expended for developing such a specialization.

(a) The Firm Can Be a Laboratory for Developing Ethical Understandings

Inasmuch as a professional code guides public accountants, public accounting firms have established policies and procedures that are monitored in a number of different ways. The experience of establishing policies and practices and of monitoring implementation can be documented in a manner that enhances understanding of many aspects of ethical behavior.

For example, considering the firm as an environment worthy of careful observation and reflection is a highly relevant strategy to gain understanding, as well as confidence, about dimensions of ethical behavior. Violations that are discovered are especially valuable in extending understanding based on candid diagnosis of motivation and expectations from such unethical behavior.

(b)   Insight from Firm Experience with Pressure in the Marketplace

Public accountants experience pressure. For example, there are clients who seek an unqualified opinion from their auditors. Some clients will use every strategy they can imagine to compel the auditors to give them a so-called clean opinion when the auditors cannot support such a conclusion to their audit. Auditors withstand that pressure and maintain the goodwill of their clients, for the most part. A careful analysis of a public accounting firm's strategy for withstanding pressure and adhering to professional responsibilities can be the basis for valuable insight. That insight has powerful transfer value in providing ethical services to all types of organizations.

(c)   Experience in Self-Regulation

Public accounting has professional status. The characteristic that is the central one and impacts all the others is that "Those in a profession regulate their own behavior." Practitioners in professions have a clear image of what appropriate behavior is at all times. Without close monitoring and outside continuous evaluation, a professional person can be trusted to adhere to the tenets of ethical behavior. Some would say that such self-regulation is burdensome. Others would say that if the professional has not internalized this responsibility, reliance on what a professional does cannot be assumed to meet standards expected. To make ethical responses a natural response assures consistency in behavior.

   A firm could learn much from studying their own staff's success in internalizing ethical behavior. Through such study much can be learned, possibly, about the factors that hasten the development of such a sense of responsibility.

2.5   THE DYNAMIC INTERACTION OF KNOWLEDGE AND EXPERIENCE

There is an impressive body of training and education that public accountants possess. The primary value of that background is that it is a foundation for further learning and enhanced insight.

   Empirical knowledge of ethical behavior in the workplace is limited. There are few generalizations supported by convincing evidence. Among the questions for which there are not convincing answers are the following:

- What factors in a work environment contribute to a high level of ethical behavior among employees?
- What characteristics are possessed by leaders of organizations who impose high ethical standards on their own behavior? How do these leaders differ from those who seem to thrive in a corruption-biased environment?

- To what extent can individuals be trusted to monitor their own ethical behavior and adhere to a code of conduct?
- How segmented is an individual's adherence to ethical standards?
- How divergent are personal ethic behaviors from public ethical behaviors?

The foregoing are just a few of many questions that can be raised. Knowledge about ethical behavior is often derived from public opinion polls. A limited amount of information from very narrowly designed studies provides no support for generalizations. Public accountants can contribute much to our understanding and, possibly, from there they can aid in the encouragement of higher ethical behavior in the workplace.

PART 2

Contemporary Ethical Environment: Problems and Demands

Chapter 3

Confusion Regarding the Value of Ethics

An early observer of life in the United States, de Tocqueville, was highly impressed with the citizens and their being driven to engage in commerce and industry. As he stated:

> Their present condition . . . is that of an almost exclusively manufacturing and commercial association, placed in the midst of a new and boundless country, which their principal object is to explore for purposes of profit. This is the characteristic that most distinguishes the American people from all others at the present time. . . . All those quiet virtues that tend to give a regular movement to the community and to encourage business will therefore be held in peculiar honor by that people, and to neglect those virtues will be to incur public contempt.[1]

The astute observer de Tocqueville, may have been somewhat optimistic about the citizens of the United States. The public judgment of behavior was perceived to be a powerful deterrent to unethical behavior. Such judgment continues to be present, but over time there has developed uncertainty of the extent of agreement about what is ethical and what is not. Yet, throughout the history of the United States, there has been strong support for high ethical standards. Respect for person of "sterling character" has been a historically central attitude among U.S. citizens.

The attention at this point is on the climate of the U.S. business society during the last two decades of the twentieth century. During this period, a number of massive frauds in major organizations has intensified concern about ethical behavior at work. However, between the mid-1980s and the end of the 1990s, success in implementing high ethical standards has yet to be supported by empirical evidence. To date, there has not been definitive objective support that the quality of ethical behavior at work matches the rhetoric about commitment to ethical standards enunciated by company officials during this period. There have been extensive efforts at training employees to company expectations. The task has not been simple. For example, *The Wall Street Journal* noted that "ethical training gets a boost at many companies." A Stanford University professor, who

---

[1]Alexis de Tocqueville, *Democracy in America,* Vol. 2, *The Henry Reeve Text* as revised by Francis Bowen and Phillips Bradley (Alfred A. Knopf, 1945), 237.

was quoted in the story, concluded that "companies must overcome an assumption by many employees that top management wants profits, however they have to be achieved."[2]

3.1 THE OVERRIDING PROBLEM

An overwhelming persistent problem related to ethics is that hypocrisy is not readily observed. What is promulgated as an organization's values and what is actually demanded of employees are often irreconcilable.

The silence that engulfs an entity where unethical practices are pervasive can be maintained for long periods. The conspiracy of cover-up has powerful support primarily because of the contemporary confusion about the value of ethical standards and the perceived short-term rewards that can be realized if "rules are bent." Leaders of organizations can enunciate elegant statements about what is expected in the company; those same leaders later can appear stunned at ethical lapses discovered in their own organizations. To establish who knew what was going on is difficult; frequently, the whistle-blower is dismissed for some technical failure.[3]

3.2 LEVELS OF ATTITUDES AND COMMITMENT TO ETHICAL STANDARDS

The cases of unethical and illegal behavior in U.S. society during the past two decades reveal a number of dominant attitudes and commitments that are essentially mutually exclusive and are responsible for the contemporary confusion. Only the last one reflects a firm, good faith belief that ethical standards are to be maintained. The four levels are as follows.

(a) Ethical Standards Are Irrelevant

Generally, there is no acknowledgment that the prevailing attitude is that there is no place for ethics in this company. Close observation—which is difficult for anyone except a sensitive insider—can disclose the consistent disregard for any thought to the ethical implications of decisions and actions. What is really conveyed is that there is no need to consider ethical standards at work. The business arena is about success—visual success reflected in command of sufficient funds to live affluently. Who cares? As long as an individual's behavior can enhance the bottom line, there is no improper behavior. The bottom line is the objective; ethics are rhetoric.

---

[2]*The Wall Street Journal,* (September 9, 1986).
[3]"He Told, He Suffered, Now He's a Hero," *The New York Times* (May 23, 1994), Business, 1.

(b) Ethical Standards Are Only Pronouncements

Somewhere in a policy making office, officials have realized that in today's society some kind of statement about ethics is good public relations. Carefully worded codes of conduct may be distributed to all workers; there may be workshops and seminars; there is some talk about ethical standards in appropriate places and at the right time. There is a paper trail for the company's good faith concern with ethical standards. Yet, the reality—the unspoken evaluation—is that there is no effort or expectation of making judgments within the framework of the pronouncements. Window dressing is sufficient; there is no worry that there is no substance to what is being proclaimed. If any problems develop, officials in the company are skilled in appearing sincere and concerned. They have the ability to convey a proper attitude.

(c) Ethical Standards Have Low Priority

Some companies have codes of conduct that employees conscientiously accept and attempt to implement. However, such standards are followed to the extent that no problems develop. If there is conflict, ethical concerns are relegated to low priority. Many who are caught in ethical violations point to a superior who dictated the action to be taken. Such persons feel that they could not behave independently; they believe they would have lost favor with a superior or even been dismissed from their position for insubordination. The total process—from policy to follow-up when there are alleged violations—has not been carefully developed to assure employees of the commitment of the company. Some in such an environment would like to see ethical standards honored, but no framework exists to implement such standards.

(d) Ethical Standards Guide All Actions

Some companies have accepted the responsibility for ethical behavior that begins with "the tone at the top" and continues throughout the company with all operational employees understanding what implementation of the company's ethical standards means.

In such companies, there is an openness to grievances reflecting problems with implementation. Questions about behavior are considered thoughtfully. The companies where ethical behavior would meet this description are limited. Many who have observed businesses believe there are too many pressures that large numbers cannot handle in an ethical matter. The long-run horizon for consideration of behavior is not currently popular; there is so much at stake in "looking good" now, even if unethical practices have been condoned.

Companies that function with this attitude toward ethical behavior often relate the value of such an attitude to their economic success. Some leaders believe that good ethics can enhance customer satisfaction and employee productivity, and reduce costs.

3.3 PERCEPTIONS OF ETHICAL CONDUCT
IN THE UNITED STATES

Currently, there is considerable discussion whether the United States has a reliable moral compass. There is no sense of a higher authority that guides individuals, as persons and as employees in the workplace. There is an expediency to choice making.

Such dire statements appear to have been made again and again throughout the ages. Unfortunately, there is no empirical evidence to identify the quality of ethical behavior now or earlier. Drucker reminds his readers that "the new realities . . . call for perception as much as for analysis."[4] The efforts to identify what is actually happening—and what people believe—about ethical behavior during the final two decades of this century lead many to believe that enhancing the quality of ethics at work would contribute markedly to the quality of work life— and, in the end, the quality of life.

(a)   What Polls Report

Crittenden, in an article, commented that "Many are alarmed that America's corporate chiefs are losing sight of moral standards in the new frenzy to get rich."[5]

A Louis Harris poll in 1983 which measured public confidence in corporate executives showed that only 18 percent placed "great confidence" in American executives; it was 29 percent in 1973 and 55 percent in the mid-1960s. The Opinion Research Corporation found in 1983 that only 29 percent rated corporate executives "excellent or good" in ethical practices; the percentages were 33 percent in 1981 and 36 percent in 1975. Polls are not comparable; however, these figures appear not to be significantly different from the Gallup poll results discussed in Chapter 1. In the Gallup polls, the combined categories were "very high" and "high," while the Opinion Research Corporation combined "excellent and good."

A *Time* cover story entitled "Whatever Happened to Ethics?" referred to "a time of moral disarray. . . ." "Most ethics becomes important when the roof falls in," said TV producer Fred Friendly recently as he plunged into the making of a PBS series designed to examine the tangled state of American ethics. His task could not have been more timely or more daunting, nor could his comment have been more appropriate. Large sections of the nation's ethical roofing have been sagging badly, from the White House to churches, schools, industries, medical centers, law firms, and stock brokerages—pressing down on the institutions and enterprises that make up the body and blood of America.[6]

The same article reported the results of a poll conducted for *Time* by Yankelovich Clancy Shulman in which 90 percent of the respondents agreed that

[4]Peter F. Drucker, *The New Realities* (New York: Harper & Row, 1989), 264.
[5]Crittenden, *The New York Times* (August 19, 1984), Section C, 1.
[6]"Whatever Happened to Ethics," *Time* (May 25, 1987), 26.

morals have fallen because parents fail to take responsibility for their children or to imbue them with decent moral standards; 76 percent saw lack of ethics in businessmen as contributing to tumbling moral standards; and 74 percent decried failure by political leaders to set a good example.

A panel of academics, business ethicists, and insurance executives participating in a discussion entitled, "Ethics in the Competitive Financial Services Business" concluded that in today's competitive marketplace, the constant push for growth and profits contributes to ethical lapses. One study cited was a survey of employees in the financial service industry which was undertaken by the Society of Chartered Life Underwriters and other professional organizations. Fifty-six percent of the respondents felt pressure to behave unethically and 48 percent admitted that they had engaged in an unethical act.[7]

(b) One Company's Program—and Its Inadequacies

It was in this environment where there began to be heightened attention to ethics—the 1980s—that a sophisticated system for monitoring ethical conduct was developed at Dow Corning. As reported in *Business Week,* Dow Corning's Ethics System included the following:

- A Business Conduct Committee of six managers who serve three year stints. Each member devoted up to six weeks a year in fulfilling this obligation.
- Two members of the Committee audit every business operation every three years. The panel reviews up to 35 locations annually.
- Three-hour reviews were held with up to 35 employees. Committee members use a code of ethics as the framework and encourage employees to raise ethical issues.
- Results of audits are reported to a three-member Audit and Social Responsibility Committee of the board of directors.[8]

Dow Corning was considered a pioneer in corporate ethics. It was among the first to establish an ethics program, which many believed to be the most elaborate in corporate America. The quality of what was designed for Dow Corning was considered worthy of study. The distinguished Harvard Business School professor Kenneth Goodpaster had prepared a trio of case studies on the company's ethical strategy. The program had been introduced in the early 1970s after the Watergate disclosures. The company chairman at the time wanted to create a corporate culture that emphasized high ethical standards. It was the extensive commitment to ethics that attracted Goodpaster, whose case studies were read and reviewed by thousands of MBAs and managers in executive-education courses.

[7]National Underwriter Life & Health Financial Services Edition (May 5, 1997), V101, N18, 26(1) [http://web3.search_bank.com/infotrac/Session/259/743/981/1833w3/4!xr n_14&bkm].
[8]*Business Week* (March 9, 1992), 67–68.

Yet, this program—monitored and reviewed by an outside expert in business ethics so impressive to many—seemingly failed to pick up any signs of controversy over the safety of breast implants during four separate audits conducted after 1983. Even the review of the unit that made the implants, which was completed in October 1990, did not reveal the safety issue. Yet, in 1976—the year the ethics program was launched—an engineer questioned the product's safety. The engineer resigned from the company in protest. There were internal documents that showed that there were company officials who knew about the problem. In a company with a heightened sensitivity about ethical concerns, it does seem disappointing that the engineer who questioned the safety of the developing product felt no support for at least a good faith review of the questions raised. Silence prevailed until sometime later.

A *Business Week* story included the comment: "Ethics programs aren't designed to deal directly with complex problems. Instead, they are there only to help cultivate an overall environment of proper conduct. In Dow Corning, issues of product safety or efficacy typically go through normal management channels."

The confusion is evident in this commentary. Who implements an ethics program? What does it mean to have a culture of honesty and integrity? Furthermore, even an astute outsider intent on understanding the ethics program in effect failed to discover the attitude toward safety. Yet, a company manufacturing devices with potential health hazards would be expected to be sensitive to safety factors.

Here was a company that was able to communicate a positive, highly favorable perception of an extensive ethics program. That program was reviewed by an outsider, who was a specialist in ethics. The account of the program was developed for a case available to professors throughout the world who wanted students to understand what a good ethical program is like. Yet, there was disclosed a serious flaw. Unfortunately, the type of discrepancy observed between what is stated and what appeared to be the reality of the situation is far too common in U.S. organizations.

An absolutely impeccable record of high ethical behavior is no more realistic than factory output with zero defects. In dealing with a subject as subjective as ethics, there must be allowance for lapses. The ethical program in an organization must be developed and implemented realistically and with flexibility. Focus needs to be on good faith belief in enhancement of the climate to assure fairness and justice throughout the environment.

(c) Anecdotal Revelations

Considerable attention is being given to quality-of-life issues, especially in the work environment. In exploring the implications of the ethical environment vis-à-vis quality of life, several businesspeople, in moments of candidness, away from their workplaces, have disclosed the following observations or circumstances.

An early experience: "As a new staff member in an insurance company— shortly after I graduated from college—I was assigned the job of serving as an assistant to a senior vice president on a business trip throughout the western part of the country. The trip took approximately two weeks. At several sites, the executive planned parties for large groups that seemed to be social parties—and not related to business, but I was not one to pass judgment on the motivation for the parties. I was stunned at the expenditures; I couldn't believe what I was observing. Then, when we arrived back at our local airport, he said to me: 'Let me have your expense form; I'll fill it out for you; you will share the reimbursement with me.' I didn't study business in college; this was my first job. I wanted to believe that people in business were honorable. At the time, I didn't respond to the final request; I talked with the senior vice president the next day to be sure I understood what he had requested. He explained that padding travel accounts was standard practice; he would take the responsibility if there was any problem. I merely had to sign the form. I told him I would have to think about the matter. Later that day, I wrote a brief note of resignation. I was a beginning assistant; I was confident I could get another job. Fortunately, I have not encountered ethical problems in my present job—I have been in this job for about a year only, though!"

A staff member, who had been hired about a year before, reported this incident: "The vice president said I would have to go to Paris for a week's work. There were to be three of us on this trip. It was fine with me. I don't mind working in Paris. However, three days before the date of departure, the vice president called to say that there had been some changes and I would not have to go. That was fine; I understand changes are inevitable. When the vice president returned, he handed me travel forms and said: 'Just fill these out as though you went on the trip.' I was stunned; I made him quite unhappy when I said I couldn't fill them out. I learned later that his girlfriend had gone on the trip; he was seeking reimbursement for her expenses. It wasn't long until I was recommended for transfer to another department. I declined the offer and left the company."

A member in public relations of a major telecommunications company commented: "While we were reviewing the fluff for the forthcoming annual report—and putting in all those good sounding words about integrity and honesty—a staff member was out at one of the city's fanciest stores buying a birthday present (she could spend as much as $5,000 of the company's money) that the CEO and his wife could take to the birthday party of a friend, who was also a CEO. Oh, how very nice it would be if words really reflected what the company officials believed. I realized that this kind of behavior is common; I just accepted it; I like my job in public relations."

A member of the internal audit staff of a major conglomerate commented about relations with the company's board in these words: "All this talk about responsible members of boards of directors . . . is not reality! In our company, we must do whatever the board wants. If board members want to attend a tennis tournament in England or France, we must schedule a meeting convenient for such diversion. Talk about independent boards; I wonder where they are? My friends and I could keep you stunned at the stories we have personally experienced—all behind a facade of 'representing the shareholders.' "

As the persons responsible for the foregoing comments discussed their disappointment with what they had experienced in their organizations, they each were asked "Why is such behavior tolerated?" These were their responses:

- Executives know that there is no clearly organized, honorable way for subordinates to register a complaint about what is done. Furthermore, they know that there is acceptance among the higher ranked individuals that their behavior would be defended, if there was a challenge.
- Success is the goal . . . at any cost. Companies are rewarded when success is reported. The gullibility of the public—and even the business community—merely encourages the persistence of unethical behavior.
- Responsibility seems to be tied to power—power to make decisions "as I want to make them"; power to be above rules such as ethical standards which could be inhibiting.
- Awareness of the limited, negative consequences—if any—that would be forthcoming because of the general attitude of the relevance of ethical standards in the society.
- A general sense that rules of ethics are old-fashioned; we live in a permissive society; to pass judgment on another's decision or behavior is judgmental and not in vogue.

3.4 PREVAILING PROBLEMS PERCEIVED IN THE LATE 1970s

Sensitivity to ethical problems was heightened with the revelations that led to the passage of the Foreign Corrupt Practices Act in December 1977. The Act imposed on U.S. companies operating abroad the need to behave ethically and avoid the practice of bribing foreign public officials. Furthermore, the Act amended the Securities and Exchange Act of 1934 by adding the requirements for maintaining books, records, and accounts in sufficient detail to accurately and fairly reflect the transactions and dispositions of the resources of the entity. There is also the requirement to "devise and maintain a system of internal accounting controls" sufficient to provide reasonable assurances that transactions are executed in accordance with management's authorization, recorded so as to permit the preparation of financial statements in conformity with generally accepted accounting principles (GAAP) and to permit disbursement of assets in accordance with management's general or specific authorization. Additionally, the recorded assets should be compared with existing assets at reasonable intervals, with appropriate action taken when differences are found.

The revelations of widespread bribery in what had been perceived to be honorable, ethical American companies raised serious questions about the assumptions that had not been earlier challenged: (1) American companies operated in ethical fashion and (2) external auditors would uncover misrepresentations in financial reporting, including the use of company resources for bribery. The questions raised about the quality of external audits at the time led to the first Federal investigation of the accounting profession. That investigation raised serious questions about audit quality. While the initial report recommended that the government take on the responsibility of auditing publicly owned companies, that recommendation was eliminated and the Securities and Exchange Commission accepted a new monitoring program that began with a newly created Public Oversight Board, which began functioning in 1979.

So, the 1970s ended and the 1980s began with some awareness of ethical problems, but the visibility of problems seems not to have been quickly highlighted in the public consciousness. The developments relative to fraudulent financial reporting will be used as an illustration of what was happening.

(a) Momentum Leading to Commission on Fraudulent Financial Reporting

The attitudes toward financial reporting reflect an organization's ethical standards in a most realistic manner. A look at just a few observations will illustrate what was perceived to be the situation relative to this matter.

(i) Evidence of Cooking Books. In a presentation to the Institute for Corporate Counsel in Los Angeles, California, Treadway, a commissioner on the Securities and Exchange Commission, noted the increase in cases of *cooked books*. His assessment was based on a review of instances of misrepresentation of financial information:

> Recent cases of "cooked books" have been egregious and have involved major companies. By and large those who participated in the improper activities apparently believed that the manner in which they acted was in the best interests of the company. In some cases, it was an admitted feeling of "team effort." Granted, these activities may have led to bonuses, promotions, or good standing in the eyes of the company and the "team." But they have not involved direct, immediate, personal gain from theft, kickbacks, bribes, or diversion of assets.

(ii) Establishment of a Commission. In 1985, the National Commission on Fraudulent Financial Reporting was established. Five accounting associations joined in establishing the Commission in an acknowledgment that the problem of fraudulent reporting was pervasive.[9]

Barely a week goes by without some revelation of corporate infidelity. The insider-trading scams that have rocked Wall Street in the past 12 months are but the latest in a long legacy of schemes dating back to Ponzi's pyramids. Fraud damages the credibility of not only the company involved but also—as in the case

---

[9]*CFO* (April 1987), 38.

of the E.S.M. Government Securities scandal—the accounting firm that audited its books.

In an interview, Treadway was posed the following question: "You've said that the main determinant of fraud is corporate culture. How does a company's corporate culture get set, and how can it be changed if it is found wanting?"[10] He responded as follows:

> It gets set by the people at the top. That means they should view their job as managing the assets of others; they are accountable to the others and should take their accountability seriously. If the people in the lower management tiers look at the top to see the way they conduct themselves that's the best communication of all.
>
> But if your top managers are prone to cutting corners, rationalizing their behavior, or falling into some of those other traps, then no matter how many rules and regulations you have, the word gets out quickly that they wink at [fraudulent practices]. If management does not effectively demonstrate a commitment to proper practices—and if the guy in the fifth tier of the company doesn't believe what top management says—then it won't work. That's why we have recommended that all companies adopt, publicize, and enforce written codes of conduct. They should deal with things like perks and the use of company assets.[11]

(iii) A Professional Organization Establishes an Ethical Code.   In 1983, for the first time, the National Association of Accountants (NAA; later renamed the Institute of Management Accountants) issued Standards of Ethical Conduct for Management Accountants. The statements are considered philosophical and identify the major elements of professional conduct as *competence, confidentiality, integrity, and objectivity.* (See Appendix B.)

When past presidents were asked about the motivation—or perceived need—for a code of conduct, the responses were enlightening. One question raised was: "The NAA Standards of Ethical Conduct for Management Accountants were promulgated in 1983 after several years of effort. The Association started in 1919. Why did it take so long to codify the Standards that all of you have endorsed and complied with during your professional careers?" The responses were as follows:

Joe Brumit: Our Association started as a cost accountants' group and evolved over time to its present status. Our members grew up in a generation that accepted ethical standards as "granted."

Grant Meyers: Ethics always has been part of the character of the Association. In 1919, the founders established 12 standing committees, one of which was a Committee on Ethics. . . .

Ethics was understood and accepted. Therefore, the need for codification was not apparent. Drastic changes in the corporate environment over the past 15

---

[10]Id., 40.
[11]Id., 41.

years, caused by the intense pressure resulting from emphasis on earnings, corporate takeovers, "get-rich-quick" schemes, and a variety of questionable accounting practices made it apparent that there was a breakdown in the previously accepted principles and standards of the profession. The Association recognized that the management accountant needed support. An *ad hoc* committee was appointed in 1981, and its members determined quickly that the profession needed a *written* code of ethics.

Lee Ellis: For most of those years between 1919 and 1983, most of us thought that reducing ethical standards to writing was unnecessary. . . . Rules of ethical conduct, responsibility, and accountability—rules going beyond basic legal requirements—were handed down orally from generation to generation.

We saw the system serving us well, although over time, we had increasing concern about those who exploited the excesses of our system's virtues and violated the spirit, if not the letter, of the law. The violations served as the basis for many of the shouts and protests of the '60s, continued as we staggered through the '70s, and arrived at what we hope was the peak in the '80s—the "decade of greed.". . . Finally we came to recognize the need to codify ethical standards.

Bob Donachie: Your first question implies that NAA [now IMA] may have been delinquent in promulgating the standards of ethical conduct. I don't believe this is the case at all. The term *accounting* and the title *accountant* historically have carried a very strong implicit assurance of integrity, truth, and accuracy in the recording and disclosure of data. . . .

Charlie Smith: It seemed necessary to *finally* do something. The media were focusing on political corruption, illegal political contributions, foreign corrupt practices, payoffs, unethical business practices. . . . In prior years, many people wondered what good a code of ethics would do because everyone knew right from wrong anyway. They thought a code of ethics was strictly damage control and/or a public relations ploy.[12]

(iv) The Report of the Commission on Fraudulent Reporting. In October 1987, the Commission under Treadway's leadership issued its report. Without any qualifying terms, the Commission concluded that fraudulent financial reporting was a serious problem. Furthermore, the Commission identified the importance of the tone at the top and the responsibility of a company's leadership in the prevention and early detection of fraudulent financial reporting.

3.5 FRAUDULENT BEHAVIOR DISCLOSED

A number of highly publicized cases of fraudulent behavior have occurred during the period beginning with the mid-1980s. Only three cases will be described at this point.

---

[12]"Past Presidents on Ethics," *Management Accounting* (June 1990), 23–29.

(a) Dennis Levine: The Insider Strategist at Drexel Burnham

Levine began his business career as a management trainee at a salary of $19,000 a year (1977). By 1986, he was a managing director at a salary of more than $2 million. The introduction to the excerpt of his book which appeared in *New York* magazine noted:

> Dennis B. Levine was an emblematic man of the eighties. He plunged into the superheated corporate finances of the decade and fashioned a brilliant Wall Street career that brought him all the things that were supposed to matter—the right apartment, the right cars, the right business connections, and millions of dollars. At the same time, Drexel Burnham's M&A star was leading a secret, criminal life, piling up insider-trading profits in an offshore bank account. Then one morning, Levine's lavish and carefully constructed world fell apart.[13]

In his book, Levine acknowledged that "making money was my passion, and the $10.6 Million in my secret account represented points on the board." Levine found co-conspirators, who were also implicated later. Levine moved to Smith Barney and then was heavily courted by Drexel Burnham in 1984 and 1985. Only after he was promised a chance to meet Michael Milken did Levine express interest in the position. In his words, Levine described the introduction to the job:

> Several people [at Drexel's] preached that the offer of a high-level Drexel job was akin to stumbling upon a pot of gold. Quite apart from the salary and the annual bonus, they said, was the opportunity offered by the matrix of private investment partnerships that would be offered along the way. Within two or three years, I was told, "You will have personal investments worth at least $10 million."[14]

After serving a jail term, Levine was released. He wrote about his experiences, noting how his unethical strategies had begun. During his first year at Citibank, he met a colleague who shared a stock tip with him. This colleague had cracked the code that the bank was using for a company involved in a pending merger. His colleague told him that he had bought a position in the company through his mother's stock account. His colleague told him the procedures were easy and that everybody does it. In his book, Levine revealed his recollection of his response:

> Only in retrospect would I realize that something snapped at this very moment, something that caused me to cross the clear lines of morality delineated by my father and my late mother. Ethical behavior was a routine component of my youth.

---

[13]Dennis Levine, "The Insider," *New York* magazine (September 16, 1991), 36 (article excerpted from *Inside Out: An Insider's Account of Wall Street,* G. P. Putnam, 1991).
[14]Id., 44.

While I resisted the temptation for a while, somewhere between Queens and Wall Street I was losing track of those values. Throughout my college and graduate studies, I believe, I did not even hear the word *ethics*. In the big-business environment of the late seventies, morality was not an issue.[15]

When Levine reflected on why he had gone astray, he concluded:

Ambition eclipsed rationality. I was unable to find fulfillment in realistic limits. One deal was piled atop the next. The hours grew longer; the numbers grew bigger; the stakes grew more critical; the fire grew ever hotter. By the time I became a managing director of Drexel, I was out of control. So was Boesky; so was Milken; so was Drexel.[16]

The firm of Drexel Burnham had earned a profit of more than $500 million in 1986; four years later, on February 13, 1990, the company filed for bankruptcy.

(b) Joseph Jett, the Bond Trader at Kidder, Peabody

Kidder, Peabody & Co. ceased business in December 1994, and most of the firm's assets were sold to PaineWebber Group Inc. The demise of the company was attributed, according to a story in *The Wall Street Journal,* to "a double whammy: a costly bond-trading scandal last April [1994] that has focused on Joseph Jett, a onetime star bond trader, and eventually entangled Edward Cerullo, a former top Kidder executive; and the collapse of Kidder's risky strategy to dominate the market for mortgage-backed bonds. Kidder might have survived either crisis alone. But the combined effort was to focus intense scrutiny on the company at precisely the wrong moment."[17]

Kidder, Peabody & Co. had promised to implement a compliance system designed to help the firm detect complex trading crimes as a part of its 1987 settlement of civil insider-trading charges. The revelation in April 1994, therefore, that a 36-year-old managing director who had headed the government-bond trading desk since 1991 had beat the proclaimed compliance system was surprising. The allegation was that Jett had executed thousands of phony trades that resulted in inflating Kidder's income by $350 million for the year, all in an alleged bid to boost his performance-based bonus.

General Electric officials had undertaken to assure an effective compliance system. As *Time* reported, management experts think ethics should start at the top. That may have been what General Electric officials had in mind last week when they shook up the management at GE's Kidder Peabody investment division in the wake of

[15]Id., 42.
[16]Id., 49.
[17]*The Wall Street Journal* (December 29, 1994).

insider-trading charges against two former employees and a third employee who is now suspended. The chief executive of ten years was replaced by the former chairman of Illinois Tool Works, in a move that may be designed to inject a dose of heartland ethics into the Wall Street firm.[18]

Yet, a few years later, a relatively new trader, whose success was beyond reasonable expectations of top performers, seemed to have considerable freedom. The alleged ruse lasted over a year and was uncovered when there was an attempt to reconcile the government-strips trading. Jett maintained that his strips trades were made only to offset some other trades. As reported in *The Wall Street Journal:*

> The trading fiasco [Jett's] raises questions about the risks in the performance-based system Wall Street firms use to pay traders and others. In some way, paying such enormous sums of cash based on volume of business encourages abuses . . . .
>   Intense visibility is given to top achievers. Jett, received the chairman's award as star employee for 1993. Early in January 1994, Jett made a presentation to 130 Kidder senior executives at a meeting in Boca Raton, Florida. His remarks included these words: "This is war; you do anything to win. You make money at all costs."[19]

His basking in glory for having received a $9 million paycheck in 1993 was shortlived. In the tale as reported in *The Wall Street Journal,* there had been some inquiries about Jett's success. However, none of the inquiries led to a comprehensive review that would have provided an answer to how Jett was able to earn from $5 to $10 million per month when previous highest earnings had been only $20 million for a full year.[20]

(c) Nicholas W. Leeson, the Young Man with Two Hats at Barings

Leeson, the young trader responsible for $1.36 billion of losses at Barings, noted that in a single day he could make or lose more than $50 million and that he was astonished that his superiors in London continued to provide funds. Ultimately, the 233-year-old bank was sending him huge sums of money, as he requested.
   Leeson began with back office responsibilities and then added trading activities to his daily work. With virtually no controls in effect, Leeson was able to lose $1.3 billion trading derivatives that were, in effect, bets on the direction that Japanese stock prices would move. The losses led to the collapse of the 233-year old bank. In the report of Britain's central bank to Parliament, the spectacular collapse was attributed to "total collapse of management control." The report concluded that "if Barings had had an effective system of management, financial and

---

[18]"Having It All and Throwing It Away," *Time* (May 25, 1987), 23.
[19]*The Wall Street Journal* (April 6, 1997).
[20]Id.

operating controls such a massive unauthorized position could not have been established."[21] Leeson reported that he was stunned at how readily the home office provided him with the large sums of money he needed to maintain his positions in trades.

3.6 IMPLICATIONS OF CASES FOR ETHICAL STANDARDS

Many levels of analysis could be derived from the three cases briefly discussed and from other cases that have been reported in the business press. At the macro level, these three cases illustrate the priorities of business.

(a) Exceptional Success Is Not Suspect

Companies strive to be successful. The individuals who can outshine others— even at rates that seem out-of-line (in hindsight)—are given considerable latitude to take matters in their own hands. Internal controls are too weak to impose barriers to star performers. So, as was the case, questions about Jett were not fully investigated; Levine's success at earlier companies was not challenged; Leeson's double responsibilities were not undermined by headquarters.

(b) An Ethical Brake Was Not Functioning

Apparently, no one in authority to follow through challenged the basic behavior of these individuals. For example, even the impassioned words of Jett at the Florida meeting seemed not to have raised some question about whether this young man could be adhering to the rules of trading. Leeson seemed to have to provide no explanation for the large sums of money he asked to be transferred to the Singapore office.

(c) Internal Controls Were in Name Only

All of these companies were in financial services, where internal controls are perceived to be critical. Yet, in all three instances there was no power either to the controls themselves or to implementation. There was no will to meet the control requirements. For example, even though GE's Kidder Peabody was reportedly reorganized in 1987, as a part of civil insider-trader charges, there was not adequate follow-up to assure proper accounting for complex transactions. While there were superiors to whom the executives reported, there appears to have been no substantive monitoring of what was happening. To what extent was the realization that there was no actual oversight a factor in the reckless strategies put into play?

[21]"Barings Managers Share Blame for Collapse, Britain Says," *The New York Times* (July 19, 1995), D2.

3.7 THE CONTEMPORARY CHALLENGE

What is the economic cost for flagrant failure to strive to maintain an ethical environment? In extreme cases, there is the end of entities—as happened to Kidder Peabody, Drexel Burnham, and Barings. There have been other companies where corruption was identified as a factor in their demise.

Of course, many organizations have been able to survive in the presence of considerable fraudulent actions. No clear evidence exists of the relationship of ethical behavior and profitability, especially in the short-run. Ethical behavior does not assure success; unethical behavior does not predict the end of the entity. However, there is a general sense among astute observers that some level of adherence to ethical standards does have long-term value. Adhering to ethical standards introduces a degree of stability that is missing in a corrupt environment where the ability to predict becomes virtually impossible.

Has the level of tolerance for unethical behavior been reached? Have the consequences of failure to adhere to ethical standards been sufficient to encourage companies to earnestly strive to not only build an ethical environment but also monitor that environment to assure compliance? Assuring compliance includes full understanding that human beings err in judgments not only in relation to the technical aspects of their work but in ethical matters, too. An appropriate ethical environment is one where there are no barriers to behaving ethically. At the same time, mistakes are understood; the improvability of human behavior is assumed.

Rushworth Kidder, the president of the Institute of Global Ethics, was asked in an interview what he considered the central ethical issue of our time. He stated:

> The continuity of the human race. I am concerned that we may not survive the twenty-first century with the ethics of the twentieth century. I say this because of the way that technology today enables us to leverage individual decisions in such a way that the consequences can be disastrous. Chernobyl, Exxon Valdez, the Barings Bank collapse, and the recent scandals in the copper market all point in this direction and this leaves out the horrific consequences that would arise if ever nuclear weapons were used in anger, or by mistake. In all these cases, a small group of individuals, or in some cases one person, have the power to make some profoundly unethical decisions which are not corrected before they result in far reaching consequences for large numbers, sometimes very large numbers of people.[22]

---

[22] "Ethics for the New Millenium," *Leadership and Organization Development Journal* (February–March 1997, Vol. 18, n2), 145.

Chapter 4

Regulatory Demands

All organizations, as well as individuals, in the United States are responsible for adhering to a wide range of laws and regulations. Businesses, regardless of their products and services, must establish policies and procedures to assure that relevant laws and regulations are indeed reflected in decisions and actions.

Increasingly, organization leaders have perceived that it is good business to comply with laws and regulations. Compliance officers, internal audit staff, legal counsel, and other personnel participate in the task of understanding the rules and monitoring the extent of adherence. Yet, assurance of compliance is enhanced with an independent assessment. Here is where the public accountant can make a notable contribution to the well-being of the entity as well as to the society.

Throughout the history of the United States, there has been a question about the balance between personal freedom and the public good. Does the average U.S. citizen have the ability to do whatever he or she wishes? Not really. One has to pay taxes and if caught for committing a crime, then one will have to pay the penalty. What if what one does does not harm anyone else? One could list a multitude of "victimless" crimes, including the use of illegal drugs and gambling.

The point is that our government has evolved from striving to save us from harming one another to saving us from ourselves; for example, you must wear seat belts. Irrespective of one's personal perspective of drinking, the law in the 1930s against drinking (Prohibition) was a glaring example of the government's attempt to legislate the personal rights of citizens. What this shows is that for laws to be obeyed, they must be laws that the public will accept and comply with—*from an ethical perspective.*

The intersection of the legal/government role and one's own personal ethics is a difficult one. While it may generally be considered ethical to pay one's taxes (versus cheating on taxes) and to obey laws, it is difficult to make absolutes, such as that one must obey his or her government's laws in order to be considered ethical.

What is the role of government and ethical conduct?

A firm manufacturing a well-known mouthwash was accused of using a cheap form of alcohol possibly deleterious to health. The company's chief executive, after testifying in Washington, made his comment privately: "We broke no law. We're in a highly competitive industry. If we're going to stay in business, we have to look for profit wherever the law permits. We don't make the laws. We obey them. Then why do we have to put up with this 'holier than thou' talk about ethics? It's sheer hypocrisy. We're not in business to promote ethics. Look at the cigarette companies, for God's sake! If the ethics aren't embodied in the laws by the men who made them, you can't expect businessmen to fill the lack. Why, a sudden submission to Christian ethics by businessmen would bring about the greatest economic upheaval in history!"[1]

Irrespective of the private views of some businesspersons, our point here is to show the CPA and the government's role in the development of business ethics. There has been an evolution in this process. There is a speculation that in an ethical environment there is less need for laws and law enforcement. For example, if businesses had enough principles not to market harmful products, would there be a need for the Consumer Product Safety Commission? Or if businesses cared enough about their employees and environment, would the Occupational Safety Health Administration (OSHA) and Environmental Protection Agency (EPA) be necessary?

The failure of passing laws and trying to enforce them (as, for example, with Prohibition) has evolved to encouraging self-regulation with professionals such as CPAs and lawyers monitoring themselves. Another example of the evolution towards self-regulation is the carrot (vs. stick) approach of the Federal Sentencing Guidelines, whereby self-reporting of offenses reduces the penalty a corporation will receive.

A CPA is required to follow standards. Consider what standards a CPA may be obligated to follow or verify in a typical financial audit.

* Financial Accounting Standards Board (FASB) Statements
* Statement on Auditing Standards (SAS)
* Securities and Exchange Commission (SEC) regulations
* Internal Revenue Service (IRS) regulations
* State Tax regulations
* State Board of Accountancy Rules
* American Institute of Certified Public Accountants (AICPA) Professional Ethics Code of Conduct
* State Society Professional Ethics Standards

Currently, the CPA is most noted for performing the attest function in the area of financial statements. The CPA needs to examine compliance in other areas besides the financial. While training may be necessary in some of these areas, we have shown in previous chapters that the CPA has the skills to perform other types of compliance audits. Depending on a CPA's scope, in an ethics audit the CPA could provide assurance that a company is in compliance in such areas as the following:

[1]Albert Z. Carr, "Is Business Bluffing Ethical," In *Essentials of Business Ethics,* edited by Peter Madsen and Jay Shafritz (New York: Meridan, 1990).

- Equal Employment Opportunity Commission (EEOC)
- Minimum wage standards
- Workplace Safety
- Environmental Quality
- Labor Relations
- Occupational Safety and Health

The question is that with government relinquishing oversight power (as demonstrated by the Federal Sentencing Guidelines—companies encouraged to monitor themselves), will this enhance the responsibility of the CPA for monitoring and providing assurance services?

The discussion of this chapter takes a national perspective and focuses on federal regulations as a basis for illustrating what is happening with respect to the regulatory environment of businesses and the ramifications for CPAs. Some of the key regulations will be briefly described.

4.1 PERCEPTIONS OF REGULATORY BURDEN

Most federal regulations begin with an act of Congress. Therefore, the members of Congress are sensitive to the impact of such regulations on the society. Because of the interest in encouraging economic growth, the lawmakers in the United States are reluctant to impose new laws that impede progress. At the same time, lawmakers have a public trust responsibility that requires astute assessment of benefit of laws and regulations under consideration. The task of maintaining an optimum balance between extent of regulation and freedom to function with self-regulation is a critical responsibility that publicly elected members of Congress assume.

The public accountant who chooses to provide professional services related to compliance has a challenging engagement. The challenge is illustrated, for example, by some of the conclusions of a General Accounting Office (GAO) study on regulatory burden which was issued in November 1996.[2] The study was done in response to a request from several persons in Congress who wanted information on the impact of federal regulations on business. The GAO was asked to describe (1) what selected businesses and federal agencies believed were the federal regulations that applied to those businesses, (2) what those businesses believed was the impact—cost and other—of those regulations, and (3) the regulations those businesses said were most problematic to them and relevant federal agencies' responses to those concerns.

The investigators encountered difficulty in undertaking the study and were unable, in the final report, to provide any generalizations. Most of the companies

---

[2]United States General Accounting Office, "Regulatory Burden: Measurement Challenges and Concerns Raised by Selected Companies—Report to Congressional Requesters (U.S. General Accounting Office, November 1996).

contacted declined to participate. In the end, there were 15 companies that did participate, of which 10 did so with the agreement that their names would not be made public. Initially, 15 promised to provide a list of applicable federal regulations. In the end, however, none of the businesses provided a complete listing. Furthermore, none could provide comprehensive data on the incremental costs of regulations.

The investigators found that federal regulatory agencies themselves had difficulty determining the applicability of their regulations to particular companies without a detailed knowledge of the companies' situation and affairs. Some agencies noted that sufficient information was available to the public so that businesses themselves could determine their regulatory responsibilities.

Company concerns about regulatory issues were grouped under 10 themes, which were as follows:

1. Costly compliance and cost-benefit issues
2. Effect of compliance costs on competitiveness
3. Unreasonable regulations
4 Lack of understanding of regulatory requirements
5. Rigid and inflexible regulations
6. Paperwork and process issues
7. Severe penalties imposed on business
8. Regulators' "gotcha" enforcement approach
9. Regulators' lack of knowledge and assistance
10. Regulatory coordination and duplication

The report on regulatory burden ends with no recommendations. The agencies also indicated that they make extensive amounts of information available to the public, so the businesses themselves could determine their regulatory responsibilities. However, these sources of information often appear to be fragmented both within and across agencies. As a result, a business attempting to determine its regulatory responsibilities may find it necessary to contact multiple agencies, and sometimes multiple offices within particular agencies, to collect the information it needs. In some cases, responsibility for an issue may be spread between two or more agencies, making it difficult for companies to determine which agency or agencies should be called regarding that issue. The increasing complexity of the federal regulatory environment makes effective communication between regulatory agencies and the community even more important, and some agencies are taking steps in that direction.

The difficulties businesses and agencies experienced in developing applicable regulations also suggest two other conclusions—one is an issue of compliance and the other is a research concern. First, a business that finds it difficult to list its regulatory compliance responsibilities may not be fully aware of those responsibilities. As a result, the business runs a risk of being out of compliance with regulations that it did not know were applicable. Second, the development of a list of a company's compliance responsibilities is the first step in determining the impact of all regulations on that company. If the list of regulations applicable to a company is incomplete, any assessment of the impact of regulations on that company will be equally incomplete. The difficulties businesses and agencies described in developing company-specific lists of regulatory compliance responsibilities suggest that the development of information on the costs and benefits of regulations to those companies will be at least as difficult.

4.2 OPPORTUNITY FOR THE CERTIFIED PUBLIC ACCOUNTANT

Compliance with rules and regulations is a basic ethical responsibility in the United States. As noted in the GAO study, for example, companies face many problems in meeting their obligations. It appears that, at times, companies are not fully aware of what their obligations are.

Public accountants who develop expertise in relation to regulations can provide wise counsel to clients. Possibly, one of the most valuable public service contributions public accountants can make in relation to regulations is to interact with agencies in providing the real life situations that will help refine rules and regulations so that their meaning is clear and implementation will not require extensive attention to interpretation. The range of conditions and environments in which federal regulations are relevant should impose on an agency the need to be sure of the relevance of what is being required to a varied population of businesses.

4.3 SELECTED LAWS AND REGULATIONS THAT ILLUSTRATE RANGE OF COMPLIANCE EXPECTED IN THE UNITED STATES

External public accountants were clearly identified as participating in determining whether an audit client had been involved in illegal acts with the passage of SAS No. 17 in 1977. That statement was superseded by SAS No. 54 in 1989. The essence of responsibility is noted in the statement: "It is the auditor's responsibility to detect and report misstatements resulting from illegal acts having a direct and material effect on the financial statements."

Illegal acts may relate to any one or more of a wide range of regulatory requirements. The standard even notes "Whether an act is, in fact, illegal is a determination that is normally beyond the auditor's professional competence. . . . The determination as to whether a particular act is illegal would generally be based on the advice of an informed expert qualified to practice law or may have to await final determination by a court of law."[3] This range of violations refers to violations of state, local, or federal laws or other governmental regulations including relevant acts as OSHA violations, EPA violations, EEOC violations, or insider trading.

---

[3] Statement on Auditing Standards 54, par 317.03.

"It is the auditor's responsibility to detect and report misstatements resulting from illegal acts having a direct and material effect on the financial statements."[4]

Statement on Auditing Standards 54 indicates that the following may cause the auditor to raise a question regarding illegal acts:

- Payments for unspecified services
- Excessive sales commissions
- Not filing tax returns
- Large cash payments
- Unexplained payments to officials

The standard then continues by suggesting some procedures for following up potential illegal acts, such as performing additional procedures, consulting counsel, reviewing supporting documentation, and determining if a transaction has been authorized. All of the various federal and state agencies have authority to step in and take action when someone has violated the rules they promulgated. Perhaps the most notable—the ones that make the most headlines—are the SEC, the Federal Trade Commission (FTC), the Food and Drug Administration (FDA), and the EPA. However, most of the agencies have limited staff and limited resources. Thus, unless the violation is egregious and material, the agency will probably not get involved.

It is interesting to note that most actions taken by regulatory authorities would never have gotten started if there had not been a lapse in ethical conduct. A stock scam, a boiler room operation run illegally, illegal price fixing, tampering with the results of experimental drug tests, or dumping effluents which poison the well water are all examples of improper ethical conduct. Regulatory authorities usually pursue these cases, first to stop the illegal conduct, but also to serve as an example to others. Unfortunately, some cannot see or do not want to stay on the right path.

The Wall Street Journal described how a dozen people were indicted by a federal grand jury in Miami for allegedly taking part in a $15 million Medicare-fraud scheme. The federal government is taking increasingly aggressive action to try to curb various forms of medicare fraud involving the federal healthcare programs for the elderly.[5]

Texaco Inc. reacted very promptly to the scandal in 1996 resulting from racially biased comments. To put teeth into its plan, Texaco signed an agreement with the EEOC which requires Texaco to report on its progress annually for the next five years. In addition, Texaco amended its bonus plan for top management so that 20 percent of the annual cash bonuses will be linked to increasing work-

---

[4]Id.
[5]*The Wall Street Journal* (August 8, 1997).

place diversity. Other companies, such as General Mills, Polaroid, and Allstate Insurance, have also instituted incentive compensation for managers who meet diversity goals. Texaco agreed to have an independent "Equality and Fairness Task Force" review all human resource programs and policies, evaluate and provide recommendations to improve existing or newly added programs, and monitor progress in achieving their diversity goals. In addition, Texaco also implemented a mentoring program, an ombudsperson program, and a new alternative-dispute-resolution program to resolve all issues quickly. This is also backed up by the public statement of the chairman, who stated that there will be no tolerance of intolerance at the company.

Texaco is not an isolated case. Look at a sampling for 1996, which includes Bankers Trust Company and its derivatives group. The New York law firm of Cadwalader, Wickersham and Taft released a report that sharply criticized the bank for lax internal control. Mitsubishi Motor Manufacturing of America Ltd. brought in former Labor Secretary Lynn M. Martin to examine its workplace policies. Astra, a Swedish drug maker, commissioned a probe of the firm by a New York law firm because of a sexual harassment scandal that resulted in the firing of Chief Executive Lars Bildman.

Business Week reported the story of Orange & Rockland Utilities in Pearl River, New York. The ethics overhaul cost them some $7 million. However, President Larry S. Brodsky stated that the investment had paid off. The article also quoted Winthrop M. Swenson, a former deputy general counsel at the U.S. Sentencing Commission, who later joined KPMG Peat Marwick. He stated, "They'll do enough training to say that they do training, but they wouldn't really analyze their training techniques to see if they are reaching people. They'll have a hot line, but there's no effect to assure people that there wouldn't be retaliation." Other critics contend that many companies are simply looking for window dressing.[6] These kinds of stories do not help CPA firms provide the public with ethical programs.

In *The Wall Street Journal,* the headline screamed, "The Ethical Mess of the FDA." It made the point that political considerations sometimes overruled considerations of public health.[7] Political pressure should not be allowed to set corporate cultures. Rationalizing away ethical values does not make good business sense. Providing ethical programs does make good business sense. Regulation sometimes walks a very thin line deciding between individual needs and the overall public good.

There are many reasons to begin or improve an ethics program from the perspective of deterring illegal acts. The publicity surrounding sexual harassment cases is an example of why more and more businesses are turning to preventative measures. It is natural for CPA firms to market corporate codes of conduct to their clients. The selling may be easier because the corporation wants to avoid litigation

[6]*Business Week* (July 15, 1996).
[7]"The Ethical Mess of the FDA," *The Wall Street Journal* (January 16, 1997).

or wants to minimize the damage resulting from litigation. Independent ethics audits are needed services that CPAs have the ability and skill to provide.

Environmental liabilities pose another problem in ethical behavior. Demands have increased for corporate account liability for toxic wastes and the EPA has increased its oversight. For instance, a firm may have used a licensed waste hauler and complied with all disposal requirements. However, the EPA can investigate abandoned waste sites. Under federal law, the liability for cleanup costs can be significant and who can be held responsible can be ambiguous.

Ethical reasoning does not help from the perspective of accounting for contingent and unasserted environmental claims. The AICPA has issued Standard Operating Procedure (SOP) 96-01 on Environmental Remediation Liabilities. It does give some guidance in FASB 5, "Accounting for Contingencies," but it offers no help with the moral dilemma. Management may have believed it did everything it was supposed to under the law, but now finds itself with potentially significant liabilities. While life may not always seem fair, it still pays to do what is morally right.

Frequently, government tends to react to a crisis by setting up a set of rules which supposedly corrects the abuses. Businesses react the same way. Thus, when ethical lapses become material, a Code of Ethics or a Code of Conduct is established by the entity. Unfortunately, the implementation of the program and the continuous monitoring is not given much thought. The actions do not always follow the words.

4.4 SEC OVERSIGHT RESPONSIBILITIES

A basic ethical premise is that citizens abide by the rules made by society. For CPAs in public practice, one of the most important regulatory agencies is the SEC. Violations of SEC regulations can cause a CPA to be brought before an administrative hearing.

The SEC is an independent regulatory agency that administers the securities laws of the United States. The SEC was established by the Securities Exchange Act of 1934. There are five commissioners that sit on the SEC, with one designated as Chairman by the President of the United States. The terms of the commissioners are staggered over a five-year period with one expiring in June every year. No more than three commissioners may be of the same political party.

The SEC has both investigative and regulatory responsibilities. The SEC is currently organized under several divisions. Division of Corporation Finance has responsibility for ensuring that disclosure requirements are met by publicly held corporations registered with the SEC.

The Division of Investment Management basically administers three statutes: the Public Utility Holding Company Act of 1935, Investment Company Act of 1940, and the Investment Advisers Act of 1940. The responsibility includes monitoring of sales and advertising practices of investment advisors, including examining new products.

The Division of Market Regulation has responsibility for registering broker-age firms, monitoring the securities markets, and for overseeing the securities self-regulatory organizations, such as the stock exchanges. The Office of Compli-ance Inspections and Examinations conducts compliance inspection programs of self-regulatory organizations, investment advisors, brokers, and dealers. The objective of the office is to protect the investors. The Division of Enforcement is responsible for enforcing federal securities laws. This division investigates viola-tions of the securities laws.

Clearly, the SEC is organized to protect the public interest. As such, it has even described the qualifications for accountants to be recognized by the SEC. Such qualifications include being a CPA who is registered and in good standing under the laws of the state of his or her business office or residence. The CPA must be independent of the organization he or she is performing the services for.

From the perspective of the accountant's report, the report is to include the following:

- The date
- Signature of the accountant
- City and state where issued
- The financial statements covered by the accountant's report
- Whether the audit was made in accordance with generally accepted auditing standards (GAAS)
- Any auditing procedures deemed necessary by the accountant which have been omitted and an explanation for their omission
- The opinion of the accountant

From the origin of the SEC, the auditor was held accountable for his or her work. The SEC Act of 1933 (Section 11a) provided that ". . . any part of the reg-istration statement . . . [that] contained an untrue statement of a material fact or omitted to state a material fact required to be stated therein . . . to make the state-ments therein not misleading, any person acquiring such security . . . may . . . sue . . . every accountant . . . who has with his consent been named as having prepared or certified any report or valuation which is used in connection with the registra-tion statement. . . ."

While section (a) holds the CPA liable for any misleading statements, section (b) provides exemption from liability upon proof of issues. One part of section (b) states regarding the accountant (among others associated with the registration statement) that the accountant will not be held liable if "he had, after reasonable investigation, reasonable ground to believe and did believe, at the time such part of the registration statement became effective, that the statements therein were true and that there is no omission to state a material fact required to be stated therein or necessary to make the statements therein not misleading. . . ."

The burden of proof is on the accountant and Section 11 (b) provides that the accountant can establish his or her due diligence defense. While civil liability in general has motivated the actions of the accountant, it should be remembered that criminal liability in extreme cases (Equity Funding, Continental Vending, National Student Marketing) can be sought.

While criminal penalties are infrequent, the SEC has other penalties that it may impose. The SEC may as per Rule 2 (e) indicates: ". . . deny, temporarily or permanently, the privilege of appearing or practicing before it in any way to any person who is found . . . to be lacking in character or integrity or to have engaged in unethical or improper professional conduct, or . . . to have willfully violated or willfully aided and abetted the violation of any provision of the federal securities laws. . . ."

The SEC is aggressively trying to provide the investor with full disclosure not only from just the accountant's perspective, but also from the director's. A report on the disclosure violations by W.R. Grace & Co. highlighted the officers' responsibility to go beyond merely adopting corporate procedures.

Specifically, the SEC determined that W.R. Grace made inadequate disclosure of retirement benefits paid to a former CEO, Peter Grace. It also found that there was a lack of disclosure on the sale of properties to Mr. Grace's son. While the directors had provisions for collecting this type of information, the SEC concluded that certain directors knew of the transactions and yet no steps were taken to disclose these issues.

While the SEC has its own sanctions and provides for civil penalties for accountants, it should be remembered that CPAs are licensed by the *state,* and as such for violations of accounting standards or serious departures from the code of conduct CPAs can be suspended by the state or are subject to revocation of their license by the state board of accountancy.

4.5 FOREIGN CORRUPT PRACTICES ACT

In 1977, the United States enacted the Foreign Corrupt Practices Act. Alleged payments by U.S. corporations to foreign officials in order to secure contacts in the mid-1970s was the motivation for the Act. While most governments had some type of provision against governmental officials taking bribes, the Foreign Corrupt Practices Act (FCPA) made it illegal to *give* a bribe.

The Act made it illegal to offer a payment in order to obtain or retain business to such entities as a foreign official, foreign political party, or candidate for office. The Act applies to all types of organizations—not only corporations, but also to partnerships, associations, unions, governments, and nonprofit organizations. It should be noted that an individual did not have to give a bribe; the mere offering of one was sufficient to be in violation of the Act. Bribes can also be in the form of retaining services at inflated prices.

The FCPA has guided our business entities, but there are many who contend that we are handcuffing our own businesses in competing with foreign firms.

International trade wars erupt periodically. The efforts of the United Nations General Assembly and the International Monetary Fund at the World Bank to eliminate these problems seem to be gaining momentum. Various countries are also working on legislation to bar the tax deductibility of bribes.

Penalties for violation of the Act can be as high as $2 million for organizations and up to $100,000 plus up to five years imprisonment for individuals.

From the CPA's perspective, an accounting requirement was added to the act which required organizations to devise and maintain internal controls, record transactions as necessary, and permit access to assets only with management's authorization.

It has to be emphasized again how unique it is to have a regulation to not *offer* bribes and requiring companies to maintain sufficient record keeping. From the legislative perspective, the FCPA raised the standard of ethical practices for U.S. companies and organizations.

What has been the impact of the Act? This is difficult to respond to since it is impossible to know if U.S. corporations have lost business to other international competitors or if there has been some way the Act has been circumvented. It should be noted that companies have been penalized due to maintaining insufficient records under the accounting provisions of the Act.

4.6 FEDERAL SENTENCING GUIDELINES

The Federal Sentencing Guidelines were enacted because of injustices that had been noted within the criminal justice system. For example, it was noted that for the same violation of law a person might receive a harsher penalty in the south than a person in the north. The guidelines were created in order to bring more uniformity into the sentencing process from a national perspective. Subsequent to developing guidelines for criminals violating federal laws, the U.S. Sentencing Commission enacted corporate sentencing guidelines as of November 1, 1991.

Clearly, since corporations cannot be incarcerated, the penalties that the judge may impose on a corporation found guilty can include restitution, remedial orders, fines, and probation.

The court strives to have the organization remedy any harm caused by the offense. If the court deems that the guilty party is a criminal purpose organization, the court may divest the organization of its assets.

Upon hearing a guilty verdict, the steps a judge would take in determining a penalty would include the following:

- Determining a base fine
- Establishing the organization's culpability score
- Implementing the multipliers corresponding to the culpability score
- Imposing the fine

Clearly, the fines are based upon the seriousness of the offense and the culpability of the organization. Culpability is determined by the actions taken by the company prior to the offense (e.g., is a compliance program in place?), the level of involvement by senior management, and the company's response after the offense is committed (e.g., was the violation self-reported?).

From an ethical perspective, the progressive aspect of the Federal Sentencing Guidelines is that the severity of a company's penalty is up to the company itself. Two vice presidents in identical companies could perpetrate similar offenses, such as insider trading, but the companies may under the Federal Sentencing Guidelines receive different fines based on aggravating or mitigating factors. The culpability of the organization and response to the violation are also determining factors.

As indicated earlier, one of the steps is determining the culpability score of a company. The culpability score is an attempt to establish an organization's responsibility for the crime. Culpability scores are calculated by establishing aggravating factors and mitigating factors.

Aggravating factors increase the crime and include the following:

- Obstruction of justice
- Previous criminal history
- Involvement of criminal activity
- Violation of judicial order

Obstruction of justice could include such items as impeding an investigation or stalling in turning over requested evidence. Regarding previous criminal history, the court would look at what has been the track record of this organization—what pattern has the company established for itself; have there been previous violations of a similar nature? Involvement of criminal activity points toward establishing if the company was developed for illegal gains (i.e., was an organized crime effort the motive for creating the company?). Violation of judicial order means that the organization will be found more culpable if prior to the act the organization was under some judicial order.

Mitigating factors reduce the fine and include the following:

- Self-reporting
- Cooperation
- Acceptance of responsibility
- Implementation and maintenance of an effective program to prevent and detect violations of law

Regarding the last mitigating factor (frequently referred to as a compliance program), the *United States Sentencing Guidelines Manual* states "The hallmark of an effective program to prevent and detect violations of law is that the organization exercised due diligence in seeking to prevent and detect criminal conduct by its employees and other agents."[8]

The U.S. Sentencing Commission indicates that a compliance program would include elements such as the following:

- The organization develops, updates, and maintains compliance standards and procedures.
- Employees known to have a criminal background are not given substantial discretionary authority.
- Organization makes a good faith effort to comply with the standards and enforces them consistently.
- Procedures, policies, and rules are communicated to all employees via publications or training courses.
- A high-level individual is responsible for oversight of the compliance program.
- Upon detecting an offense, the organization must take steps to prevent similar offenses from re-occurring.

In order to be eligible to receive a reduced penalty for having a compliance program, the program had to be operating before the violation occurred. Elements that a court might look towards to determine that a program exists might include the following:

- Code of ethics
- Fraud policy
- Hotlines
- Training programs
- Monitoring of program by internal audit
- Screening of employees, phoning references or making background checks when necessary
- Uniform disciplinary measures (does the compliance program have teeth?)

How important is having a compliance program? Larry Ponemon, CPA, CMA, stated, "None of the 86 companies convicted in 1994 of federal crimes was judged to have effective programs in place. . . . The U.S. Sentencing Commission estimates that eventually there will be more than 400 organizations per year that are found guilty of federal crimes. Last year's fines averaged $419,028, and restitution averaged $353,999."[9] While the benefit of having a program is a reduced

---

[8]*United States Sentencing Guidelines Manual*, 362.
[9]Larry Ponemon, CMA, "Ethics," *Management Accounting* (December 1995).

fine for some potential future violation, a compliance program can have other beneficial effects on companies, such as the following:

- Enhancing the ethical level of all employees
- Strengthening the internal controls of organizations
- Deterring potential violations (the mere presence of the compliance program may act as a deterrent)

Clearly, the U.S. Sentencing Commission is using a "carrot and stick" approach to having corporations self-police themselves—the carrot being a reduced penalty for an organization having a compliance program, self-reporting violations, and accepting responsibility; the stick being an increased penalty for organizations not having a compliance program, obstructing justice, and violating judicial orders.

The Federal Sentencing Guidelines represent an evolution in governing from a couple of perspectives. First, the government is clearly requiring the corporations to monitor their own employees' actions. Secondly, whereas before the Guidelines, penalties for violations were the same, regardless of the circumstances, now the circumstances are clearly taken into consideration.

A clear illustration of this is the FCPA. In the late 1970s or early 1980s if there was an illegal payment, the company received a fine—regardless of whether or not that company was culpable. Now if the company had a compliance program it could receive a reduced sentence or if the company obstructed justice, then it could receive a higher sentence.

4.7   REPRESENTATIVE REGULATORY AGENCY REQUIREMENTS

The focus on this section is to provide representative regulatory agency requirements and suggested methods of how CPAs may review these areas in an ethics audit. Regulatory agencies selected include one that strives to promote ethical business practices including such areas as safety of employees, proving equal opportunity, prevention of sexual harassment, and promoting fair trading and marketing practices.

(a)   Occupational Safety and Health Administration

Originally, OSHA was an agency within the Labor Department and was created in 1970. Created in order to reduce the number of deaths and injuries that can occur in companies and business places, OSHA can require employers to keep records on injuries by workers and perform inspections of work areas.

Other representative responsibilities include the following:

- Reducing hazards in the workplace
- Developing and enforcing health and job safety standards

- Monitoring federal safety programs
- Assisting small businesses to meet OSHA standards

Each business covered by OSHA is subject to inspection by OSHA safety and health compliance inspectors. Business management and owners can apply to OSHA for a variance from a standard or regulation. Usually, this means that they can show that their means or methods are at least as effective as OSHA in providing employee protection.

This is not to say that a CPA has the skills of an OSHA inspector. Ethically, however, a company or organization should provide a safe and healthy workplace. In an ethics audit, representative steps that could be reviewed by the CPA could include the following questions:

- Has management considered compliance under OSHA requirements?
- Have OSHA records been maintained?
- Has the staff been trained by OSHA, state, or other safety officials?
- Has the company had any OSHA citations?
- When was the last OSHA inspection and have any comments by inspectors been addressed?
- Do policies and procedures support a safe working environment?

So prevalent are questions about OSHA that Deloitte and Touche included representative questions that might be posed to the board in their booklet *Questions at Stockholders' Meetings 1998:* "What has the company done to promote workplace safety and accident prevention? Were there any serious injuries to employees or others during the year? Have there been any fines or penalties imposed by the Occupational Safety and Health Administration (OSHA)?"

(b) Equal Employment Opportunity Commission

Certainly one ethical trait is fairness. Every employee wants to be treated fairly and have an opportunity for advancement. The EEOC was established in 1965 subsequent to noticing unfair discrimination by employers. The thrust of the legislation was to provide equal employment to all candidates, ruling out discrimination practices by employers based on race, national origin, religion, or sex.

Representative responsibilities include the following:

- Coordinating federal equal employment efforts
- Addressing discrimination against disabled individuals within the federal government
- Enforcing laws prohibiting discrimination based on race, national origin, religion, or sex
- Enforcing laws to protect against pay discrimination based on sex

While the CPA is not an EEOC compliance official, the CPA can determine if there has been compliance with regulations and policies and make certain observations to answer questions, such as the following:

- Does the company have an EEOC policy?
- Have there been any EEOC investigations?
- Are there any outstanding lawsuits against the company?
- In a review of payroll records, does there appear to be any discrimination based on sex, age, or national origin?
- In review of payroll, does there appear to be any notice of age discrimination (unusually high termination of workers between 40 and 70 in violation of the Age Discrimination in Employment Act of 1967)?
- In interviewing employees, does there appear to be any violations of EEOC regulations?

Pivotal in the realization of sexual harassment in this country was the Navy's "Tailhook" problem and the Clarence Thomas/Anita Hill hearings. When the country faces such problems that are widely publicized, it behooves companies to ask "Why couldn't this be a problem at our organization?" Clearly, the CPA should be proactive by addressing such issues with his or her clients.

Sexual harassment is a problem in business. Generally, sexual harassment falls into two categories. The first is tangible job benefit or "quid pro quo" harassment. In the second category, an employee's career path is impacted by a manager's request for sexual favors and it is understood that denial of such requests would unfavorably affect the employee's career.

Another form of sexual harassment is a hostile work environment. In order to show that an environment was hostile, an individual would have to show elements of the following: that he or she belonged to a protected group, he or she was subjected to unwelcomed sexual harassment, and the harassment complained of affected the conditions or privileges of his or her employment. It should be recognized that hostile work environment harassment from a legal perspective is actionable even if there has not been an economic impact on an employee's position. Representative of this is that the federal court has held an employer liable because of existing female "pin-ups" in an office about which newly hired women complained.

With respect to sexual harassment, the CPA may determine the following:

- Is there a policy addressing the issue of sexual harassment?
- Is staff aware of the policy (i.e., policy is posted or is in the employee manual)?
- Has anyone kept track of the number and types of sexual harassment (or complaints) in the past year(s)?

- Are there preventative and post-loss strategies on how to handle these issues?
- Is there a means of communicating problems of sexual harassment (grievance procedure)?
- If a sexual harassment problem is noted, does management and human resources know what appropriate steps to take?
- Have there been any training programs presented to staff to address the issue?
- Can it be determined if policies and grievance procedure are in effect and enforced?
- Take a tour of the client's facility—are offensive pictures, calendars, or magazines noticeable? Are federal and state guidelines posted on bulletin boards?
- Can it be determined if management is "tuned in" to these issues?
- Is management aware of the cost of harassment—in financial terms and in the morale of employees?

In summary, prevention of sexual harassment is best. When an incident arises, executive management must promptly take the necessary steps to handle such problems by training all managers in how to appropriately deal with them.

(c) Federal Trade Commission

The FTC is an independent agency that promotes free and fair competition via interstate commerce. The FTC attempts to prevent the restraint of trade through illegal combinations of businesses, price fixing, and unfair trade practices. The FTC follows up on deceptive and false advertising practices.

Representative responsibilities of the FTC include the following:

- Monitoring deceptive labeling and packaging
- Prohibiting credit discrimination
- Upon learning of mergers and acquisitions, the FTC may stop the merger based on antitrust reasons.
- Protecting the public from unlawful price discrimination
- Protecting the public from actions that may create monopolies

The FTC also has a number of practices aimed at allowing the consumer to have a chance at making a fair purchasing decision, including giving customers for door-to-door sales and telephone sales three days to cancel such sales, prohibiting the mailing of unordered merchandise, prohibiting collection agencies from using obnoxious practices, and requiring 900 phone services to disclose fees.

Representative questions in an ethics audit may include the following:

- Is there pending or ongoing litigation regarding deceptive pricing?
- Based on review of the credit approval process, does there appear to be any pattern of rejection of credit based on age, national origin, race, or sex?
- Are there any ongoing investigations by the FTC?
- Are any potential acquisitions or mergers pending that may be challenged by the FTC on the basis of antitrust?
- For any "gray" areas, have there been any inquiries made by the company to the FTC to render an advisory opinion?
- In a review of sales, is there any indication of price discrimination?
- Are there policies and procedures supporting fair trade practices (including a code of conduct addressing fair trade practices)?
- In reviewing sales, are customers who order by fax, mail, or telephone notified if merchandise cannot be delivered by the promised date and given an opportunity to cancel the sale or concur with a new delivery date?

4.8 THE CPA'S REQUIREMENT FOR FINDING UNETHICAL/ILLEGAL BEHAVIOR (SAS 82)

Should CPAs provide ethical services such as an ethics audit? It can be argued that currently the financial audit involves some key ethical matters. Examining, analyzing, and testing the ethics of a corporation is an evolutionary step for CPAs. The regulatory body for CPAs is the Auditing Standards Board of the AICPA. The Auditing Standards Board requires the auditor to consider the possibility of unethical or fraudulent activity. "Consideration of Fraud in a Financial Statement Audit" (SAS 82) became effective for audits of financial statements for periods after December 15, 1997. Clearly, if CPAs are obligated to look for unethical behavior, it is not such a large leap to look for ethical behavior. What are the requirements now for CPAs looking for unethical or fraudulent behavior?

Statement on Auditing Standards 82 indicates that CPAs can only provide reasonable assurance that material misstatements due to fraud will be detected. It should be noted that this detection responsibility is not substantially different from SAS 53, "The Auditor's Responsibility to Detect and Report Errors and Irregularities." What is different is that SAS 82 explicitly states that an assessment of the potential for fraud and a response to any fraud risk factors are required. It provides the following:

- A definition of fraud
- A requirement that the auditor assess the risk of material misstatement due to fraud

- Guidance on how to respond to the results of the assessment
- Documentation and communication requirements

Statement on Auditing Standards 82 describes fraud as having two components: (1) fraudulent financial reporting and (2) misappropriation of assets.

1. **Fraudulent Financial Reporting**—is the intentional misrepresentation or omission of disclosures or dollar amounts with the objective to deceive financial statement readers. This includes the following:
   - Manipulation, falsification, or alteration of accounting records
   - Misrepresentation or intentional omission of events or transactions
2. **Misappropriation of Assets**—is the theft of a company's cash, inventory, or other assets, causing the financials not to be in compliance with GAAP.
   Examples of misappropriation of assets would include the following:
   - Embezzlement
   - Stealing supplies, plant property, or equipment
   - Shipping inventory to a co-conspirator without purchasing it

The first part of the process is to perform a risk assessment. Requiring the auditor to perform a risk assessment regarding the possibility of fraud is a key element in the new standard. The risk assessment needs to consider both misstatements due to fraudulent financial reporting and misstatements from misappropriation of assets. It should be noted that risk factors do not indicate the existence of fraud. However, these factors tend to be present when frauds do occur.

The assessment needs to be developed in the planning stage of the audit, when audit procedures are being designed and the risk factors should be reassessed throughout the audit. Consider the following:

- Reviewing last year's workpapers, were there any potential areas that now could be determined a potential risk area?
- Has this been a bad year for the industry as a whole?
- Have there been new governmental regulations that have increased competitiveness?
- Is there new management?

Questions such as the above should be asked at the beginning stages of the audit. Other questions that should be asked of management to determine if there are any risk factors present would include the following:

- Have there been any changes to the internal control structure?
- Have there been any major internal control breaks?

- Have there been any changes to the accounting/financial reporting system?
- Have any of the ratios (i.e., gross margin) been off this period?
- Have there been any changes in personnel in sensitive positions?
- How have results compared to budgeted expectations?

According to SAS 82, auditors should assess risk factors that relate to both fraudulent financial reporting and misstatements from misappropriation of assets. Three fraudulent financial reporting risk factors are discussed:

1. Management characteristics
2. Industry conditions
3. Operating characteristics and financial stability

With misappropriation of assets, there are two categories of risk factors:

1. Risk due to susceptibility of assets to misappropriation
2. Risk due to control

Representative risk factors noted include the following:

- Management's compensation tied to performance
- Management dominated by one individual
- Disregard for regulatory authorities
- High turnover by top management
- Disputes with the auditor
- Large declines in customer demand
- Possible bankruptcy
- Lack of segregation of duties
- Poor safeguards over cash and inventory

One approach for applying SAS 82 in a financial statement audit would be the following four steps:

1. Conduct a complete risk assessment.
2. Adjust/tailor audit based on the risk assessment.
3. Evaluate impact of findings on overall audit conclusion.
4. Document/communicate findings.

Chapter 5

Private Sector Response to Regulatory Oversight of CPAs

In Chapter 4, there were discussions of governmental and regulatory attempts at addressing ethical problems in the financial realm (i.e., Foreign Corrupt Practices Act [FCPA], Securities and Exchange Commission [SEC], Federal Sentencing Guidelines). However, the concerns of maintaining integrity in the financial reporting process were not only those of the government, but also the private sector.

Paramount in having those concerns were the certified public accountants themselves. The impetus for some of the private sector initiatives was the CPAs noting that if there was lack of integrity in the financial reporting process and they were found to be responsible for that, then the specter of increased governmental regulation of the profession could become a reality.

Public accountants in the United States have an enviable history of responsibility for the public interest. In the ending years of the 1800s, there were accountants who were willing to provide the type of accountant's report that a client wanted. Such accountants were operating commercial enterprises. As noted in a discussion which was presenting support for *only* CPAs having the right to practice public accounting, Goodloe noted:

> We regret to say, persons calling themselves accountants . . . are not adverse to making false statements as to financial matters—at the request of the management or for the purpose of misleading the stockholders—if by the making of such false statements, their fee be increased.[1]

In contrast, there were accountants who early in the development of the field in the United States believed that public accounting must be a professional pursuit. As stated by Goodloe:

> The services of professional public accountants have become a necessity to the business world of today and the statutes regulating the practice of accounting should restrict such practice to accountants of known integrity and good character, who

[1]Goodloe, *Journal of Accounting* (December 1905), 10.

have proved their fitness and ability to be trusted in matters requiring ability and technical knowledge.[2]

The accountants who believe that public accounting should be a profession won the battle and ultimately all states in the United States established requirements for entry into the practice of public accountancy.

To the present day, public accountants belong to a self-administered profession. Commitment to professional leadership is reflected in a number of initiatives undertaken in the final decades of the twentieth century.

Those initiatives include the following:

- Report of Commission on Fraudulent Financial Reporting (Treadway Commission)
- Committee of Sponsoring Organizations
- Peer Review
- American Institute of Certified Public Accountants (AICPA) Practice Committees
- New York Stock Exchange (NYSE) and American Exchange (AMEX) guidelines regarding Audit Committees

5.1 THE NATIONAL COMMISSION ON FRAUDULENT FINANCIAL REPORTING (TREADWAY COMMISSION)

In the 1980s, the profession became aware of the perception that there was extensive fraudulent financial reporting. This led to the establishment of a commission charged with studying the claim. The outcome of the commission's deliberations and study was the *Report of the National Commission on Fraudulent Financial Reporting*. Also known as the Treadway Report after the chairman of the group, James C. Treadway, Jr., the report was released in 1987. This was a private sector initiative that was developed by the following sponsors:

1. American Institute of Certified Public Accountants (AICPA)
2. American Accounting Association (AAA)
3. Institute of Internal Auditors (IIA)
4. Financial Executives Institute (FEI)
5. National Association of Accountants (which changed its name to Institute of Management Accountants as of July 1, 1991)

The objectives of the Commission were the following:

- Consider the extent to which acts of fraudulent financial reporting undermine the integrity of financial reporting.

[2] Id.

- Examine the role of the independent public accountant in detecting fraud.
- Identify how corporations may contribute to fraudulent financial reporting.

Among the recommendations of the Treadway Commission were the following:

- The proper tone must be set by top management to deter fraud.
- Public companies must have an internal audit function that is effective and objective.
- Audit committees should exercise vigilant and informed oversight of internal controls and the financial reporting process.
- Generally accepted auditing standards should be revised to indicate the CPA's responsibility for detecting fraud.

The Commission confirmed that the CPA who audits the financial statements of a public company also has a public obligation. As the U.S. Supreme Court has recognized, when the independent public accountant opines on a public company's financial statements, he or she assumes a public responsibility that transcends the contractual relationship with that client to the stockholders, creditors, customers, and so forth. The regulations and standards for auditing public companies must be adequate to safeguard that public trust.

While the Commission was not able to quantify the amount or significance of fraudulent financial reporting, it did note that there were three relevant factors:

1. The seriousness of the consequences of fraudulent financial reporting
2. The risk of its occurring in any given company
3. The realistic potential for reducing that risk[3]

The Treadway Commission's report was noticed and got results. The recommendations of the Commission highlighted the multidimensional nature of financial reporting. Based on the recommendations regarding CPAs, new auditing standards were developed and a private sector study on internal control was established.

The recommendations of Treadway report provided guidance for CPAs concerning errors, irregularities, and illegal acts. As a result, new auditing standards were developed, specifically "The Auditor's Responsibility to Detect Errors and Irregularities" (SAS 53) and "Illegal Acts by Clients" (SAS 54). These standards were issued and effective for audits beginning on or after January 1, 1989. These two statements were part of a group known as the "expectation-gap" standards, with the mission of trying to bridge the gap between what auditors could "deliver" versus what the public expected.

[3]*Report on the National Commission on Fraudulent Financial Reporting,* 4–5.

5.2 COMMITTEE OF SPONSORING ORGANIZATIONS (COSO)

One of the recommendations of the Treadway Commission was that a study be undertaken on internal control. The same sponsoring organizations that worked on the Treadway report united once again to deliberate and study internal control. The organization this time was called COSO. The Committee developed a study entitled "Internal Control–Integrated Framework" which was released in 1992 and was utilized as the foundation for SAS 78.

The study noted that the goals of an internal control system included the following:

- Minimizing the exposure to loss of assets
- Promoting effective and efficient operations
- Compliance with regulations and laws
- Issuance of reliable financial statements

Internal control was defined by COSO as "a *process,* effected by an entity's board of directors, management and other personnel, designed to provide reasonable assurance regarding the achievement of objectives in the following categories:

- Effectiveness and efficiency of operations
- Reliability of financial reporting
- Compliance with applicable laws and regulations"[4]

The Committee enlarged the concept of controls for the accounting community. It should be noted that control was defined as a *process.* Controls were not just stagnant, separate checks on records, but rather a dynamic process. According to COSO, internal control was comprised of the following five interrelated components:

1. Control environment
2. Risk assessment
3. Control activities
4. Information and communication
5. Monitoring

Under COSO, the basis for the control environment includes ethical values, integrity, and management's philosophy. Again, we are seeing the broadening of the concept of internal controls—internal controls not only being authorizations and reconciliations, but also a company's philosophy and principles.

---

[4]*Internal Control–Integrated Framework,* 1.

The Auditing Standards Board (ASB) issued SAS 78, "Consideration of Internal Control in a Financial Statement Audit," and made it effective for all audits after January 1, 1997. This SAS amended SAS 55 and utilized much of the same terminology as was in the COSO report. The ASB acknowledged the importance of the work of the COSO by stating, "The ASB believes the COSO report is rapidly becoming a widely accepted framework for sound internal control among United States organizations and its acceptance and use will continue to grow." With SAS 78, the ASB has now codified addressing ethical values as an integral part of every audit. Auditors must now perform procedures to help them understand the client's integrity, ethical values, and commitment to competence. Both the COSO and SAS 78 recognized the *direct* correlation between ethical values and the strength of an internal control environment.

5.3 PEER REVIEW

Who audits the auditors? One basic premise of auditing is that anything that is not monitored is subject to abuse or at least being uncontrolled. Professionals are expected to evaluate their own performance. As an additional oversight responsibility, some professional groups have introduced systematic policies and procedures to guide in this evaluation. Ethics requires that there is quality in the service being provided by CPAs.

Quality control is vital to every CPA practice. Elements included in quality control at public accounting firms include the following:

- Hiring qualified candidates
- Continuous training of personnel
- Having engagements be reviewed by other CPAs in the firm before signing off
- Keeping up-to-date with new innovations and technology
- Knowing the latest accounting standards and pronouncements

The AICPA, in conjunction with the state CPA societies, has developed a Peer Review Process. Certain state CPA societies have elected to administer the program in cooperation with the AICPA. In a Peer Review, one CPA firm examines the work of another firm. The objective of the review is to provide a basis for expressing an opinion on whether the firm met quality control standards and complied with professional standards. Peer Reviews may be administered on-site or off-site. If the CPA performs audits, an on-site peer review is required. If the CPA only does reviews or compilations, then an off-site peer review may be performed.

In an off-site review, the CPA provides information about the types and number of the engagements performed. The reviewer indicates the types of engagements selected. Under new standards, in an off-site Peer Review, the following three criteria must be met for engagements selected:

1. One engagement reviewed in each of the following areas: reviews, compilations with disclosures, compilations without disclosures, attestation engagements
2. One engagement reviewed for each owner of the firm who issues a compilation or review
3. Review of at least two engagements

For engagements selected by the reviewer, the CPA is requested to submit a copy of the financial statements plus an engagement questionnaire.

It should be noted that peer review does not cover other aspects of a CPA's practice such as consulting or tax engagements.

In an on-site Peer Review, the firm's quality control policies will be examined. Representative steps that may be included in this process could be as follows:

- Examining work papers
- Reviewing administrative records
- Interviewing firm personnel regarding procedures utilized
- Reviewing compliance with quality controls

Upon completing the review, an exit conference is held and a report is drafted to the state CPA society administering the review. The Peer Review program is designed to be tailored to the CPA's practice and the nature of his or her clients. According to the AICPA, CPAs conducting the reviews should be independent, have integrity, be objective, and conduct the review with due professional care.

Just as clients pay for their audits, CPAs pay for the Peer Review. Peer Reviews are normally charged on a per hour basis. Some recommendations for CPAs to make the reviews as economical as possible would include the following:

- Make sure all audit work papers and administrative files are neat and complete
- Provide timely and accurate data to the reviewer
- Have an effective quality control system implemented that partners and staff adhere to
- Designate a manager or partner to be in-charge of quality assurance
- Conduct in-firm reviews

In summary, there has been a variety of public sector initiatives to assure the public of not only integrity in the financial statement process but also that there are CPAs who are not only ethical, but also of a high quality. Even the NYSE has been striving to ensure integrity of financial reporting by its members by requiring audit committees to be composed solely of directors independent of management. It is because of measures such as these that the public has been able to rely on the CPA. These are measures that the CPAs place on themselves to maintain the public's confidence. In Chapter 7, there is a discussion of the responsibility of the CPA in maintaining high ethical standards.

Chapter 6

Ethics Survey Reports
on CPAs

6.1 BUSINESS ETHICS: SOME SURVEY RESULTS

Two small scale surveys were undertaken to get some contemporary information about perceptions of ethics in modern day businesses. One survey solicited perceptions of key officers in businesses, directors of State Boards of Accountancy, and directors of state societies of CPAs. The second was a survey of evening students in MBA programs and final portions of undergraduate business programs at an urban university in downtown Manhattan, New York City. This latter survey was entitled "Integrity in Contemporary Organizations."

6.2 SURVEY OF ETHICS: PERCEPTIONS

In order to get a contemporary view of ethics and the certified public accountant in the U.S. society, a Forbes survey investigation was designed and completed in late 1996 and early 1997. The responses of the survey were to answer, in general, the following questions:

1. How do perceptions of State Boards of Accountancy, CPA State Societies, Forbes 500 company Chief Financial Officers (CFOs), and CFOs of the best small companies of America differ relative to ethics?
2. What are perceived to be deterrents to unethical behavior?

6.3 SAMPLE SELECTION AND QUESTIONNAIRES USED

Random selection strategy was used for selecting 486 of the companies listed in the Forbes 500 companies and for the 193 listed as the best small companies in America. The total population of 54 State Boards of Accountancy in the jurisdiction of the United States (50 states plus Guam, Puerto Rico, the Virgin Islands, and the District of Columbia) were included. The total population of 54 State CPA Societies were also included in the group solicited for comments.

82

Covering letters and questionnaires designed for each of the four groups were prepared and forwarded by mail to CFOs of the businesses included and to the directors of the State Boards of Accountancy and of the CPA State Societies.

(a) Overview of Responses

Of the 54 surveys sent to State Boards of Accountancy, 22 or 37 percent responded; of the 54 sent to CPA Societies, 20 or 36 percent responded; of the 486 surveys sent to Forbes 500 companies, 46 or 9.47 percent responded; and of the 193 surveys sent to the best small companies in America, 30 or 16 percent responded. Overall, there were 118 responses or 15 percent.

(b) Companies Represented in Responses

Below are details for the respondents from large and small businesses:

Forbes 500 Companies

Industry	Companies	Employment Avg
Manufacturing	10	20,749
Telecommunication/Computers	7	13,692
Finance/Banking	10	8,755
Insurance	1	5,000
Retail	5	36,400
Utilities	4	5,200
Other	6	9,283

Note: Three respondents gave no company information.

Small Companies

Industry	Companies	Employment Avg
Manufacturing	14	1,246
Telecommunication/Computers	6	828
Finance/Banking	1	1,300
Other	5	1,246

Note: Four respondents gave no company information.

Although not overwhelming, the results suggest that ethical problems exist in the business environment. Implicit from the results was a necessity to magnify the important role high ethical standards play in the business environment. Accordingly, attention needs to be turned to finding solutions that will assure that ethical standards are given appropriate attention throughout organizations. The combined results follow.

6.4 GENERAL PERCEPTION

1. Across all four categories of respondents, there was strong support for the position that "there is a problem because of the lack of ethics in our society." Approximately 68 percent of the total group checked "definitely." Only five (4 percent) checked "not at all." One can conclude that this problem is perceived present by both those from businesses and those who serve key professional groups in public accounting.

2. In response to the comment, "There is a problem because of the lack of ethics in the CPA profession today," 69 percent of the total group checked that no problem existed. When the responses are disaggregated, approximately 76 percent of the business respondents indicated that there was no problem while only 62 percent of those related to the CPA societies had the same opinion. Thus, the business respondents appear to hold the CPAs in higher esteem than the CPAs themselves do.

3. Respondents were split in responding to the comment, "CPAs' ethics are being effectively monitored today," with 39 percent saying that they definitely agreed with the statement and 41 percent checking "3, average." However, 68 percent of the respondents from state boards of accountancy checked "3, average."

4. A total of 81 percent of the respondents agreed that "CPAs need no more government regulation." No debate is needed on this issue based on the responses. Only six of the respondents (5 percent) felt more regulation was needed.

5. Respondents were split in responding to the comment, "CPA's need more self regulation." Thirty-six percent agreed by checking "definitely." However, 35 percent of the total group checked "3, average." Approximately 28 percent checked that more self-regulation was not needed.

6.5 CPAs' BEHAVIOR IN PRACTICE

Respondents from large and small businesses were asked to make a judgment about the extent to which each of five practices were observed among CPAs. As noted in Table 6.1, the respondents reported, to a great extent, that they had not observed the practice at all. Such perception supports the public accountants' sense of professional responsibility. At the same time, 24 percent of the respondents observed that "sometimes" public accountants charged for time/work not performed; 20 percent noted that sometimes CPAs did not adhere to professional standards or were negligent in performance of work.

The 42 respondents associated with state boards of accountancy and state societies of CPAs were given the same practices that were listed on the questionnaire to the business respondents. However, these 42 were asked to indicate the extent of prevalence of each of the practices. Additionally, they were asked to

Table 6.1 Prevalence of Selected Practices among CPAs as Perceived by Business Respondents

	Extent of Observation		
	Not at all	Sometimes	Frequently
	(Number = 76; percentages shown*)		
Charging for time/services not performed	61	24	3
Taking engagement when firm is not qualified	74	18	7
Not adhering to the AICPA code of ethics	82	13	4
Not adhering to professional standards or being negligent in performance of work	74	20	5
Not adhering to state/federal laws	87	8	4

*Percentages do not add up to 100, because of nonresponses.

Table 6.2 Perceptions of Selected Practices by Representatives of Public Accounting Associations

	Extent of Practice		
	Low	Moderate	High
	(Number = 42; percentages shown)*		
Charging for time/services not performed	71	17	10
Taking engagement when firm is not qualified	38	38	24
Not adhering to the AICPA code of ethics	43	36	17
Not adhering to professional standards or being negligent in performance of work	57	29	14
Not adhering to state/federal laws	62	29	7

*Percentages do not add up to 100, because of nonresponses.

judge the public perception of CPAs when compared with other professions. The responses are shown in Table 6.2.

When the responses of the two groups—businesses and those who administer professional societies—are compared, there are some interesting differences. While 61 percent of the business respondents had not observed public accountants "charging for time/services not performed," 71 percent of the directors of professional societies believed that the extent of such a practice was "low." Approximately three-fourths of the business respondents believed that public accounting firms did not take engagements for which they were not qualified; yet, only 38 percent of the administrators of public accounting societies had the same judgment. The business respondents believed to a far greater extent than did the representatives of public accounting associations that CPAs were not likely to violate the American Institute of Certified Public Accountants' (AICPA) code of ethics or fail to adhere to professional standards.

6.6 ETHICAL BEHAVIOR IN BUSINESS

All respondents were asked a series of "yes"/"no" questions related to ethical behavior in business. Table 6.3 summarizes the responses. As noted in the table, a considerably higher percentages of respondents of public accounting professional societies had knowledge of a business operating fraudulently than did the business respondents. Public accountants would have had far more experience in a variety of businesses than would have been the case of the respondents from busi-

Table 6.3   Knowledge of Unethical Behavior

		Responses from		
	Businesses N = 76	Accounting Societies N = 42	Businesses N = 76	Accounting Societies N = 42
		(Percentages shown)*		
	Yes	Yes	No	No
Knowledge of a business operating fraudulently?	21	38	79	62
If yes, did the fraud have a material effect on financial statements?**	13	31	13	7
Have you knowledge of a business operating unethically at the senior management level or above?	39	40	59	60
Did the organization (where fraud was noted) have a published code of ethics?***	7	7	32	24
Have you been requested by a superior to do something you considered unethical?	22	69	70	24
Have you seen intentional misstated financial statements?	13	19	78	33

*Percentages do not add up to 100, because of nonresponses.
**Percentages shown are based on total group; if based on the number saying "yes" in the preceding question, there were 56 percent who said "yes" and 41 percent who said "no."
***Percentages shown are based on total group; if based on the number saying "yes" in the preceding question, there were 17 percent who said "yes" and 72 percent who said "no."

nesses. As noted in the footnote related to the "yes" of the first question, in a majority of instances (56 percent) the fraud was judged to have a material effect on the financial statements.

Approximately the same percentages in the two groups had knowledge of businesses operating fraudulently at the senior management level or above. As reported in the footnote, of those indicating that they had knowledge of fraudulent behavior at the senior management level or above, only 17 percent reported that the companies had a published code of ethics.

Marked differences occur in response to the question about whether the respondent had faced a request from a superior to do something considered unethical. While 69 percent of those representing the public accounting societies said "yes" to the question, only 22 percent of the business respondents did so. The percentages who said "yes" to having seen intentionally misstated financial statements were not significantly different (13 percent of business respondents; 19 percent of public accounting societies respondents).

When those who said "yes" to having seen intentionally misstated financial statements were asked to describe the situation, several added comments. These included the following:

- "As the Executive Director of a State CPA Society, we have seen a small number of abuse cases in our ethics enforcement."
- "Wholly owned subsidiary inflated profits for performance enhancement."
- "In the borrowers' case . . . inventory levels and values were overstated."
- "Inappropriate accounting practices overstated earnings."
- "I've read about a number of companies. Miniscribe is a classic example."
- "Bill and hold transactions in the electronic business."
- "Nonprofit company—boost public perception of the ability of top management. Allowed this management to set up a 'for profit' service company."
- "Overstated assets and equity."
- "Misstatement of segment data to hide failures of executive management to address issues in a particular division."
- "I have seen this in disciplinary cases handled by this Accountancy Board more than once."
- "Very aggressive recognition of auto lease revenue."

6.7 DISCRIMINATION AND SEXUAL HARASSMENT

When asked if they were aware of discrimination in their organizations, the overwhelming response was "no." The responses are combined for the two groups of

Table 6.4 Extent of Discrimination in Respondent's Organizations

	Responses from			
	Businesses N = 76	Accounting Societies N = 42	Businesses N = 76	Accounting Societies N = 42
		(percentages shown)*		
	Yes	Yes	No	No
Discrimination based on				
Age	0	12	95	86
Gender	7	26	88	71
Race	3	5	89	93
Religion	1	0	93	98

*Percentages do not add up to 100, because of nonresponses.

business and for the two public accounting societies. The responses are shown in Table 6.4. Those responding from public accounting societies noted age and gender discrimination to some extent. Twenty-six percent said "yes" to gender discrimination; 12 percent to age discrimination.

All respondents were asked the question: "Are you aware of any incidents of sexual harassment in your organization?" Thirty-nine percent of business respondents and 19 percent of public accounting societies' respondents reported "yes."

6.8 PREVENTION AND DETERRENT TO UNETHICAL BEHAVIOR

Respondents were asked the degree to which each of a list of proposals would deter unethical behavior, judging from "effective" to "ineffective." The results are shown in Table 6.5. There were significant differences in the judgments between the two groups as to which proposals would be effective in deterring unethical behavior. The respondents from business were less likely than respondents from public accounting societies to believe that codes of ethics, written policies, and ethical training would be effective deterrents. Public accounting societies are very much involved in professional training; the response related to ethical training may reflect such ongoing experience. Eighty-three percent of the respondents from the public accounting societies believe that ethical training would be effective; only 51 percent of the respondents of business had the same judgment. Respondents from the public accounting societies felt that state or federal laws would be helpful far more than the respondents from businesses indicated. The two groups were not significantly apart in assessment of the effectiveness of "monitoring" or "tone at the top" and "co-worker or peer pressure."

Table 6.5 Respondents' Judgment of Proposals to Deter Unethical Behavior

	Responses					
	Effective	Effective	Moderate	Moderate	Ineffective	Ineffective
Proposal	Businesses N = 76	Accounting Societies N = 42	Businesses N = 76	Accounting Societies N = 42 (percentages shown)*	Businesses N = 76	Accounting Societies N = 42
Code of ethics	55	69	22	24	21	2
Written policies and procedures	62	81	28	14	9	5
Monitoring or "tone at the top"	97	88	1	7	0	2
Co-worker or peer pressure	82	86	16	10	1	2
State or federal law	18	52	53	36	28	12
Ethical training	51	83	33	12	13	5
Parents' guidance	80	93	5	5	1	2

*Percentages do not add up to 100, because of nonresponses.

Table 6.6   Respondents Opinions Regarding Ethical Beliefs and Practices

	Businesses N = 76	Responses from Accounting Societies N = 42	Businesses N = 76	Accounting Societies N = 42
		(Percentages shown)*		
	Yes	Yes	No	No
Should business adhere to the highest form of ethical conduct?	88	100	5	0
Should allowance be made for human nature?	29	24	36	43
Should top management set an example and follow through on a code of ethics?	97	100	0	0
Should management support a code of ethics but not make "big waves"?	9	10	31	55
Does your organization ask if vendors have a code of conduct?**	18	n/a	56	n/a
Does your company have a written code of conduct?**	49	n/a	49	n/a

*Percentages do not add up to 100, because of nonresponses.
**Question not asked of respondents of public accounting societies.

Further questions about ethical behavior were asked in a "yes"/"no" format. Those questions are shown in Table 6.6. Note that some questions were asked only of business respondents. All respondents believe that businesses should adhere to the highest form of ethical conduct and that management should set an example and follow through on a code of ethics. It is interesting to note that respondents are not inclined to "make allowances" for human nature, with 29 percent of the business respondents and 24 percent of the public accounting society respondents stating "yes" to the question. Only approximately half of the business respondents noted that their companies have a written code of ethics.

All four groups were asked if they believed CPAs could assist in enhancing ethical conduct in organizations. The responses are shown in Table 6.7. While there were more than a third of the business respondents who believed that CPAs could be of assistance for all three types of services, the CPAs were far more positive on the assistance they could provide.

Table 6.7 Respondents' Opinion of Ethical Assistance from CPAs

	Businesses N = 76 Yes	Responses from Accounting Societies N = 42 Yes	Businesses N = 76 No	Accounting Societies N = 42 No
		(Percentages shown)*		
Type of assistance				
Drafting codes of conduct	36	81	57	5
Performing ethics audits	37	71	55	12
Providing ethical training	47	88	43	5

*Percentages do not add up to 100, because of nonresponses.

6.9 SOLUTIONS TO UNETHICAL BEHAVIOR

The business respondents were given an open-end question which asked: "What solutions do you believe will resolve the ethics situation?" Among the "solutions" written in were the following:

• "The only long-term solution will be adherence to a strong unwavering moral compass by all citizens."
• "Education."
• "Question 22 is critical—top management must set an example and follow through on a code of ethics."
• "I believe there should be a code of ethics and periodic reminders (ethics training or counseling)."
• "Management must set the highest standards."
• "There is no solution—human nature creates deviations from the norm from time to time."
• "I'm not sure whether you are referring to a 'situation' in the profession or in society. I don't think there is a major problem in the profession. There is in society, but I don't have any solution(s) for it."
• "Executive management commitment to the highest standard of ethics. I do not believe our outside (independent) accountants have a role to play in this issue."

6.10 AN OVERVIEW OF THE FINDINGS

The results of the overall survey responses led to one conclusion—an ethical problem exists. Finding a solution for the ethical problem, from the survey results, was as elusive as trying to determine the source of the ethical problem and who is responsible for taking action. For example, 68 percent of respondents believed that there is a problem in our society because of the lack of ethics. However, 69 percent believed there is no problem in the CPA profession today because of the lack of ethics. In addition, 81 percent of the respondents stated that CPAs needed no more government regulation. Yet, only 39 percent of the respondents believed that CPAs were being effectively monitored today.

When asked to give a solution, only a few of the respondents attempted to give one. Solution responses ranged from "education" to "executive management's commitment to the highest standard of ethics." These responses have laid a foundation for the development of a solution to the problem of lack of ethics in the business environment. A solid integrated approach can be used to solve the ethical dilemma in the business environment. This approach would begin at the basic educational level and work its way into the core of the business operations.

Business disciplines such as management, marketing, finance, accounting, and others are taught to students in colleges and universities as the key fundamentals to business operations. As students become business professionals, they are constantly challenged to put the disciplines they have learned into practice in order to make businesses function successfully. Missing from the equation are business ethics. The problem of ethical behavior, or the lack thereof, can be recognized as a critical component of running a business successfully and should be integrated into the overall business equation similar to other business disciplines. Nationally and internationally, business disciplines are taught and reinforced in the business environment to determine success. Similarly, business ethics can be integrated into the college and university curriculum and eventually enhance the business environment. Graduates of colleges and universities where ethics were an integral component of their studies should implement a style of behavior that gives appropriate attention to ethical concerns.

6.11 IMPLICATIONS OF FINDINGS

There are some tentative implications to be made, even though the overall response rate was only 15 percent, from this survey of opinions related to ethics in business and among CPAs.

Respondents support the general impressions expressed in the business press and in popular periodicals that there is an ethical problem in the United States. At the same time, the long-term perception that "CPAs are ethical" seems to be persisting as three out of four of the business respondents checked definitely not to the item, "there is a problem because of the lack of ethics in the CPA profession today."

The extent of violations of what are perceived to be ethical expectations is not assessed as widespread. However, the extent of such violations is sufficient to raise questions about what might be done to reduce the incidence of practices that result in ethical violations.

Respondents were in agreement to a significant degree in their judgments of proposals which would deter unethical behavior. There was considerable support for the contemporary efforts to enhance ethics in the workplace, including codes of ethics, written policies and procedures, and ethical training.

The findings support the premise of this book, which is that there are ethical services that CPAs can provide. The responses from accounting societies were significantly higher than those from business about their opinion of ethical assistance from CPAs. However, approximately half of the business respondents believed that CPAs could provide ethical training; slightly more than a third of the business respondents believe that CPAs could assist in drafting codes of conduct and in performing ethics audits.

6.12 ETHICS IN CONTEMPORARY ORGANIZATIONS: THE VIEW FROM YOUNG WORKERS

What is the perception of younger workers about the ethical environment in which they work? That was the question for which an answer was sought from students studying on a part-time MBA program or in their final year as part-time students in an undergraduate business program. They were all studying in an urban university located in the financial district of New York City.

(a) The Questionnaire and Student Participants

A simple questionnaire of eight questions was developed which asked respondents whether their organizations had codes of ethics, whether they had received any training or orientation about the organization's ethical values, and their own experience related to ethical problems at work.

Students in eight classes were asked to fill out the form if they were employed, either part-time or full-time. A total of 228 students filled in the questionnaires and submitted them anonymously.

(b) The Respondents

The students were asked to identify their current position as support staff, technical staff, or management staff. The respondents comprised of:

Support staff	120
Technical staff	56
Management staff	52

Students were employed in a wide range of organizations, including banks, financial services, utilities, communications, telecommunications, nonprofit health centers, investment banking, brokerage, fashion, and public accounting.

The range was wide. A review of responses by type of organization did not reveal any differences. Therefore, the responses were classified by the three types of staff, which was a significant variable.

(c) Code of Ethics and Orientation to Company Ethical Values

The initial question was: "Does your organization have a code of ethics?" As noted in Table 6.8, the majority said "yes" to this question. There is the possibility that some employees who said "no" did not know whether or not there was a code of conduct. It is interesting to note that those classified as management staff reported to a greater percentage than the other two groups that their organizations did have codes. Overall, 25 percent of the respondents either said there was no code of ethics or they did not know if there was.

The second question asked if they personally had a copy of the code of ethics. The responses are shown in Table 6.9.

While the majority said that their companies had codes of ethics, it is interesting to note the extent (32 percent) to which the staff reported that they did not have a copy of such a code.

When the total group of respondents is considered, far more employees had no orientation or training in the organizations' ethical values than did have such training. Table 6.10 reports the responses. The management staff had received orientation or training to a far greater extent than had the other two groups. Yet, even in the management group, 42 percent reported that they had had no training. For the total group, 65 percent reported that they had had no training or orientation.

Table 6.8 Extent to Which Companies Have Codes of Ethics

	Yes		No		Don't Know	
	N	%	N	%	N	%
Support staff	88	73	16	13	16	13
Technical staff	40	71	10	18	6	11
Management staff	42	81	8	15	2	4
Group as a whole	170	75	34	15	24	10

Table 6.9 The Extent to Which Respondents Had Copies of Code of Ethics

	Yes		No	
	N	%	N	%
Support staff	52	59	36	41
Technical staff	30	75	10	25
Management staff	34	81	8	19
Group as a whole	116	68	54	32

Table 6.10 Extent of In-Company Orientation or Training in Organization's Ethical Values

	Yes		No	
	N	%	N	%
Support staff	34	28	86	72
Technical staff	16	29	40	71
Management staff	30	58	22	42
Group as a whole	80	35	148	65

Table 6.11 Extent of Involvement in Ethical Problems or Dilemmas

	Personally Involved		Have Observed Such Situations		Have Not Observed Such Situations	
	N	%	N	%	N	%
Support staff	32	27	28	23	60	50
Technical staff	16	29	6	11	34	60
Management staff	30	58	16	31	6	11
Group as a whole	78	34	50	22	100	44

(d) Experience with Ethical Problems or Dilemmas

The respondents were asked "What is the extent to which you personally have been a participant in a situation that presented an ethical problem or ethical dilemma?" They were given the following alternatives:

1. Personally involved
2. Have observed one (or more) in the organization
3. Have not been involved or have not observed any ethical problems

As noted in Table 6.11, 34 percent of the total group reported that they had been personally involved in situations that presented an ethical problem or ethical dilemma.

Far more of the respondents had never observed situations where there were ethical problems or dilemmas than had been personally involved in or observed such situations. The management staff reported twice as often as the other two groups that they had been personally involved in such situations.

Those who stated that they had been personally involved were asked to assess their judgment of the resolution of the problem or dilemma. The question provided these alternatives:

1. The problem (dilemma) was reviewed fairly and the decision seemed the best under the circumstances.

Table 6.12   Judgment about Resolution of Ethical Problem (Dilemma)

	Reviewed Fairly and Decisions Seemed Best		Not Properly Reviewed or Resolved Appropriately		Unsure About What Should Have Been Done	
	N	%	N	%	N	%
Support staff	15	48	14	45	2	7
Technical staff	7	50	6	43	1	7
Management staff	22	79	6	21	0	0
Group as a whole	44	60	26	36	3	4

2.   The problem (dilemma) was not properly reviewed nor appropriately resolved.

3.   Unsure about what should have been done.

Only 73 of the 78 who checked that they had been personally involved responded to the question about the resolution of the problem. Their responses are shown in Table 6.12.

When the total group of 73 respondents is reviewed, 60 percent of those who stated that they had been personally involved felt that the problems were fairly reviewed and an appropriate decision had been made. A considerable percentage of both support staff and technical staff responding believed that the review and the decision were not optimum. Few, though, reported that they were unsure. There were five nonrespondents to this question, however.

(e)   Overall Assessment of Adherence to Policies and Practices

Respondents were asked to judge on a scale of 1 to 10—with 10 representing the best assessment—their company's adherence to policies and practices that assure that decisions reflect integrity. The mean averages for the three groups were:

Support staff	7.48
Technical staff	6.13
Management staff	7.09

The weighted average for all respondents was 7.06. All three assessments were above the average and reflect a reasonable degree of optimism about the ethical environment in which they work. This judgment does not appear to be out of line with the judgment of the 60 percent who had been personally involved in ethical problems who concluded that their problems had been reviewed fairly and the decisions seemed the best in the circumstances.

6.13 IMPLICATIONS OF FINDINGS

It is not clear if the results reflect a lack of communication on the part of companies or the reality of attention to ethics in companies. Although this was a survey in a limited population and generalizations are not appropriate, some interesting questions are raised. Among such questions are:

1. To what extent do companies have codes of ethics, but fail to communicate the information to all staff, especially newer workers?
2. To what extent are codes of ethics published and distributed to all staff?
3. To what extent is there specific training about a company's core ethical values?

Although a limited survey, the results are in line with other experiences with younger workers in all types of organizations. There appears to be justification for turning attention to explicit actions related to the ethical environment at work.

6.14 CONSIDERATION OF THE FINDINGS OF THE TWO SURVEYS

The populations of the two surveys were different. In the first survey reported in this chapter, executives in top management responded; in the second, employees who were enrolled in university studies participated.

The questions in the two are not parallel and cannot, therefore, be directly compared. However, some indirect comparison may be in order. For example, 59 percent of the respondents of the ethics survey had knowledge of a business operating fraudulently. In the survey of workers were also students, the question about the extent to which the respondent had participated in an ethical dilemma resulted in 56 percent checking that they had either been personally involved or had observed such situations.

In the first survey, 22 percent of the business respondents answered "yes" to the question "Have you been requested by a superior to do something you considered unethical?" When the employees who were also students were asked to indicate on a scale of 1 to 10, with 10 the highest rank, their company's adherence to policies and practices that assure that decisions reflect integrity, the overall average ranking was 7.06. If that is converted to a percentage, it is approximately 71 percent adherence.

There is perceived to be an ethical problem in the workplace and at the same time respondents believe ethical behavior in the workplace is to some extent adequate. There is not, however, the overwhelming sense that there is no opportunity for improvement. The opportunity for the CPA to make a contribution seems a reasonable assessment of the contemporary environment.

PART 3

Promoting Value-Added Ethics Services

Chapter 7

Promoting Ethics in the CPA Firm

The premise of this book is that certified public accountants can be leaders in providing ethics services to all types of organizations. Clearly, to provide such services, the CPA needs to *be* a model and perceived as a model of ethical standards. (See Chapter 5 for a discussion of the standards established for the profession.) In other words, if the CPA is assisting an organization in being ethical, then the CPA, in order to avoid hypocrisy, should also be ethical. The CPA needs to "walk the talk."

To "practice what you preach" is perceived to be a far more positive circumstance than to pronounce support for one style and yet practice a very different style. The optimum world in which CPAs function is one where their firms exemplify high ethical standards. Many observers note that we do not have that optimum world presently. (See Chapter 6 survey results.) Such observers of professional performance in the contemporary world are wary of the extent to which any professional group, including accountants, adheres to its own professional ethics standards.

What is likely, for example, to be the quality of an ethics audit performed by a firm in which thoughtful staff members within the firm believe higher-level personnel function in a flagrantly unethical manner?

It is the position reflected in the discussion in this chapter that a public accounting firm that strives to meet professional ethical standards is likely to perform ethical services most effectively. This, of course, does not mean that a CPA who finds it difficult to adhere, and does not adhere, to professional standards could not also perform an ethics engagement. In this latter situation, the practitioner has the unenviable conflict that a basic sense of right and wrong imposes on his emotional well-being.

In the contemporary world, where decisions are frequently driven by the short-run possibility of success, omissions of ethical considerations are revealed in the long run. The tenets of professionalism that were enunciated in clear language in the early decades of the twentieth century appear, at times, to be set aside as opportunities for material gain arise. The following account illustrates the point as it relates to one aspect of ethical standards—conflict of interest:

A public relations officer of a state insurance division resigned, in part, because he did not believe the agency was doing an effective job of regulating the industry. He followed up by criticizing the agency and recommending that the agency undertake an audit of its enforcement activities.

The former public relations officer was pleased when he learned that the agency would have an audit as he had recommended. However, he was surprised when he learned that an industry law firm was to do the audit. Many of the complaints were made against some of the key clients of the law firm selected. The former public relations officer wondered about the quality of audit that would result since there appeared to be a conflict of interest.

Turn now to the law firm invited to undertake this audit of the effectiveness of the agency's enforcement activities. A review of what transpired revealed that the law firm had applied for this audit assignment. The partner assigned to the audit had formerly headed the California Insurance Department's enforcement division. It was this partner's opinion that the work of his team would in no way be influenced by the realization that his firm provided services to key insurance companies, which were the subject of many of the complaints. This partner also pointed out that a legal ethics professor in one of the major law schools in the United States had been engaged to make a judgment about the possibility of a conflict of interest. The law professor concluded, as had the law firm partner, that there was no conflict of interest present. However, a second professor of legal ethics—not participating in any way in the case—concluded that the situation created a clear conflict of interest. Later, the law professor hired by the law firm was interviewed. At this point, he revealed that the law firm officials had not told him that some of its clients were subjects of many complaints the firm would be reviewing.

What are the critical ethical concerns revealed in this brief account? What is likely to be the assessment made by a reasonable person with a level of skepticism that would lead him or her to raise questions about professional people such as lawyers, accountants, and doctors? What could be the assessment of a person who made accurate judgments about ethical behavior and knew well the parties involved in this case were people of impeccable ethics?

The answer to the first question is that without persuasive evidence of the integrity of the law firm, the conclusion is that there is sufficient potential for serious misrepresentation of the findings because of the conflict of interest. One fact revealed in a follow-up by a reporter—that there was no knowledge that clients of the law firm were named in complaints—raises serious question about the due professional care evident in making a judgment about conflict of interest. The law professor hired to make a judgment acknowledged that certain information had not been provided to him. Why was that information not revealed? Did the professor have a due care responsibility to ask about relationships that were critical to the judgment regarding a conflict of interest he had been asked to make? Why was that information not revealed? Did the firm have a responsibility to indicate the extent to which its clients were the subjects of many complaints in the state? Why did the professor fail to raise questions for which he needed answers to provide an expert judgment about the potential for conflict of interest in the case described to him? A reasonable person would conclude that limited confidence, if any, should be given to the conclusions of the audit.

On the other hand, it is theoretically possible that there are individuals who know the integrity of the law firm. Assume, for purposes of this illustration, that such individuals have objective evidence that the firm's personnel would in no way be influenced by the possible financial repercussions to the firm if the audit conclusions did indeed reveal material violations of their insurance client's obligations to customers. These individuals would have no qualms about the appearance of conflict of interest. Appearance is irrelevant if there is such strong professional integrity that conflicts of interest just do not arise. Would not those individuals who have confidence that they *know* the integrity of the firm raise some question about their assumption? Might there be some hesitation about the firm because of the failure to reveal relevant information to the law professor? Questions about the ethical standards of both the firm and the outside expert, the professor of legal ethics, would be raised.

The foregoing case is an illustration of just one factor of professional ethics—conflict of interest. The fact that such a factor is identified in professional codes reveals that the ability of individuals to behave ethically in the presence of such a conflict requires that the professional person decline an engagement or withdraw from an engagement when such a potential conflict arises. The practical conclusion is that there is sufficiently high probability of bias when there is a potential conflict of interest to undermine the validity of any conclusions or recommendations made by the professional person. In a utopian environment, where individuals behaved according to the highest ethical standards of the society, there would be no awareness of conflict of interest, and its possibility would not ever be considered.

In this chapter, there will be a discussion of some of the key considerations as CPAs review their own behavior. Over the years, the profession has developed and instituted basic tenets, principles, rules, and interpretations that many CPAs honor unfailingly.

7.1 KEEPING ONE'S OWN HOUSE IN ORDER

The task of serious self-assessment is not simple. It requires candidness in facing reality; it requires continuous vigilance. Public accounting firms have multiple divisions. They provide a wide range of services. That range is being extended through the rapid change in the society that leads to new types of assurance services. Whether a public accounting firm is managed with a centralized or decentralized structure, there must be an overriding firm philosophy of ethical behavior if the total firm is to establish and sustain an image of a quality professional organization. The task of assuring a firm-wide philosophy of ethical behavior is not a simple one in an organization in which essentially all resources are human assets and services are labor intensive.

The Securities and Exchange Commission (SEC) is the governmental agency responsible for the oversight of the self-regulating public accounting profession. The SEC reviews the extent to which there is implementation of the rules and regulations related to behavior and substance of the profession.

Periodically, this strategy is tested, particularly when there is a major fraud perpetrated on the public such as was revealed in the PharMor and Lincoln Savings Bank cases. Subsequent to such revelations, the question "Where were the auditors?" is raised. The oversight agency, the SEC, is charged with assessing the evidence to answer the question.

To date, there has not been a candid review of any major alleged audit failure. The strategy of review of the McKesson-Robbins fraud, for example, is not one that has been used in any instance of alleged audit failures during the past two decades. Public accounting firms have made large financial settlements, without acknowledging or denying failure to adhere to professional standards. The explanation for settling out of court is that to do so is the most economical decision in the circumstances. Thus, the question of quality of professional behavior remains unresolved.

There continues to be concern about the ethical behavior of public accountants, as evidenced by the pressure from the SEC about the independence of public accountants. As a result of that pressure, a new board was established—the Independence Standards Board. This board was established in May 1997. Shortly thereafter, a White Paper was presented to the board, on behalf of the American Institute of Certified Public Accountants (AICPA). That paper's Introduction and Executive Summary state the following:

> Independence is one of the most deeply ingrained values of the accounting profession. No one has greater interest in upholding the independence of auditors . . . than members of the profession, as the reputation of all professionals engaged in auditing public entities depends on it.

The skepticism of realistic practitioners does not lead to applause in confirmation of such a statement. At the same time, the statement has the possibility of representing reality, if public accounting firms seriously undertake to be sure their own firms are reflecting such pronouncements. A profession is made up of individuals who have joined together in organizations. There must be a steadfast resolution to live up to public expectations of ethical standards. Opportunism does not undermine the proclaimed responsibility of the practitioner. Standards do not have to be lowered to reach the financial goals of the entity. Maintaining high standards is not a simple task; however, over the long run, the costs of such maintenance can prove to be an invaluable investment that produces higher levels of profitability.

As of mid-1998, there was no conclusion as to the implementation of the White Paper as presented. (See Chapter 9 for further discussion of the Independence Standards Board.)

7.2 "WINDOW DRESSING"

Public accounting firms must be on guard that they are not used for show or window dressing (used to put up a good image or front). There is a growing trend to hire a CPA firm to help a client during a scandal. The question arises: What is such a company buying? Is it buying consulting services or is it buying the ethical reputation of the CPA firm? Certified public accountants provide a service to society because of the tradition of professional independence. They are not customarily in the business of providing public relations services to firms in trouble—in this type of role, a firm specializing in public relations would be more beneficial. The CPA firm must make sure it is not being used solely for window dressing. Practitioners should take responsibility for ensuring that the motivation for the engagement is substantive and not merely a positive spin on the company's position.

How can a public accounting firm determine whether the prospective client is seeking "window dressing"? How can it determine whether its conclusions have already been determined by the client and a rubber stamping is all that is required? Here are four questions to guide the public accounting firm in assessing the good faith motivation of a prospective client:

1. Is the problem (task) described in clear, candid words?
2. Is the problem (task) supported by top management as well as the board of directors?
3. Does top management understand the extent and depth of the investigation and study to be done if the public accountant is to complete the engagement effectively?
4. Does the client reflect a willingness to accept conclusions that are not favorable?

The irony of performing ethics-related engagements in an environment in which only form rather than substance is of interest leaves the client, the public accountant, and those outsiders interested in the outcome with a meaningless, hollow conclusion.

7.3 CONFLICTS OF INTEREST

In a world in which we cannot assume high ethical standards, there must be practices that will aid in reducing unethical behavior. The professional requirement that there be no potential conflict of interest between the CPA and the client is to be honored at all costs.

The AICPA Professional Ethics Executive Committee has assessed a wide range of situations wherein conflict of interest might arise. Operationally, lines have been drawn. For example, CPAs are perceived to face a potential conflict of interest if they provide services in which they essentially are functioning in managerial aspects of the client's business.

The profession has determined that consulting services provided to audit clients do not constitute a conflict of interest. The professional guidance in the performance of engagements is assessed to be sufficient to ensure proper actions. Thus, the CPA firm is not perceived to have a conflict of interest if it performs an ethics-related engagement for an audit client. Generally, as a safeguard, a public accounting firm's policy is that different personnel will be assigned to audit and nonaudit engagements.

The most critical potential for conflict of interest arises from the fact that clients provide payment for services and also make decisions about continuing and additional services with their public accounting firms. Public accounting firms must make clear the ultimate responsibility of every professional staff member in the face of pressures or incentives present in a relationship with a client.

> An audit client asks its public accounting firm to undertake an ethics audit. The ethics audit would be provided by a different division of the public accounting firm. There is intense pressure in the firm to increase revenues—and, thus, to hold on to all clients and to extend services to them. In fact, it was the skillful marketing efforts of an audit manager who realized the client had problems in implementing its ethical program that resulted in the ethics audit engagement.
>
> In a firm culture where enhanced revenues are the goal, questions can be raised about the extent to which staff involved in this extended service—the ethics audit—will be influenced by an attitude that keeping the client happy is something we must not forget!

It is the CPA's mental attitude, grounded in professional responsibility that overrides consideration of business outcome, that is perceived to persist. It is the role of all CPAs and their firms to see that there is constant support and implementation of such an attitude. Public accounting firms, to a considerable extent, reinforce this demand through training and small group discussions among staff about problems that arise and how they are effectively handled.

Concern about conflicts of interest is recognized by the Institute of Internal Auditors (IIA). In the IIA's statement of its code of ethics, members and certified internal auditors are reminded that they "shall refrain from entering into any activity which may be in conflict with the interest of their organization or which would prejudice their ability to carry out objectively their duties and responsibilities."

7.4 SUBSTANCE VERSUS IMAGE

Image is never to be a substitute for substance for ethical standards in a public accounting firm. Top management must indeed "walk the talk." The realization that the "tone at the top" determines the quality of ethical behavior applies not only to the clients of CPAs, but also to the CPAs themselves.

There are many ways to be sure that there is reality to a CPA's ethical standards. Public accounting firms must provide workshops, seminars, and other forms of continuous education. Topics fully explored in meaningful fashion should include sensitivity and awareness of every aspect of the firm's own code of conduct. Role playing is an effective activity for identifying attitudes and beliefs and exploring how they are influenced and how they can be modified. An ethics program must be comprehensive and involve all professional staff. It is the responsibility of managing directors and partners to demonstrate the benefits that accrue from striving for high ethical decision making in all circumstances.

A good faith monitoring program is needed to identify vulnerabilities and lapses. Senior management must maintain an active interest in monitoring and in following up constructively to the observations and facts disclosed from monitoring activities.

7.5 CODE OF PROFESSIONAL CONDUCT

Being a professional means a variety of things, including maintaining a higher standard. Certainly, one evaluating the ethics of others must also have a high standard. The ethical framework for the CPA is presented in the Code of Professional Conduct. The Code "consists of two sections: (1) the Principles and (2) the Rules. The Principles provide the framework for the Rules, which govern the performance of professional services by members. The Council of the American Insitutue of Certified Public Accountants is authorized to designate bodies to promulgate technical standards under the Rules, and the bylaws require adherence to those Rules and Standards. . . . Compliance with the Code of Professional Conduct, as with all standards in an open society, depends primarily on members' understanding and voluntary actions, secondarily on reinforcement by peers and public opinion, and ultimately on disciplinary proceedings, when necessary, against members who fail to comply with the Rules."

The Principles are what CPAs are striving to implement as they provide professional services. The Rules are enforceable standards.

7.6 PRINCIPLES OF PROFESSIONAL CONDUCT

The Principles of Professional Conduct are identified as follows:

- Responsibilities
- The public interest
- Integrity
- Objectivity and independence
- Due care
- Scope and nature of services

The Preamble sets the tone for the Principles by stating, "By accepting membership, a certified public accountant assumes an obligation of self-discipline above and beyond the requirements of laws and regulations. These Principles of the Code of Professional Conduct of the American Institute of Certified Public Accountants express the profession's recognition of its responsibilities to the public, to clients, and to colleagues. They guide members in the performance of their professional responsibilities and express the basic tenets of ethical and professional conduct. The Principles call for an unswerving commitment to honorable behavior, even at the sacrifice of personal advantage."[1]

The Principles are the altruistic objectives to be worked toward by all members. The Preamble calls on its membership to exhibit such traits as the following:

- Self-discipline
- Obligations beyond what the law requires
- Responsibility to the public
- Ethical and professional conduct
- Honorable behavior
- Personal sacrifice

What do these traits mean to the CPA? Clearly, a line can be drawn between *legal* and *ethical.* They do not necessarily have to be parallel actions. For example, lying (except when under oath or to defraud someone) usually is not illegal; however, it is usually considered to be unethical.

The Preamble also indicates that the member will have a commitment to honorable behavior "even at the sacrifice of personal advantage." In the context, it would seem that *personal advantage* would include economic gain. Representative types of dishonorable behavior that would include economic gain are billing for time not worked, selling an opinion (when little or no audit work is performed), and not performing a thorough audit.

Each of the sections of the Principles is succinct. The section on responsibilities admonishes members to "exercise sensitive professional and moral judgments in all their activities. . . . Members of the American Institute of Certified Public Accountants have responsibilities to all those who use their professional services. Members also have a continuing responsibility to cooperate with each other to improve the art of accounting, maintain the public's confidence, and carry out the profession's special responsibilities for self-governance."[2]

Some items that may be included in the responsibilities to those using their services would include the following:

- Conducting a thorough audit

---

[1] AICPA, *Code of Professional Conduct,* as amended January 14, 1992. *By Laws and Implementing Resolutions of Council* as amended June 17, 1996 (New York, NY: AICPA), 4.
[2] Id., 4.

- Resisting a client's choice of inappropriate generally accepted accounting principles (GAAP)
- Making full, fair, and adequate disclosure
- Billing only for actual hours performed
- Noting redundant or ineffective systems

Responsibilities to other members would include being honest with each other, treating other professionals fairly, and helping each other through involvement in professional memberships.

7.7 PUBLIC INTEREST

What does *public interest* mean? What exactly is in the interest of the public? The Article on public interest states, "A distinguishing mark of a profession is acceptance of its responsibility to the public. . . . The public interest is defined as the collective well-being of the community of people and institutions the profession serves. . . . Those who rely on certified public accountants expect them to discharge their responsibilities with integrity, objectivity, due professional care, and a genuine interest in serving the public. They are expected to provide quality services, enter into fee arrangements, and offer a range of services—all in a manner that demonstrates a level of professionalism consistent with these Principles of the Code of Professional Conduct."[3]

The Article defines public interest as the "collective well-being of the community," that community consisting specifically of government, employers, investors, creditors, and the business community.

The CPA has a responsibility to the public, as well as a potential liability to the public or third parties who do not engage the CPA for his or her services. This condition has led the CPA, in some cases, to perceive the facts as the client does, thus impairing his or her independence and exposing his or her firm to potential liability.

What can CPAs do to serve the public interest? Consider the following:

- Self-govern (the extent to which the profession governs itself is the extent to which governmental regulation is not needed)
- Increase professionalism (to maintain the confidence of the public in corporate financial statement reporting)
- Maintain integrity (developing a reputation that other professions would aspire to)
- Maintain independence
- Volunteer time or services to community or charitable organizations (pro bono work)

It is in the above ways and others that the CPA contributes to the well-being of the community. Clearly, there are lapses, and at times CPAs have failed in

[3] Id., 5.

meeting their obligation to the public. However, many businesspeople do hold their CPAs in high esteem and view them as trusted advisors.

7.8 INTEGRITY

Trust, honesty, public service, and integrity are all values that CPAs should reflect in all their professional engagements, according to the Principles. Article III states, "Integrity is an element of character fundamental to professional recognition. It is the quality from which the public trust derives and the benchmark against which a member must ultimately test all decisions. Integrity requires a member to be, among other things, honest and candid within the constraints of client confidentiality. Service and the public trust should not be subordinated to personal gain and advantage. Integrity can accommodate the inadvertent error and the honest difference of opinion; it cannot accommodate deceit or subordination of principle."[4]

Article III goes on to indicate that integrity can be measured by what is right and just. It advises the CPA to ask "Am I doing what a person of integrity would do? Have I retained my integrity?" The article also states that integrity calls for objectivity, independence, due care, and adherence to the form and spirit of ethical standards.[5]

Webster's Ninth New Collegiate Dictionary defines integrity as "firm adherence to a code of especially moral or artistic values; integrity implies trustworthiness and incorruptibility to a degree that one is incapable of being false to a trust, responsibility, or pledge." Therefore, the CPA is to be trusted by both the client and the public.

Why is there such an emphasis on trust and integrity? Perhaps one reason for the emphasis on integrity and ethical behavior is that the public cannot directly verify what the CPA reports. The CPA is entrusted to tell the shareholders, investors, and creditors the state of their investment. By being objective, independent, and performing his or her work with due care, the CPA will fulfill his or her responsibilities to the letter and spirit of the Code of Professional Conduct.

7.9 RULES

The Rules consist of the standards by which the CPA must comply or else face possible disciplinary proceedings. The guidance provided by the AICPA with respect to the Rules includes "Interpretations of the Rules." These interpretations provide guidance by which members can apply the specific rules.

It should be noted that there can be differences between the AICPA Rules and the individual state CPA licensing division regulations. Clearly, in order to maintain one's license, the CPA would give precedent to the state regulation. The Rules consist of the following:

*   Independence, integrity, and objectivity

---

[4] Id., 5.
[5] Id., 6.

- General standards and accounting principles
- Responsibilities to clients
- Other responsibilities and practices

It should be noted that at the time of publication, the section on "Responsibilities to Colleagues" was reserved. Therefore, there are currently no rules providing guidance with respect to the responsibilities of CPAs to colleagues.

7.10   INDEPENDENCE, INTEGRITY, AND OBJECTIVITY

Herman J. Lowe stated, "Paramount to all other issues faced by members during the last 100 years were those of independence, integrity and objectivity."[6]

The Rule regarding independence states that the CPA will be independent with respect to the services provided. Interpretations of this rule indicate that independence is impaired if there is any material or direct monetary interest in the company for which the services are provided.

Another problem for CPA firms is the outsourcing of the internal audit function by certain corporations. In some cases, the outside audit firm is used. It is easier to maintain the perception of independence when a firm other than the independent accountant is used. However, as is typical in a business situation, the CPA firm performing the attest function may be reluctant to refuse an offer to serve as a client's internal auditor.

The internal audit function is the responsibility of management. However, some CPA firms are very active in soliciting the business. Erecting a "Chinese wall" between the attest function and providing consulting services is not easy. Many people believe the perception of independence is flawed when the CPA firm is performing the audit as well as performing the internal audit function.

The fear is that the competition for the fee income will compromise independence and raise serious ethical concerns. Public accountants would like to have the additional business in the internal audit area, but can they perform internal audit functions and remain independent with respect to the financial audit? The independence problem arises when the audit team of a CPA firm performs the audit function, while the internal audit team of the same CPA firm performs the internal audit process. If the outsourcing is unavoidable, at what point does the responsibility of management begin?

The SEC has called for clarification of "how extended audit services impact auditors' independence." This outsourcing of internal audit departments or *extended audit services* is becoming more prevalent. Many companies are focusing on their core businesses. One study reports that about a fourth of 700 internal audit departments have outsourced some part of their internal audit function.[7]

---

[6]Herman J. Lowe, "Ethics in our 100-year History," *Journal of Accountancy* (May 1987), 78.
[7]Richard Anderson, "New Ethics Rules for CPA Firms," *Journal of Accountancy* (August 1996), 61.

The AICPA Professional Ethics Executive Committee has now indicated that CPAs can perform internal auditing services or provide audit services beyond the year-end audit (extended audit services) without impairing independence, as long as the auditor does not do the following:

- Act as an equivalent member of management or employee
- Perform ongoing control activities that affect the execution of transactions (e.g., loan approvals)
- Maintain custody of assets
- Prepare source documents on transactions

In other words, the services provided should be in substance of a consulting nature rather than of a managerial nature. Services that the CPA may supply include the following:

- Performing test counts of inventory
- Confirming balances in accounts receivable
- Performing analytical techniques
- Analyzing fluctuations of account balances

Continuous monitoring by the independent directors on the board as well as the outside auditing firm of the outsourcing aspects of the internal audit function is necessary to make sure that the public confidence in the independence of the CPA is not impaired.

There are those who believe that the interpretation under Rule 101 issued in August 1996 by the AICPA's Professional Ethics Executive Committee has not settled the matter.

Regarding integrity and objectivity, the Rule states, "In the performance of any professional service, a member shall maintain objectivity and integrity, shall be free of conflicts of interest, and shall not knowingly misrepresent facts or subordinate his or her judgment to others."[8] Any member who knowingly makes misrepresentations in records or financial statements is considered to be in violation of this rule.

The interpretation extends the obligation to a member who is dealing with his or her employer's external accountant, indicating that the member must not misrepresent or fail to disclose material facts.

7.11 GENERAL STANDARDS AND ACCOUNTING PRINCIPLES

With respect to General Standards, it is indicated that members are to comply with the standards issued by the "bodies designated by the Council." The body designated by the AICPA Council is the Financial Accounting Standards Board (FASB).

---

[8]Code of Professional conduct, 13.

Standards specifically addressed include professional competence, due professional care, planning and supervision, and sufficient relevant data.

Competence refers to the member's having the ability to conduct the services properly according to the professional standards.

It is also noted that a member performing auditing, compilations, tax, consulting, or other professional services will comply with the professional standards.

Rule 203, Accounting Principles, states, "A member shall not (1) express an opinion or state affirmatively that the financial statements or other financial data of any entity are presented in conformity with generally accepted accounting principles or (2) state that he or she is not aware of any material modifications that should be made to such statements or data in order for them to be in conformity with generally accepted accounting principles, if such statements or data contain any departure from an accounting principle promulgated by bodies designated by Council to establish such principle that has a material effect on the statements or data taken as a whole."[9]

It should be noted that a departure can be made if the financial statements would be otherwise misleading. However, the member must explain the departure and the resulting effects and provide reasons why compliance with GAAP would be misleading to the financial statement user.

The following are covered under Rule 203:

- Statements of Financial Accounting Standards
- Interpretations of Statements of Financial Accounting Standards issued by the FASB
- Statements of Governmental Accounting Standards
- Any Accounting Research Bulletins (ARB) or Accounting Principles Board (APB) statements not modified by the FASB

The AICPA industry audit guides and accounting interpretations are not covered under Rule 203.

7.12   RESPONSIBILITIES TO CLIENTS

The primary responsibilities to clients deal with confidentiality of client information and contingent fees. Rule 301, Confidential Client Information, states, "A member in public practice shall not disclose any confidential client information without the specific consent of the client."[10]

It should be noted that the above Rule does not exempt a member from his or her obligations in terms of compliance with accounting principles or standards, nor does it prohibit a member from fulfilling his or her obligations if subpoenaed.

[9] Id., 14.
[10] Id., 14.

Rule 302 pertains to contingent fees and states:

A member in public practice shall not
1) perform for a contingent fee any professional services for, or receive such a fee from a client for whom the member or the member's firm performs,
    a) an audit or review of a financial statement; or
    b) a compilation of a financial statement when the member expects, or reasonably might expect, that a third party will use the financial statement and the member's compilation report does not disclose a lack of independence; or
    c) an examination of prospective financial information; or
2) prepare an original or amended tax return or claim for a tax refund for a contingent fee for any client.[11]

It should be noted that contingent fees are permitted in certain instances, such as representing an individual in an examination by a revenue agent.

7.13   OTHER RESPONSIBILITIES AND PRACTICES

This section covers a wide variety of topics including discreditable acts, advertising, commissions, and forms of organization. Rule 501, Acts Discreditable, simply states, "A member shall not commit an act discreditable to the profession."[12]
    The interpretations cite the following as being discreditable acts:

- Retaining client records after a demand is made for them
- Discriminating on the basis of race, color, religion, sex, age, or national origin in employment practices
- Failing to follow standards or requirements in audits of governments
- Negligence in the preparation of financial statements
- Failing to follow governmental or regulatory requirements in performing attest or other such services
- Soliciting or disclosing a question from the Uniform CPA Examination

7.14   ADVERTISING

Rule 502 regarding advertising indicates that members may not use false or deceptive advertising or coercion in their solicitations. An example used in the interpretations is indicating that a member may have influence in a court or with a governmental official.
    Rule 503, Commissions and Referral Fees, states that a member will not recommend a service or a product to a client for a commission when the member is

[11] Id., 15.
[12] Id., 16.

providing audit, review, or compilation services or an examination of prospective financial information is performed.

Regarding referrals, any member who accepts a referral fee or who pays for a referral fee must disclose such practice.

7.15 FORM OF ORGANIZATION AND NAME

Rule 505, Form of Organization and Name, states, "A member may practice public accounting only in a form of organization permitted by state law or regulation whose characteristics conform to resolutions of Council."[13]

Previously, many accounting firms were partnerships; a relatively recent form of legal entity is the limited liability partnership (LLP). It should be noted that a member cannot practice under a misleading firm name.

7.16 CONTINUING PROFESSIONAL EDUCATION

As of January 1, 1990, all AICPA members in industry, public practice, education, or government were required to complete continuing professional education (CPE) to maintain their AICPA membership. Excluded from this requirement were retired or inactive members. Members who do not meet their continuing education requirements may lose their AICPA membership.

Members in public practice are required to complete an average of 40 hours of CPE annually, with a minimum of 20 hours each year. Members who are not in public practice are to have an average of 30 hours annually, with at least 15 hours completed each year.

To date, no detailed reporting of CPE hours was required; however, members were to retain documents and records to affirm that they were complying with the requirements. The documentation to be retained includes the following:

* Sponsor providing the CPE
* Course title and description of content
* Date course was taken
* Location
* Number of CPE hours

The AICPA's policies for CPE may not necessarily comply with the individual state CPA Society's requirements or even with the state boards of public accountancy. There may be differences as to the continuing education requirement's covering a 1-, 2-, or 3-year period. Some organizations may require certain courses such as auditing, accounting, or tax, or some courses may be permitted by one organization and excluded by another.

[13] Id., 17.

Do CPE courses have any effect? Regarding ethical considerations, S. Douglas Beets indicated, "To determine whether CPE ethics courses have an appreciable effect on familiarity with conduct rules, the responses of those who had attended such courses were compared with those who had not. Those practitioners who had participated in some sort of post-college ethics education were significantly more familiar with the Code than those who had no additional training. Post-college ethics education, therefore, may be effective in enhancing CPAs' familiarity with conduct rules and improving their ability to evaluate ethics situations."[14]

Regardless of the AICPA Code of Professional Conduct and related Rules, practitioners must be familiar with the codes for the states in which they are licensed. Some state codes may be more restrictive than the AICPA rules, and therefore noncompliance at the state level could result in license suspension or revocation.

7.17 BUILT-IN PROCESS OF REVIEW

A public accounting firm that believes its mission is to function in accordance with the highest professional ethical standards will have a built-in process of review. The ethical environment of the firm is not a "sometimes concern." The amount of attention required to establish a procedure of review is justified because of the long-term benefits that are realized.

Although the questions appropriate for a candid review may vary from firm to firm, the following general questions are basic and useful in beginning the design of a firm's own questionnaire:

- Is there a strong ethical message communicated by the senior partners to all managers, seniors, and staff?
- Are there seminars and discussions about ethical issues on a timely basis?
- Has the accounting firm established a compliance program as defined in the Federal Sentencing Guidelines? (See Appendix G.)
- Does the accounting firm conduct a client evaluation that includes assessment of integrity before accepting an engagement?
- Is an independence questionnaire completed by all partners, managers, seniors, and staff before starting an audit or engagement?
- When an ethical problem is noted, does the firm address it directly and resolve it appropriately?
- Are conflict of interest forms completed by all staff on an annual basis?
- Does the accounting firm conduct internal reviews of its ethics program?
- Is the firm's ethics program examined when a peer review is performed?

[14]Douglas Beets, "The Revised AICPA Code of Professional Conduct: Current Considerations," *The CPA Journal* (April 1992), 32.

Chapter 8

Providing the Ethical Services

8.1 ETHICS SERVICES

(a) Consultations to Attestations

The certified public accountant is able to provide many useful ethics-related services to all types of organizations. As consultants to clients and as auditors, CPAs have given careful attention to ethical matters. From the initial consideration of a prospective client, CPAs have had to make judgments about the integrity of management. CPAs realize that the effectiveness of their services requires that they understand in considerable depth the quality of the ethical environment of each client.

It is this knowledge and detailed experience with a variety of clients that a CPA can leverage in providing services related to ethics. Those services cover a wide range, from serving as a consultant for the design and implementation of a new ethics program to performing an audit of the effectiveness of an ongoing program. Between these two services are many other types of engagements, including reviews of programs or aspects of programs and assessment of the adequacy of training programs and of effectiveness of policies and procedures.

Consulting services can relate to a variety of foci, including the following:

- Design of a comprehensive ethical program
- Redesign of a current program judged to be ineffective
- Evaluation of the adequacy of the design of a program
- Introduction of an ethics program or updating employees about the company's ethics program
- Conducting surveys and other types of investigation to form a conclusion regarding the implementation of a code of conduct or program
- Undertaking an analysis of the adequacy of the administrative structure for ethics

Attestation services also can relate to a range of services, including the following:

- Examination of effectiveness of a total program or a component of a program in accordance with attestation standards (AT 100, paragraphs 1–55)
- Review of effectiveness of a total program or a component of a program in accordance with attestation standards (AT 100, paragraphs 56–58)
- Completion of agreed-upon procedures related to ethical considerations (AT 600)

In this section, representative engagements illustrating the range of services will be discussed.

(b) Consulting Services

Public accountants have been consultants to businesses from their earliest experience as independent professionals. Consulting services may be provided for a wide range of purposes. Those services related to all such engagements, including those related to ethics, must adhere to the professional standards of the profession.

Public accountants are familiar with standards for auditing, such as the General Standards (adequate training, proficiency, independence and due professional care), Standards of Field Work (adequate planning, understanding of internal control system, obtaining sufficient competent evidence), and Standards of Reporting (presentation in accordance with generally accepted accounting principles [GAAP], consistency, informative disclosures, expression of opinion taken as a whole). Other guidance relates to the following:

- Compliance with Financial Accounting Standards Board (FASB) pronouncements
- Compliance with Statements on Auditing Standards (SAS)
- Compliance with Internal Revenue Service (IRS) rulings
- Compliance with state, local, and/or federal taxation laws

As CPAs know, the profession has standards for consulting services, which are stated in the American Institute of Certified Public Accountants' *Statement on Standards for Consulting Services*[1] (SSCS). The CPA engaged in consulting is performing a different service from the audit, which is an attestation service and, as such, must adhere to different rules. A consulting engagement does not include attestation services and can meet a range of purposes. The standard indicates, "In

---

[1] American Institute of Certified Public Accountants, *Statement on Standards for Consulting Services* (AICPA, 1991).

a consulting service, the practitioner develops the findings, conclusions, and recommendations presented. The nature and the scope of the work is determined solely by the agreement between the practitioner and the client. Generally, the work is performed only for the use and benefit of the client."

The standard goes on to define various terms such as the *consulting process* and *consulting services*. The statement also notes that the general standards of the profession apply to all services performed by members, including professional competence, due professional care, planning and supervision, and obtaining sufficient relevant data. The CPA is also advised to serve the client's interest while maintaining integrity and objectivity, establish an understanding of the services to be provided, and inform the client of any conflicts of interest, reservations regarding the scope, and any significant findings.

What types of consulting services may the CPA provide relating to ethics? The Statement on Standards for Consulting Services addresses such engagements as consultations, advisory services, implementation services, transaction services, staff and other support services, and product services. The accountant will find it beneficial to identify the objective of the engagement in the initial stages.

1. *Consultations.* An engagement in which the CPA provides advice in a brief time frame. The advice is generally based on the CPA's existing knowledge of the company and the situation (i.e., no in-depth research is requested). Accountants rendering ethical services may undertake short-term consultations, such as the following:
   - Assessing the description for the new position of ethics officer and providing strategies for identifying promising candidates both internally and externally
   - Evaluating a proposal for a code of conduct that is to be presented to the board of directors for the purpose of determining its adequacy in the company

2. *Advisory services.* An engagement that results in findings, conclusions, and recommendations to assist the company in decision making. Among such engagements are the following:
   - Evaluating the effectiveness of the ethics program at the company as a whole
   - Evaluating the merits of implementing a hotline
   - Evaluating the strategy used by the grievance committee as a basis for determining its effectiveness

3. *Implementation services.* An engagement in which the accountant can put an action, service, or strategy into effect, such as the following:
   - Implementing a grievance procedure for the company
   - Implementing a hotline system
   - Implementing an annual program of ethics training

4. *Transaction services.* An engagement in which the accountant's services pertain to a specific transaction of the company (usually with a third party, i.e., mergers, acquisitions, valuation services), such as the following:
   - Determining which hotline service would be the most cost effective

5. *Staff and other support services.* An engagement in which the CPA's function is to provide staff for tasks requested by the client company, such as the following:
   - Supporting the activities of the ethics officer
   - Supporting the activities of the ethics committee

6. *Product services.* An engagement in which the accountant provides the client with services in support of a particular product (i.e., implementing various software programs related to ethics), such as the following:
   - After implementing an ethics program, providing the training of the employees in that program and monitoring the system.

The type of service requested will determine the nature of the engagement. Providing the ethics services as a consulting engagement gives the CPA fewer constraints than is the case in an attestation engagement.

In an attestation engagement, the CPA must have adequate knowledge in the subject matter of the assertion, whereas in a consulting engagement, the practitioner must utilize due professional care. In an attestation engagement, an assertion has to be made and evaluated against some criteria, whereas in a consulting engagement, no assertions are required to be made. In an attestation engagement, the conclusion must be written, whereas in a consulting engagement, the communication of the results, while preferably in writing, may be provided orally. There is no impairment of independence, in and of itself, if a consulting engagement is performed for an audit client.

The AICPA's *Comparing Attest and Consulting Services: A Guide for the Practitioner* includes the following statement regarding attestations:

> An attest service requires *reasonable criteria.* Even when reasonable criteria exist, the practitioner should consider whether the assertion is capable of reasonably *consistent* estimation or measurement using the criteria and whether competent persons using the same criteria should be able to obtain materially similar estimates or measurements.[2]

How effective is a company's ethics program? Can an *objective* measurement be made whereby two practitioners would come to approximately the same conclusions? With respect to performing an attestation engagement, certainly such objective criteria could include the following:

---

[2]American Institute of Certified Public Accountants, *Comparing Attest and Consulting Services: A Guide for the Practitioner* (AICPA, 1993), 2/115.14 (emphasis added).

- Extent to which employees know the ethical policies of the company
- Extent to which calls received by the hotline are resolved to the complainant's satisfaction
- Extent of adherence to regulations

The above could objectively be supported by such means as number of signatures obtained to verify receipt of the company's ethics policy, number of calls received by the hotline, number of civil suits incurred, and number of regulatory violations. The question then becomes: Does reduction of violations point to a strong ethical program? How do you measure improved adherence to regulations due to implementation of an ethics program?

In contrast to a consulting arrangement, the CPA may also perform an attestation of the existing ethics program of a company. An attestation, per AICPA Attestation Standards, requires the following:

- An assertion capable of being evaluated against some criteria established by a recognized body or stated in a clear and comprehensive manner
- An assertion that is capable of consistent measurement or estimation
- A practitioner having adequate knowledge in the subject matter of ethics
- A practitioner having an independent mental attitude
- A report identifying the assertions, the practitioner's conclusions regarding the assertions, the CPA's reservations about the engagement, and that the report has been prepared in conformity with the agreed-upon criteria or agreed-upon procedures, and limiting the use of the report to parties who have agreed on the criteria or procedures

There are times when all the above requirements are not present and a practitioner is, therefore, unable to complete an attestation engagement. In these instances, a consulting engagement is appropriate and sufficient. As always, the AICPA's Code of Professional Conduct applies to any engagement undertaken by a CPA.

In a consulting engagement, the practitioner must maintain objectivity, whereas in an attestation engagement, the CPA must be independent. Consulting requires different skills from those required in providing attest services. In rendering conclusions from consulting, a CPA is assessing, classifying, summarizing, and interpreting data. In contrast, in an attestation engagement, the CPA is "gathering evidence to support the assertion and objectively assessing the measurements and communications of the asserter" (AT 100.07). Attestation standards require a specific type of report; in contrast, consulting service standards are more general. The nature, extent, and form of report is not specified.

While the CPA is there to provide services to the client, careful consideration should be given to the type of engagement provided.

(c) Engagement to Design an Ethics Program (Example 1)

An example of an ethics consulting assignment is the design of an ethics program. Initially, the client may wish to have the CPA develop or review only a portion of an ethics program. For illustrative purposes, this section provides guidance on how the CPA can assist a client in developing an entire ethics program from the ground up.

Assume that a client has grown rapidly in the last five years. The founder and a relatively small staff functioned in an informal manner. However, the total number of employees has increased from 100 six years ago to 3,500 now. The founder has announced plans to step aside. The incumbent chief executive officer (CEO) and outgoing founder feel they must "institutionalize an ethics environment." What does the CPA need to do?

The first part of this engagement would be to gather any relevant information on the existing program, even though informal and mostly unwritten. The guiding questions are: How are ethical issues currently handled? What are the primary beliefs (values) that guide resolution of problems? Interviews are helpful in the preliminary phase. Personnel in management, human resources, and legal are likely to be helpful in providing an overview of the current situation.

From information gained from these interviews, the CPA will be able to determine the degree to which management is interested in designing an effective ethics program. Management not only sets the policies, but allocates the resources. If management only establishes policies, but is unwilling to allocate the resources necessary for an effective program, then the accountant may suspect that his or her work may be for "window dressing." For our illustration, we will assume management has a sincere interest in the ethics program.

Elements of effective programs include the following:

- Commitment by top management ("tone at the top")
- Code of ethics
- Functional responsibility (ethics officer)
- Training of employees
- Communication mechanism (hotline, review committee)
- Plan for review of the effectiveness of the program (ethics committee/ oversight)

The process has to "fit" the environment and culture of the organization. Representative factors that could influence the scope of the above activities include the following:

- Size of organization (large, multinational corporation versus small, regional company)
- Legal entity (corporation, partnership, sole proprietorship)

- Nature of operations (manufacturing versus service)
- Industry (banking, hospitality, accounting)
- Profit versus nonprofit

A key point for the CPA to keep in mind is that an ethics program must be tailored to the particular organization. The CPA must become aware of the uniqueness of the client and how that uniqueness must influence the ethics program. The type of ethics program for a large, global manufacturer is not likely to be the same as that for a small, regional accounting firm.

Organizations develop techniques to provide employees with guidance. There are many effective techniques in use. A common technique is to reduce the overall process to simple, direct language. One illustration of a direct, easily understood process is that at Texas Instruments. This company uses the following seven-step process:

1. Is the action legal?
2. Does it comply with our values?
3. If you do it, will you feel bad?
4. How will it look in the newspaper?
5. If you know it's wrong, don't do it.
6. If you are not sure, ask.
7. Keep asking until you get an answer.[3]

The preceding is one representative process. The CPA can assist a company in developing a simple, clear, concrete process that will capture the attention of all employees and become valuable in instilling an understanding of what the company is striving to achieve in its ethics program.

(d) Designing the Code of Ethics

Codes of ethics are longstanding in many organizations. Codes for professionals may have begun with the Hippocratic Oath, believed to have been drafted in approximately 500 B.C. One of the first steps in developing an ethical environment is establishing a code of ethics. Although companies have functioned with an oral code of ethics that appeared sufficient, many are now establishing written codes.

The first step in this process is for the accountant to understand the reason for the company to develop and maintain a code of ethics. Should the code not be formally written, then the accountant will want to understand the implicit code that is to guide behavior in the company.

---

[3]Gillian Flynn, "Make Employee Ethics Your Business," in John E. Richardson (ed.), *Business Ethics 96/97* (Guilford, CT: Dushkin Publishing Group, 1996), 40.

Many companies seek assistance in reconsidering their existing code of ethics. There may be a need for the CPA to provide general information about what codes generally include. It should be recognized that the code of ethics will have substance only if there is a willingness by top management to support, communicate, and demonstrate the code.

Increasing attention to formal programs is encouraging organizations to make their codes more explicit. The content and nature of presentation can vary considerably from company to company. Interest in written codes was intensified in the report of the National Commission on Fraudulent Financial Reporting (Treadway Commission). One of its major recommendations was that companies develop and enforce *written codes of conduct*. The recommendation stated the following:

> Public companies should develop and enforce written codes of corporate conduct. Codes of conduct should foster a strong ethical climate and open channels of communication to help protect against fraudulent financial reporting. As a part of its ongoing oversight of the effectiveness of internal controls, a company's audit committee should review annually the program that management establishes to monitor compliance with the code.

The preparation of a code of ethics as part of a comprehensive ethics plan must take into account the strategic and operating plans of the entire organization. Thus, responsible corporate managers must become aware of all possible aspects and initiate the necessary input.

For example, the executive of a global corporation headquartered in New York City should not develop specific ethical guidance without the input from all units of the organization. Information must be elicited from local managers from all parts of the company so that the final policies can be a product of the corporate family. However, general traits of fairness, honesty, and ethical treatment of employees and customers tend to be universal.

The incentive system should reward and penalize accomplishments and failures other than those related to economic gain. As an example, one company provides for 20 percent of the bonus pool to go to managers who make gains towards their diversity goals. The policy of the company should take into account that employees may be demoted or discharged for failure to behave responsibly toward their subordinates, vendors, clients and co-workers, even if they are successful in economic terms.

If organizations support high standards of profit and of ethics and believe such standards can be met simultaneously, then much is required of the character, general education, and professional competence of managers who must provide moral leadership. The CPA should note that awareness of the problem usually generates its solution. The accommodation of the bottom line should not be the only aim of business. People should never be so apprehensive of their superiors or of losing their jobs that they can rationalize inappropriate, unethical, or illegal behavior. No one should ever feel so pressured that they act in a manner inconsistent with their own moral beliefs. It should also be acknowledged that it takes a certain amount of courage to stand up to one's superior and risk demotion, loss of income, or termination for standing on one's principles. An organization's code of ethics should support an employee's decision to take such a stand.

Among the general considerations for a code of ethics are the following:

- Easily readable (make it understandable by all employees, not a legal document to protect the company)
- Compatible with the philosophy of the company
- Visionary (give a direction to where the company wants to go or should be)
- Current
- Accurate
- Easily applicable
- Positive (leave the negative "any employee who . . . will be terminated" for the code of conduct policy)

The basics must be stressed. Integrity is imperative. The corporation cannot communicate a vision if people believe integrity is lacking. Trust, honesty, keeping one's word, and commitment to excellence are all vital. Other specific topics to be included in the code of ethics could be developed by the CPA in the research and interview process.

Internal ethics policies must be embraced by senior managers with honesty and enthusiasm, and not just with words. Subordinates learn to read their superiors and unless the corporate conscience is embraced, preached, and practiced from the top by actions as well as words, the code of ethics will become a hollow shell. This was reinforced in an article by Hill, Metzger, and Dalton, which stated the following:

> A recent empirical study, for example, found no statistically significant evidence that corporate codes have had any impact on the number of corporate regulatory violations. In another recent survey of management, the respondents saw no positive differences in corporate behavior attributable to the adoption of a corporate ethics code. In fact, researchers found that the perceived pressure to achieve income and return-on-investment targets was *greater* in companies which had adopted a code, a fact they tentatively attributed to the larger size of the companies that had adopted ethics codes . . . one study found that 91% of the codes examined mentioned the company's legal responsibilities as the primary basis for the code. . . . If managers who achieve "good" results by questionable means are rewarded rather than punished, other employees quickly learn the "real" organizational rules. As one observer wryly noted: "Values are what you say you believe. Ethics are how you actually behave."[4]

[4]John W. Hill, Michael B. Metzger, and Dan R. Dalton, "How Ethical Is Your Company?" *Management Accounting* (July 1992), 60.

The article went on to note that virtually no company had a reward program for achieving ethical goals.

The board of directors must be directly involved in supporting the code of ethics. The board may communicate that message when executive compensation is considered, making clear that more than the bottom line will be considered. The board must join with senior management in taking responsibility. When the right tone is not set, it is easy for subordinates to view ethical guidelines as a negative to productivity and the bottom line. Deceptive sales practices and customer fraud can claim a very high price in reputation and in income in the long run.

It is interesting to note that various studies have found that strong ethical guidelines can lead to more rapid growth and increasing returns on investment. However, it is not uncommon to find senior executives who are unaware of how their attitudes permeate their companies and give lower management little incentive to spot risks or investigate complaints. Senior management must take personal responsibility for ethical conduct and be sensitive to the possible impact of their own actions.

Codes of ethics represent the best goals established by an organization. The codes discuss the altruistic qualities that companies aspire to. Representative elements that should be considered in developing a corporate code of ethics include the following:

- Objective of the code
- Applicability (emphasize that it applies equally to everyone)
- Employees striving to exercise honesty
- Adherence to state, local, and federal laws
- Adherence to regulatory authorities
- Employees always doing their best, striving for the highest goals possible
- Recognition that the spirit of the policy needs to be demonstrated individually
- Developing a solid reputation for the individual and organization for integrity
- Maintaining the confidentiality of the organization
- Performing responsibilities with due care
- Continually striving to improve one's skills
- Demonstrating loyalty first to ethical principles and then to the organization
- Providing equal opportunity
- Utilizing diversity hiring
- Reporting unacceptable behavior (whistle-blowing)

The preceding suggestions are frequently addressed in various codes, but not necessarily covered in every code of ethics. Other areas that could be considered as *separate* policies include promotion, raises, complaint procedures, whistle-blower protection, ombudsman, hotline program, resolution of conflicts, hours of work, dress code, sick leave policy, sabbatical policy, trade secrets, use of company equipment, improper use of insider information, gifts and entertainment, and privacy issues.

Inclusion of every topic addressed would make the policy cumbersome. It is strongly recommended to have a code of ethics addressing the major concepts that guide ethical behavior in the company. The detailed policies and practices can then be addressed in other documents. It is also recommended that companies include a code of conduct (discussed later in this section); the company could then clearly delineate behavior that is unacceptable and would subject an individual to termination. Likewise, another policy may indicate that any political affairs must be done on an individual's time and at an individual's expense and that no company funding of any candidate or political party may be made.

Frequently, the terms *code of ethics* and *code of conduct* are used interchangeably. Although there are no set rules, codes of ethics tend to describe the qualities an organization aspires to achieve, while codes of conduct describe expected behavior and what is considered unacceptable behavior. There are many reasons for having *both* types of codes.

A code of conduct addresses the issues and clarifies the organization's position, and sends a message that the company is serious regarding unethical and illegal acts. Topics that a code of conduct may address could include the following:

- Lying
- Stealing
- Not accepting gifts or bribes
- Requiring employees who uncover illegal activity to report it
- Not engaging in any actual or perceived conflict of interest
- Prohibiting sexual harassment
- Prohibiting preferential treatment
- Providing for drug testing (if permitted by law)
- Prohibiting use of illegal drugs in workplace
- Allowing for reporting of illegal or unethical behavior (and description of how reporting may be done in confidence)
- Prohibiting the disclosure of confidential and proprietary information

Other areas that the CPA may want the company to address as separate policies (depending on the industry the company is in) could include the following:

- Adherence to Occupational Safety and Health Administration (OSHA) rules and procedures

- General health and safety factors
- Insider training
- Internal purchasing of stock
- Purchasing of corporate products
- Handling of gratuities, gifts, and commissions from vendors and customers
- Community interaction
- Who may speak for the corporation to the media
- Customer relations
- Refunds, exchanges, and allowances
- Environmental policy

The organization may want to indicate the potential penalty (or penalities) for violations, such as termination of one's job. There appears to be great temptation to compromise standards to meet business objectives. Price fixing, bribery, and other ethical lapses will continue unless senior management continually communicates a firm resolve for zero tolerance.

It should be noted that both the code of conduct and code of ethics should be reviewed by corporate counsel before being issued. The firm may wish to have the code signed on a periodic (e.g., annual) basis. The objective by this procedure would be to reinforce the organization's adherence to those standards. Should a termination of a company employee become necessary, then there is tangible proof that the employee was aware of the consequences.

One area that is always challenging is requesting employees to report unethical behavior. Management needs to address this issue head-on. Representative reasons frequently given for not reporting unethical behavior include the following:

- Believing no corrective action would be taken
- Fearing retribution from employer
- Not trusting the organization to keep the information confidential

Reporting of unethical or illegal behavior is an area that should be addressed in the code of conduct. A complete code of conduct makes explicit the individual employee's responsibility.

The code of ethics is not merely a public relations or a legal document. It must be descriptive, provide guidance, and provide specific practices. Unfortunately, the existence of a code of ethics does not guarantee ethical behavior. The establishment of the code must be followed by conferences, training programs, periodic revisions, and *periodic audits* by CPA firms, all supported by senior management's playing a central role. The entire organization must be committed, and good communication is a must. Ethical sensitivity should pervade at all levels of the business. Companies committed to achieving a quality ethical environment consider their code of ethics a "living" document—one that has relevance to decisions and actions daily.

Integrity and honesty should be basic principles underlying all areas of a company's concerns, including economic, social, environmental, and political. In addition, relations with the public, customers, investors, vendors, the community, and various governmental authorities should be included in the code. Corporate social responsibility must be accepted by personnel throughout the organization, regardless of level of responsibility. Again, it must be stressed that senior management must provide leadership in integrating the entire ethical program into the culture of the firm. Management should reinforce the general principles that guide behavior, so that if a circumstance is not addressed in the code, then the standards of fairness and justice—and a sense of what is "right"—should prevail. What is this "highest sense of right"? Questions employees may ask themselves to determine if they are being ethical may include the following:

- How do I feel about this?
- What is my "gut" telling me?
- Would I be comfortable with the facts of this being on the front page of the company's newsletter?
- Is what I am doing entirely legal?
- Would I feel embarrassed to share my actions with my friends and relatives?

Generally, the company that seeks the help of a CPA in developing a code of ethics/conduct anticipates the implementation of an ethics program.

Remember, the code of ethics is *only* the beginning; it cannot exist in a vacuum. Employees should, along with the code of ethics, be given a framework for making decisions (see Section 8.9), as well as access to a hotline and a supportive ethics officer.

(e) Systematic Plan for Review of the Effectiveness of the Program

A basic tenet of auditing is that an area that is not monitored is basically not properly controlled. This saying is also true for ethics programs. An organization's ethics program must be monitored. Optimally, this would be a function performed by an independent ethics committee. However, the nature and size of the business may preclude this type of arrangement. Just as in small operations, controls are more challenging to implement because of the lack of segregation of duties; likewise, ethical practices may also be challenging to monitor in large, diverse organizations.

Suggestions for performing the oversight function include the following:

Representative Entity	Oversight Responsibility
• Sole Proprietorship	• Management
• Small company	• Small, informal ethical oversight committee with access to top management or two individuals (manager and one staff)
• Large corporation	• Formal ethical oversight committee reporting to board of directors and internal auditors

Some type of ethical oversight responsibility must be established to keep the code operational, as well as overseeing periodic revisions to maintain integrity. Helping to design the ethical oversight responsibility is another area in which the CPA may provide needed client services. The CPA could provide services in helping to develop the ethical oversight responsibility. Representative services the CPA could provide include:

- Developing a description of the responsibilities of the function
- Drawing up a representative listing of potential employees to staff the oversight function (at least one representative from each level of the organization)
- Designing a system in which reviews and reporting of any results of the oversight function may be performed

(f) Ethical Oversight Committee (Example 2)

The CPA should design the program so that the ethical oversight committee would be composed of individuals who have the trust of colleagues. For example, who should be on the ethical oversight committee? Intuitively, this is not a hard problem. Most people in organizations know which people can be trusted. Through providing ethics services, CPAs become aware of the employees who have gained the trust of their peers. However, it is not the CPA's responsibility to specifically choose the people on the committee. The CPA can provide valuable help by describing the qualifications and traits of individuals who are most likely to be effective in serving on the committee. Beyond ethical traits, the CPA involved in the selection process should consider other characteristics of potential committee members, including the following:

- Ability to maintain confidentiality
- Good communication skills
- Visionary outlook
- Ability to work within (or ability to change) the corporate culture

The ethical oversight committee should be made up of all levels of employees within the company. The company may wish to consider selecting committee members who appropriately reflect the diversity of the company's personnel. Committee members who may be considered include outside board members, customers, and possibly even vendors (outside input is always useful). The most important aspect of being on the committee is that the members chosen must have the respect and support of all underlying constituencies.

This committee is a *policy* committee with the goal of helping lead the direction of the company and making recommendations for implementing those policies. The CPA could be included as an ad hoc member of the committee to provide technical assistance from an objective point of view. The responsibilities of the committee could include the following:

- Establishing that all levels of the organization are represented by the committee (if not by actual representation, then by ability to communicate or have access to representatives)
- Establishing/implementing training programs
- Monitoring/oversight of the entire ethics program
- Reviewing results of hotline calls (maintaining confidentiality)
- Reviewing the ethical performance of management
- Ensuring that the organization maintains an ethical perspective (i.e., ethics is not something that is done once, then forgotten about)

The objective of the committee is not to decide individual cases and what the ramifications may be for employees who violate the code. A separate group is needed for this function.

The CPA should design the program so that all employees are encouraged to contribute constructive feedback to the committee, be sure that the committee meets on a regular basis, and review any minutes of the meeting to determine progress of the committee.

Ethical management should be incorporated into an employee performance appraisal. If possible, ethical compliance with the code of ethics should be part of every employee's evaluation and a factor in compensation, bonus, and promotion.

Regular meetings of the committee should be held to ensure the exchange of views and whether the code of conduct should be modified, as well as discussing the cases that have come up between meetings. Human resource people may be brought in as necessary to advise regarding personnel issues.

(g) Role of the Ethics Officer

If anything shows the increaseing interest in ethics, it is the rapid rise of the ethics officer. "Today, more than 500 companies have created official guardians of corporate rectitude—up from 200 just six years ago—with a mission of keeping employee conduct *more upright than the law requires,* if not necessarily as pure as the golden rule commands. It is hard to object to the trend."[5] (See Chapter 9 for further comment about the organization established for ethics officers.)

If the size of the organization merits having a full-time ethics officer, then one should be appointed by senior management with a direct reporting responsibility to senior management. Smaller organizations may appoint one individual who would have the role of an ethics officer responsible for organizing and guiding an ethical oversight committee. The entire organization must be made aware that the board of directors fully supports the entire process and that the ethics officer reports directly to the CEO. The ethics officer should have a direct reporting line to senior management and if necessary to the chairman of the board of directors.

Public accountants can be key in helping to develop the role of the ethics officer. Representative contributions they can make include the following:

- Formulating the role of the ethics officer
- Developing the description of the responsibilities
- Assisting in the selection of an ethics officer
- Orienting the new hire to the organization from an accounting and control perspective

For example, if a CPA took the assignment of drafting the description of the responsibilities of an ethics officer to be hired, the following might be addressed:

- Should the ethics officer be from within the company or an outsider? (Consideration should be given to this based on the history of the company. For example, if the company is just coming out of a major scandal, then the CPA may lean more toward recommending an outsider.)
- Should the position be part time or full time? (CPA's recommendation may be based on not only size, but nature of the industry.)
- What experience is necessary? (Again, depending on the industry, the CPA may believe it is necessary to have someone familiar with the industry, if it is technical in nature. In other cases, an individual knowledgeable about implementing ethics programs may be sufficient.)
- What is the tone of the company? (If the CPA is drafting the responsibilities for a client he or she has had for years, then the CPA is aware of the "corporate climate" and should incorporate that into the description of the individual to be hired.)

Why should a company hire an ethics officer? Aren't people either honest or dishonest? This question persists. However, there is evidence that to a certain

---

[5]*The New York Times* (February 8, 1998), 1 (emphasis added).

degree individuals are shaped by their environment. It is this assumption that supports all efforts to enhance ethical standards in the workplace. The ethics officer can have influence in developing an environment that supports ethics and individuals who make the right choice. Employees must be convinced that they can communicate without fear or intimidation and that privacy will be respected.

Clearly, the larger the company, the more beneficial it becomes to have an ethics officer. Representative responsibilities in such a position include the following:

- Analyzing the company's process for ethical decision making
- Creating an environment that supports ethics
- Establishing ethical standards
- Determining how best to communicate those standards
- Maintaining oversight of the ethics process

Note that the preceding list does not address being a disciplinarian or being judge, jury, and executioner. The reason for this is *that* role (disciplinarian) tends to be one of management. A good ethics officer will take a broader approach and view his or her responsibilities more as that of a systems analyst or "agent of change."

What is that change? It is to empower the employees to assist them in making the right decision. Individual employees are making more decisions on their own all the time. The more decisions one makes, then the more opportunities there are to being faced with ethical questions.

Other key roles of the ethics officer include providing perspective and asking the right questions. The ethics officer can be beneficial to the company by examining an issue from the perspectives not only of the company, but from the point of view of the public, customers, regulatory authorities, and vendors. The ethics officer can only ask questions, such as is it right to use cartoon characters to market our products (alcohol, tobacco, etc.) to young people, or if our product does not meet safety standards in one country, then should we send it to another where the standards are more lax? The ethics officer can provide valuable assistance to line managers as they strive for satisfactory solutions to problems within the framework of the company's ethical values.

Dependent on the management and/or the committee, the ethics officer may be very proactive and involved, or simply be there in the event of problem. Regardless, the role is to manage the ethical programs and be an advisor to the employees and the company. The oversight functions can range from passive to very active, and can be extremely frustrating. Michael Josephson of the Joseph & Edna Josephson Institute of Ethics stated: "When I hear them talking together, they are very, very cynical about the process, because they feel so powerless. They know about all the times they lost, all the times they were not consulted about a problem but asked how to clean it up after the fact. Most ethics officers don't even have the clout to come close to overriding the bottom-line-ism that governs most business goals."[6]

The article continues by saying that they are viewed as "prophets in a land of profits, doing the best they can . . . And the most common problem they tackle, apparently, is not larceny or licentiousness, but loss of face."

Regardless, handling the ethical problems and suggesting solutions can be important to the company. Besides the oversight committee, companies need training, implementation, and continual practice, not just theory. A process for the reporting and follow-up of incidents must also be practical and not just theoretical.

(h) The Importance of Training

The Bedford Committee of the American Accounting Association stated in 1986 that "Professional accounting education must not only emphasize the needed skills and knowledge, it must also *instill the ethical standards* and commitments of a professional."

Training programs may be an important step toward effective compliance, not only for CPAs but for companies as a whole. The employees should be mandated to attend the training program on a periodic basis. A survey was taken of Irish accountants who indicated that there was "near unanimous agreement" that ethics courses should be offered as part of continuing professional development.[7] In other words, the demand for ethical guidance is clearly there.

Education and awareness in combination, as well as communication, are in the best interests of the organization. As shown throughout this book, the code of ethics and compliance with the code can improve the bottom line over the long run.

Training does not have to be only formal classroom presentations. Informal in-house programs can be just as effective, getting small groups together to address the ethical challenges of the organization. Informal training programs can be developed and presented by the ethics officer, the ethics oversight committee, the training department, or outside consultants or trainers. Public accountants can provide ethical training sessions contingent on the following:

- Being knowledgeable in the field of ethics
- Having experienced training personnel
- Having quality materials and necessary presentation skills

Training is an integral part of a good ethics program. Training in ethics has evolved from handing the new hire a policies and procedures manual and signing off on a list of "I promise not to do such and such" to having entire organi-

---

[6]Id., 12.
[7]*Accountancy Ireland*, Vol. 28 (February 1996), 10–12.

zations taking the time to determine the company's values, understanding the ethical decision-making process, and knowing the resources and who to communicate with if there is a question. Training in ethics can result in meaningful shifts in the thinking and behavior of employees if approaches such as these are taken.

The training should have the participants attempt to use some method in order to formulate an ethical decision—the desired goal is to have an employee make an ethical decision. The process can be by a variety of means. The American Accounting Association devised a decision model, as follows:

1. Determine the facts—what, who, where, when, how. (What do we know or need to know, if possible, that will help define the problem?)
2. Define the ethical issue (make sure precisely what the ethical issue is, e.g., conflict involving rights, question over limits of an obligation, and so on).
   a. List the significant stakeholders.
   b. Define the ethical issues.
3. Identify major principles, rules, and values (e.g., integrity, quality, respect for persons, profit).
4. Specify the alternatives (list major alternative courses of action, including those that represent some form of compromise or point between simply doing or not doing something).
5. Compare values and alternatives to determine whether a clear decision is possible. (Determine if there is one principle or value, or combination, that is so compelling that the proper alternative is clear, e.g. correcting a defect that is almost certain to cause loss of life.)
6. Assess the consequences (identify short- and long-term, positive and negative consequences for the major alternatives; the common short-run focus on gain or loss needs to be measured against long-run considerations; this step will often reveal an unanticipated result of major importance).
7. Make your decision (balance the consequences against your primary principles or values, and select the alternative that fits best).[8]

Although the preceding is an excellent process for making ethical decisions, it should be recognized that it is also a good method for making any decision.

Larry Ponemon, CMA, included some of the following as being important elements in ethics training:

- Live instruction
- Small class size

---

[8]Howard L. Siers, "Ethics," *Management Accounting* (April 1991), 18.

- Powerful senior executive message
- Given to all employees
- Significant group interaction
- At least four hours of training
- New employee programs
- Follow-up communication[9]

It is important to make sure that the ethical training sessions include being proactive (meaning that they teach or fortify integrity, honesty, moral excellence, and social responsibility). By being proactive, hopefully fewer problems will occur. This approach contrasts with the typical ethical problem occurring and then reacting to it by having employees attend a training course.

How much did the employees "get out" of a training course? This is where CPA firms can provide their value-added services by performing the periodic ethics audit, ensuring that the actual practices (taught in the training courses) occur.

Training is effective when it is relevant. If an organization has just faced a well-publicize ethical problem, then an ethics training program may be warranted and should be implemented on a timely basis. The training should also be relevant to the industry and the company. The ethical challenges to a manufacturing firm can be different than those to a brokerage company.

It should be recognized that ethics training is not just one part of an orientation program that an employee gets, but rather should be a continuous process for all employees. Some organizations have regular speakers on various ethical topics. Other organizations try to incorporate an ethical component in every course they provide to their employees.

A good ethical code and training does not by itself inspire moral excellence. Consistent leadership, strong support by senior management, and an ethics infrastructure that supports the entire ethics program will lead to integrity and moral excellence. Ethics can become a cornerstone of a successful business, especially where the leadership uses every opportunity to lead by word and example.

8.2 ENGAGEMENTS TO BENCHMARK ETHICS PROGRAM (EXAMPLE 3)

Another example of providing consulting services would be where a CPA benchmarks a current/existing ethics program in an organization.

What is *benchmarking?* According to Benchmarking Network (a group of benchmarking specialists[10]): "Benchmarking is a performance measurement tool

---

[9]Larry Ponemon, "Key Features of an Effective Ethics Training Program," *Management Accounting* (October 1996), 66.
[10]Website—www.com/user/benchmar/files/general.html.

used in conjunction with improvement initiatives to measure comparative operating performance and identify best practices." Considering the definition of benchmarking, clearly CPAs can use their analytical skills (measuring and making comparisons) to determine how their client's ethical practices measure up compared to those of other companies.

In the preliminary survey phase, it may be beneficial to determine what types of ethical programs or ethical practices other companies have in the same industry. Means by which such knowledge could be gathered could include contacting the following:

- Professional associations
- Trade associations
- Companies
- Employees
- Consultants

Different companies, even within the same industry, will have different corporate cultures; therefore, after completing the benchmarking process, consider whether changes to the organization's ethics program are appropriate. Experimentation is fine; however, after implementing any changes, those changes should be reviewed a few months later to determine their effectiveness.

For example, a case that a CPA may be retained for is benchmarking a hotline service for a company's ethics program. Representative steps in this engagement could include the following:

- Reviewing the existing hotline policies
- Reviewing the procedures for responding to a call on the hotline
- Determining number of calls (per day, month, etc.)
- Determining types of calls (personnel complaints versus ethics violations)
- Determining whether there may be other similar hotline services with companies of same size and/or in same industry
- Examining the practices of these companies
- Determining the response time to the calls and comparing it to other companies
- Analyzing and comparing the performance and the practices of the company's hotline to other companies

Once the preceding steps are implemented and any deficiencies noted compared to the best practices, then improvements and corrective action to the system may be made.

Benchmarking is fine for ethical programs that have had a chance to develop; however, each company should at a minimum have the following:

Minimum Ethical Requirements

- Code of ethics
- Hotline
- Grievance procedure (reporting mechanism)
- Ethics officer (if not feasible as a full-time position in small organizations, then someone performing those responsibilities on a part-time basis)
- A board of directors and management that is involved (performing the oversight function)
- Regular ethics training
- Performance reviews that address ethical qualities exhibited by employees

8.3 REVIEWS BY INTERNAL AUDITORS

There are a variety of approaches to reviewing an existing ethics program—benchmarking, as just described, is one of them. Another means is via internal reviews or independent (or external) reviews. Internal reviews are examinations of the system performed by employees within the company, in contrast to independent reviews performed by outsiders.

Internal reviews are frequently performed by internal auditors for companies large enough to support such a function. The internal audit department is ideally suited for this type of review. Not only does the internal audit department have the technical skills for performing this type of review, but the internal audit department, more so than outsiders, understands the corporate culture of the company.

The perspective of the department may be one of several. Two approaches will be discussed here.

From a compliance audit perspective, internal audit would analyze what the ethical policies and procedures are and what ethical standards are being implemented. In terms of a compliance audit, in part of the review, internal audit would determine how well the ethical policies were being complied with. It may also address any ethical questions regarding compliance with other company policies and procedures or any state, location, or federal laws and/or compliance with regulatory requirements. In other words, a compliance audit regarding the company's ethics programs may not need to limit its scope to only the stated ethical requirements.

A *compliance* audit may address the following issues:

- Does the ethics policy properly comply with the needs of the company in this industry?

- Does the ethics program of the company facilitate compliance with the Federal Sentencing Guidelines?
- Did managers properly implement the ethics program?
- Is there an overall sense that the spirit of the policy is being complied with?
- Does the ethics program support the laws and regulations of the state, local, and federal government?

In contrast, an *operational* audit by the internal audit department of the ethics area may address such issues as how *effective* was the program and could the program be performed more *economically.* Representative issues may include the following:

- From a quantitative perspective, how much was the ethics program utilized (i.e., number of calls on the hotline this year versus prior years)?
- How quickly are calls on the hotline responded to?
- Are all employees aware of the ethics program?
- How effective was the ethics program (including what managers and staff think of the program)?
- Are employees adhering to the program (i.e., how many employees have been terminated based on ethical violations and is that number increasing or decreasing)?
- Have all employees signed a statement adhering to the ethical standards of the company?
- Are part-time employees required to adhere to the same ethical standards?
- How well did the ethics officer/department do in meeting his/their stated objectives?
- Is the ethics program run in the most economical manner (could technology reduce the cost of implementing programs—videotapes, e-mail, websites, etc.)?
- Would benchmarking be warranted/beneficial?
- Does the ethics officer/department have sufficient resources to fulfill his/their objectives?
- Are the objectives of the ethics program realistic, and is measurable progress toward them being made?

The line distinguishing between compliance and operational audit is not necessarily clearly drawn. Depending on the objective of the audit, some elements of an operational audit may be desired in a compliance audit and vice versa.

Note: The ethics officer and/or ethics department should receive periodic internal audits just as any other department would.

8.4   INDEPENDENT REVIEWS OF ETHICS

Maintaining objectivity in reviewing a program is critical. Just as it is difficult for us to see our own faults from a personal perspective, this is likewise true of companies. A highly visible ethics program, for example, may be assumed to be successful. An internal review, when such an opinion is held, may be less than vigorous and candid.

An independent ethical review is requested by management to be sure that what is believed to be true is indeed true. In 1996, Bankers Trust Company, Mitsubishi Motor Manufacturing of America Ltd., Astra (a Swedish drug maker), Texaco, and Prudential, among others, initiated independent reviews.

Public accounting firms are viewing ethics consulting as a new growth area for their firms. Practically all of the big five accounting firms have set up ethics divisions, and smaller CPA firms are also beginning to develop ethics consulting units. These CPA firms help companies design internal ethics programs to overhaul the current status quo in various companies.

Such reviews may be performed to determine compliance with existing programs, or they may be performed to determine the effectiveness of the ethics program. It must be acknowledged that companies frequently request these reviews subsequent to a well-publicized ethics problem. The more progressive organizations realize the value and are proactive in conducting ethics reviews before problems occur.

Is there a market for CPAs providing these services? The answer is yes, but the real question is: How big is that market and how big will it become? The answer to this is based on the CPAs showing the cost benefit of implementing ethics programs to management. There are tangible rewards to those who uphold their principles. Principles can boost the bottom line. Various studies have found that good ethics practices raise employee morale, which raises motivation, which increases productivity, resulting in increased sales and increasing net income.

8.5   ATTESTATION ENGAGEMENTS OF ETHICS

Clients may seek an audit of their total ethics program or a part of such a program. The CPA has sufficient professional guidance to undertake such an assignment. For purposes of illustrating an engagement, assume that a client has asked a CPA to do an ethics audit. Further inquiry by the CPA reveals that the client is interested in the general question: To what extent is our ethics program effective? Through inquiry and discussion, the CPA learns that there is a comprehensive program in the company. There is a written code of conduct, an ethics officer, a clearly stated set of procedures for review and resolution of ethics problems, and an ongoing training program. The executive committee has a clear idea of what they wish to assert.

The Attestation Standards, as issued by the AICPA, state clearly what is required:

First general statement requires that the CPA have adequate training and is proficient in the attest function.
The CPA who talked with the client had a long-term interest in ethics and had experience in providing training for staff in the firm with which the CPA had been affiliated for 14 years. Furthermore, the CPA had performed many audits and had reviewed the internal control of many companies and on numerous occasions had talked with audit committees of boards of directors about weaknesses in the control environment related to ethical factors. The CPA felt fully competent in handling allegations.

Second general statement requires that the CPA have adequate knowledge in the subject matter.
The CPA in the illustration had not only taken courses in ethics audits, but had researched professional literature regarding the subject matter. In the context of examining internal controls, the CPA had examined the codes of ethics of various other companies. The CPA had adequate knowledge of the subject matter because he took the time and the training to become proficient in it.

The third general standard is that the practitioner shall perform an engagement only if the following two conditions exist:
     a. The assertion is capable of evaluation against criteria that either have been established by a recognized body (i.e. professional association) or are stated in the assertion in a clear, complete manner for a user of the report to be able to comprehend them.
     b. The assertion is capable of reasonably consistent estimation or measurement using such criteria.

In the illustration, the assertions identified by management included the following: The majority of employees had during the past two years participated in a *continuing education* program of at least two days that was related to ethics. There is general understanding of the code of conduct on the part of employees. Complaints registered on the hotline were considered and resolved within a three-month period. Therefore, in our example, the criteria were stated in the assertion and were capable of measurement (two days of ethics education within two years and a complaint reported on the hotline is resolved within three months).

The CPA can provide ethics services as an attestation engagement. The CPA is to provide the services that the client needs; however, it should be recognized that the CPA has more flexibility and is less restricted in providing the ethics services as a consulting engagement than an attestation engagement. However, in an attestation engagement, the CPA has to attest to the written assertions of another party and those assertions have to be able to be evaluated against reasonable criteria or criteria that are clearly explained.

For example, in a consulting arrangement, a CPA may be requested to make recommendations to improve an existing ethics program. In contrast, in an attestation engagement, the CPA would have to receive a written assertion by the client or another party in order to express his or her written conclusion about that assertion. Generally, it would seem that clients would prefer a consulting engagement, rather than having to develop various assertions.

Attestation services can relate to a range of services, including the following:

- An examination of the effectiveness of a total program or component of a program (in accordance with AT 100 paragraphs 1–55)
- A review of the effectiveness of a total program or a component of a program (in accordance with AT 100 paragraphs 56–58)
- Completion of agreed-upon procedures related to ethics considerations (AT 600)

The CPA, in performing an attestation engagement, is obligated to follow the Attestation Standards issued by the AICPA. AT Section 100.01 indicates that an attestation engagement is one "in which a practitioner is engaged to issue or does issue a written communication that expresses a conclusion about the reliability of a written assertion that is the responsibility of another party." The CPA should be sure not to claim or infer that he or she was the asserter.

The first general standard for the attestation engagement is that the CPA has adequate training and is proficient in the attest function. The second general standard is that the CPA has adequate knowledge in the subject matter of the assertion. The third general standard is as follows:

> The practitioner shall perform an engagement only if he or she has reason to believe that the following two conditions exist:
>
> a) The assertion is capable of evaluation against reasonable criteria that either have been established by a recognized body or are stated in the presentation of the assertion in a sufficiently clear and comprehensive manner for a knowledgeable reader to be able to understand them.
>
> b) The assertion is capable of reasonably consistent estimation or measurement using such criteria. (AT Section 100.11)

The standards are clear about the need for relatively objective criteria when CPAs provide assurance. Subjective judgment is not allowed as the basis for assurance. The fourth general standard is that the CPA will remain independent. The fifth general standard is that the CPA will exercise due professional care. The CPA performing an ethics attestation engagement is advised to review and understand all the attestation standards issued by the AICPA, including the standards of fieldwork and standards of reporting.

Representative assertions that the CPA may attest to could include the following:

- Eighty percent of hotline calls received are responded to within one business day.
- At least 90 percent of all employees have read and acknowledged reading the company's code of ethics.
- Seventy-five percent of all employees have received some ethics training within the last year.

8.6 ATTESTATION ENGAGEMENT (EXAMPLE 4)

Taking the first example, a large corporation wants to state that 80 percent of the calls to the ethics hotline were followed up within one business day. Is this an assignment that the CPA could handle as an attestation engagement?

It appears that it does meet the appropriate criteria from the perspective that there is an asserter, an attester, interested parties (employees), and reasonable criteria.

In this attestation engagement, the attester would make a written assertion to the CPA that "Eighty percent of the calls to the hotline are followed up within one business day." The criteria appear to be specific enough to be measurable.

Representative steps that could be taken in this engagement include:

- Specify the time frame (last six months, last year).
- Review the log of the calls, noting when the calls were taken and when action was taken on the calls. (*Note:* If there was no date noted on when action was taken, then the engagement could not be performed.)
- Calculate the time between when calls were taken and when action was performed.
- Summarize results and determine whether assertion is accurate.

Note how this engagement, which uses hotlines as an example, is different from the benchmarking example, which also used hotlines. The CPA would then write a report to provide the client with a certain level of assurance regarding the assertion.

8.7 OPPORTUNITIES ABOUND

Because of the contemporary interest in enhancing the quality of life in the workplace and the perception of the importance of ethics, the CPA faces many opportunities to respond in an innovative, yet realistic, manner to a request from a client. Many organizations are searching for assistance; their executives have a sense, in many cases, of what they want to achieve but are uncertain about the most effective strategy. The CPA who can bring an open mind to a potential client and can observe and listen with no prejudgments will discover ways of assisting. The CPA's rich and varied background and education will provide confidence in completing an engagement—regardless of how it is defined—with success.

Chapter 9

CPAs Facing the Future

Public accountants do not function in a vacuum. The global environment, the national environment, and the immediate business community all influence the services that are most relevant for the certified public accountant to offer to potential clients. At the same time, CPAs have a commitment to their professional responsibilities. The CPA has a long tradition of professional integrity that is the foundation on which all other credentials are based. An unassailable commitment to independence has long been recognized as ensuring that engagements are performed with the high standards established for professional services in the United States. Public accountants must reflect by action and words that they value and support with sincerity and conviction their commitment to the public interest, as discussed in Chapter 2. They understand that their acceptance of responsibility to the public is a distinguishing mark of the profession.

The actions of CPAs must reflect commitment to the highest level of ethical behavior. This is not a simple commitment in a society in which the extent of corruption, fraud, and dishonesty is frequently highlighted in the daily press. As the century is coming to an end, it appears that Americans are facing serious ethical confusion.

During the final quarter of this century, increasing attention has been given to ethics concerns. Yet, there is not evidence of much success from such attention. It appears that codes of ethics, mission statements that begin with the importance of high ethical behavior, and well-worded pronouncements of chief executive officers (CEOs) have not been sufficient to ensure the kind of ethical behavior a fair and just society desires. There is much discussion of the breakdown of moral standards as the information revolution provides instant revelations of questionable ethical behavior among those esteemed in the society. There is serious question about the long-term effect of words spoken that are not reflective of the reality.

In May 1998, for example, a commencement speaker at a highly regarded college was introduced as a man of great character—a man of integrity and honesty. Yet, the statement about his credentials in the printed program was not clear about his present position in the U.S. federal government. Furthermore, he was under investigation for serious violations of laws related to behavior of public officials. Those among the graduates who thought about what was being said in the responsible public press and what their college leader said about the speaker would have reason to be wary about ethical behavior in the world they were soon to enter as active participants. The words rang hollow to thoughtful students; the speaker lacked credibility. How much more valuable the speaker's words would be if they came from a person who was indeed a man of integrity—who had the moral authority to communicate a message of hope and vision to the college and professional school graduates who sat in the beautiful outdoors near the center campus of the more-than-a-century-old university.

Unreconciled words and actions are generating the current interest about ethical concerns in all types of organizations. The 1997 Business Ethics Conference of the Conference Board had as its theme, "Maintaining the Commitment." Attention was given to strategies for maintaining the commitment in the context of corporate acquisitions, mergers, joint ventures, and other corporate developments; to measuring the effectiveness of business ethics programs; to revising codes of conduct; to training; and to enforcing standards.

The contemporary awareness of the value of high-quality ethical environments is leading many organizations to seek independent outsiders to provide assistance and assurance about the nature and quality of ethics programs. Herein lie fruitful opportunities for the CPA. As the new century approaches, CPAs should reassess what is unique about what they do. It is time to renew the long-standing belief in what professional conduct means. It is time to realize the fund of knowledge and skills that has been built up that has significant value in the contemporary world. It is time to realize that organizations of all types need assistance in designing, implementing, and assessing their ethics goals. Organizations are becoming increasingly aware that words about ethics, carefully pronounced at meetings and reported in annual messages to shareholders, are not sufficient.

In the following sections, the following topics will be discussed:

- Importance of ethics in the public accounting profession
- Determining whether to provide ethics-related services
- Organizations dedicated to enhancing ethics in the workplace; positive emerging developments
- Growing interest in assessing the ethical environment
- Developments to enhance the quality of the ethical environment
- Possible role for education
- Erosion of ethical standards
- Challenge to CPAs in sustaining trust and profitability
- Providing services in a techno-information age
- Public accounting firms encountering the new millennium

9.1   IMPORTANCE OF ETHICS IN
THE PUBLIC ACCOUNTING PROFESSION

In the early decades of the twentieth century, as the role of the CPA in the United States was being shaped, there was considerable tension between those who saw public accounting as a commercial service and those who believed it must be a professional service. Joplin wrote in 1914:

> In discussing the subject of the ethics of accountancy it will be necessary to recognize at the outset that accountancy has taken its place among the professions. . . . This subject is perhaps as vital to the accountant as any other subject that might be considered. It determines his attitude and procedure when practising this profession; and it is, as it were the heart and soul of his activities. . . . Aside from the responsibilities of the accountant to his client, there is his relation to the general public to be considered, and it should be remembered here that his duty to the public is perhaps even greater, if it were possible, than to the client.[1]

The people in the United States have perceived the public accounting profession as one in which practitioners can be trusted to adhere to the profession's established standards of behavior. There has been a persistent assumption that CPAs adhere to the most basic tenets of professionalism: assessing their own behavior and resisting pressures to bend the rules for independence and integrity to satisfy a short-term wish of a client. The credibility enjoyed by CPAs is an invaluable contribution to the society. For three quarters of the century, there was no serious challenge to the quality of CPAs' ethical behavior.

However, in the mid-1970s, there began to be some question about the confidence and faith in the accounting establishment in the United States. The federal government, through the Subcommittee on Reports, Accounting, and Management of the Committee on Government Operations, United States Senate, undertook a comprehensive study. The summary of the prepared report highlights the critical importance of the work of public accountants and at the same time reflects a reservation about the ability of the profession to continue as it had functioned in the past. The summary, in part, stated the following:

> Independent auditors must have the complete confidence of the public for whose benefit the Federal securities laws, were enacted. That confidence can only be maintained by strict adherence to standards of conduct which assure the public that auditors are truly independent and competent to perform their responsibilities. Even the appearance of bias or conflict of interest, by an independent auditor can erode the public confidence necessary to make the disclosure policy embodied in the Federal securities laws successful. . . . Independent auditors perform a key function in achieving the goal of the Federal securities laws because they provide the means for independently checking and confirming the information reported by corporations.

---

[1]J. Porter Joplin, "The Ethics of Accountancy," *Journal of Accountancy* (March 1914), 187, 188.

Historically, Congress and the public have regarded accounting as an arcane subject better left to accountants themselves. Continual revelations of wrongdoing by publicly owned corporations have caused a new awareness of the importance of accounting practices in permitting such abuses to occur. Unexpected failures of major corporations have led to requests for substantial assistance to such companies by taxpayers. Accounting practices ultimately involve social issues related to the nation's economic welfare.

> Because of their broad social and economic significance, accounting issues must be addressed by Congress and the public in a manner which ensures that the public interest is protected. . . . Accounting issues are too important to be left to accountants.[2]

The conclusion that "accounting issues are too important to leave to accountants" was a surprise to the profession. The conclusion that possibly the profession needed the direct supervision of a federal agency was not appealing—indeed, given the past respect for the profession, the conclusion was shocking. A considerate Securities and Exchange Commission (SEC) offered an alternative, which included the introduction of a systematic system of oversight. The key to the new structure was the establishment of the Public Oversight Board. The Senate was willing to modify its recommendation regarding supervision by a federal agency. The new structure was instituted by early 1978, when the Public Oversight Board held its first meeting.

Questions about the extent to which the profession does indeed honor its public interest responsibility were raised again in 1985 when another congressional committee began hearings on the public accounting profession. As of mid-1998, the committee had not issued a report. The profession is concerned about its public image, which has as its most powerful component the integrity of practitioners. Efforts continue to be undertaken to enhance that image, which needs to be verified by actual behavior.

As CPAs implement opportunities, such as those identified in the Report of the Special Committee on Assurance Services (the Elliott Report) and discussed in Chapter 8, they recognize that they must continue their commitment to independence and integrity, which has been the foundation block of a CPA's character and professional conduct.

The leadership of the profession at national, state, and local levels gives high priority to maintaining high ethical standards. As the century ends, the leadership is confident that the credibility of CPAs in the United States will indeed be sustained. The assumption is that practitioners will adhere to high standards in the face of many pressures.

---

[2]Subcommittee on Reports, Accounting, and Management of the Committee on Government Operations, United States Senate, *The Accounting Establishment* (Washington, DC: United States Government Printing Office, March 31, 1977), 2.

9.2 DETERMINING WHETHER TO PROVIDE ETHICS-RELATED SERVICES

The addition of new services is not a simple undertaking. A CPA firm, in today's changing business environment, has options about its range of services. As CPAs review the appropriateness of their offering services related to ethics, such as those illustrated in Chapter 8, some self-assessment is helpful. Considering whether to offer such services involves a special kind of analysis.

(a) Intense Interest in Ethics

Such services are best provided by CPAs who have a fundamental, intense, persistent interest in an ethical society and the policies and practices related thereto. Among the population of CPAs in the United States, there are varying attitudes and interests related to ethics.

Some practitioners' interest relates only to meeting the expectations of the code of professional conduct in order to continue to enjoy the privileges offered in their work. For such CPAs, adherence to the code is a pragmatic decision based on the desire to avoid violations and potential penalties. Probing such CPAs' rationale and reasoning would likely reveal limited intellectual interest in high standards of ethical behavior and little genuine emotional commitment to ethical standards. Persons who have such attitudes are not likely to find engagements related to ethical concerns interesting, worthwhile, or provocative. Their decision to bypass considering services related to ethics is probably prudent.

CPAs (and their firms) who have an abiding interest in ethical behavior and how it can be sustained throughout their work are likely to find services related to ethics appealing. Attitudes such as the following are likely to be valuable in providing effective and efficient ethical services:

- A genuine, realistic belief that high-quality ethical environments are possible
- A persistent belief in the improvability of human behavior related to ethics
- Curiosity about what circumstances, policies, and procedures are likely to be effective
- Belief that performance evaluation includes assessment of adherence to high ethical standards
- Intense interest in observing, reflecting, and imagining solutions to ethical problems
- An astute, candid, honest self-analysis of one's own ethical behavior and the implications thereof

The foregoing attitudes are relevant at both the individual and the firm level. Furthermore, as a firm contemplates extension of services related to ethics, the following 10 questions may be useful in assessing what the firm's culture actually reflects about ethics:

1. To what extent are ethical considerations, identified as policies and procedures, reviewed, modified, or changed?
2. Has there been a candid assessment of the firm culture relative to ethics? What follow-up ensued?
3. How open is the leadership of the firm to listening to problems that include ethical dimensions?
4. What is the image among the newest employees about the ethical environment in which they are working?
5. How is an alleged audit failure reviewed within the firm and communicated to all employees?
6. Is there ever acknowledgment of ethical failures? If so, how?
7. What procedures are undertaken to assure that words related to ethical behavior are reconciled with actual behavior throughout the firm?
8. What is the firm's attitude toward the professional code of conduct?
9. How is the training related to ethics provided to the professional staff described, implemented, and reviewed?
10. How is the information and knowledge of the control environment of clients evaluated by the audit staffs generalized for enhancing staff insight and behavior?

(b) Knowledge of Ethics

Another key factor in assessing the feasibility of providing services related to ethics is the extent of knowledge and understanding possessed by the professional staff. A CPA—or a public accounting firm—may, at this point, want to reassess the knowledge and competencies already developed. The following seven questions will be helpful in assessing this aspect of firm qualifications:

1. Has the firm amassed a collection of books and relevant periodicals on ethical topics?
2. What experiences have been fruitful in assisting clients in handling problems related to control environment that are directly or indirectly related to ethics?
3. What materials have been developed in-house that relate to ethics and to what extent are such materials used?
4. What kinds of procedures are in place within the firm to maintain and monitor the firm's own ethical environment that have considerable transfer value?
5. What presentations and discussions related to ethics have been made to groups outside the firm?

6. To what extent are there personnel who have an intellectual interest in the field of ethics?
7. What is the tone regarding ethics at the senior partnership level?

(c) Investment Required

Another key factor to consider relates to the investment the CPA or a public accounting firm is willing to make in order to have relevant knowledge and competencies. (See Chapter 2 for related discussion.) Two questions to aid in the consideration of this factor are:

1. What resources are available—personnel and additional funds—that can be allocated to the preparation of staff to enter the field of ethics-related services?
2. To what extent are there staff members who are willing to take their own personal time to gain knowledge and develop relevant competencies?

(d) Potential Demand

A final factor is the extent of need for ethics-related services in the community or region in which the CPA or public accounting firm provides its services. Four questions to aid in the assessment are:

1. What is the status of ethics in the organizations of the firm's current clients?
2. To what extent is there potential demand among current clients?
3. What is the extent of unmet demand for services related to ethics in the geographic area serviced?
4. What are the possibilities of identifying needs not yet recognized by various types of organizations in the geographic area serviced?

9.3 ORGANIZATIONS ENHANCING ETHICS IN THE WORKPLACE: POSITIVE EMERGING DEVELOPMENTS

The beginning of the contemporary interest in ethics can be traced to the 1970s. As an example, it was in the 1970s that Trinity Church, located at the head of Wall Street in New York City, began to realize that "in our rapidly moving business world, there are few predictable questions and no easy answers. The old rules are being rewritten by changing conditions, such as: escalating global competition, deregulation, corporate restructuring and takeovers, growth in financial and service industries, institutional ownership of equity, changing demographics and markets, and higher societal expectations of business conduct."[3]

[3]Bulletin of Trinity Center for Ethics and Corporate Policy, undated.

It was the idea of the rector of Trinity Parish to explore the possibility of a special outreach program to the major corporations and financial institutions in the corporate community located in the area of the parish. The Trinity Center for Ethics and Corporate Policy was formed in 1981 and functioned for approximately eight years. Corporate ethics projects were undertaken through working with senior executives and board members. In the 1970s, many corporations had begun writing codes of ethics, and the emphasis on ethical rules had become broader than was true in earlier times and was, therefore, related to a wide range of concerns. The Trinity Center identified the following factors worthy of attention:

- *Organization values.* Corporate culture and values, governance and policy process, management style, communications, fairness
- *Fairness in the workplace.* Employee rights and duties, reduction of forces, plant closings, hiring practices
- *Social responsibility.* Environment, product safety, contributions, health and safety, stakeholders, truth in advertising, managing crises
- *Questionable practices.* Deception, bribery, insider information, anticompetitive behavior, and trade secrets

The Trinity Center found that many executives were asking about the relation of ethics to organizational policy and business performance. The Trinity Center's bulletin noted: "A critical question today is how a corporation can manage its explicit and implicit values. From the individual ethics of the past, emphasis in the 1980s is shifting to the management of values." The Trinity Center for Ethics and Corporate Policy was a successful outreach program, which provided valuable leadership until it ended in the late 1980s.

During the late 1970s and the 1980s, a number of institutes were established. Some were independent; others were affiliated with universities. The general mission of such organizations was to advance ethics in a manner to influence individuals and their organizations to understand the importance and role of ethics in their responsibilities.[4]

9.4 GROWING INTEREST IN ASSESSING ETHICAL ENVIRONMENTS

Some organizations have engaged in internal assessment of the success of their efforts to enhance the ethical standards among all employees. In a few instances, outsiders have been engaged to perform a social responsibility audit. Illustrative of efforts to organize standards for assessment is the 1997 initiative of the Council on Economic Priorities (CEP). The efforts of the Council will be briefly described as an example of what is being offered to all types of organizations.

[4]See "Ethics Web Sites: Resources for Internal Auditors," *Internal Auditing* (March/April 1998), 23–28.

(a)   The Council on Economic Priorities' Mission

The CEP is a nonprofit, public-interest research organization with a nationwide membership. The CEP evaluates the policies and practices of U.S. corporations as well as issues affecting national security. In early 1997, the Council established the Council on Economic Priorities Accreditation Agency and named an advisory committee to draft standards addressing workers' rights. Their efforts resulted in SA 8000 as well as accreditation procedures.

(b)   The SA 8000 System

As described in the literature provided by the CEP, SA 8000 is "a comprehensive, global, verifiable standard for auditing and certifying compliance with corporate responsibility."

The SA 8000 system is modeled on established ISO 9000 and ISO 14000 standards for quality control and environmental management systems.

The standards identified in SA 8000 were based on a number of existing international human rights standards, such as the United Nations' Universal Declaration of Human Rights and the UN Convention on the Rights of the Child. There are nine areas for which verifiable standards have been identified:

1.   *Child labor.* Children under the age of 15, in most instances, are prohibited from working. Certified companies are required to set aside funds for the education of children who lose their jobs as a result of this standard.

2.   *Forced labor.* Workers cannot be required to surrender their identity papers or pay "deposits" as a condition of employment.

3.   *Health and safety.* Companies must meet basic standards for a safe and healthy working environment, including potable water, restroom facilities, applicable safety equipment, and necessary training.

4.   *Freedom of association.* This standard protects the rights of workers to form and join trade unions and to bargain collectively, without fear of reprisals.

5.   *Discrimination.* A standard establishes that there shall be no discrimination based on race, caste, national origin, religion, disability, gender, sexual orientation, union membership, or political party affiliation.

6.   *Disciplinary practices.* Corporal punishment, mental or physical coercion, and verbal abuse of workers are forbidden.

7.   *Working hours.* A working week is limited to 48 hours with a minimum of one day off each week. No more than 12 hours of overtime per week are allowed, with remuneration at a premium rate.

8.   *Compensation.* All minimum legal standards must be met in the wages paid. There is to be sufficient income for basic needs, with at least some discretionary income.

9. *Management.* There must be procedures that ensure effective management implementation and review of SA 8000 compliance, which includes designating responsible personnel to keep records, addressing concerns, and taking corrective actions.

The CEP notes that SA 8000 "represents a major breakthrough; it is the first auditable social standard, created through a process that is truly independent. It is not a government project, nor is it dominated by any single interest group or constituency."

(c) The Required Audit of Compliance with SA 8000

The CEP's Accrediting Agency also accredits individuals or groups that wish to perform audits. Potential accreditors must submit an application. It was noted that "most [auditors] are likely to be accounting firms, which see a great opportunity for new business, but CEP also will approve auditing units set up by unions or nonprofit groups."[5]

The effort does have skeptics. A *Business Week* story noted: "Human rights and labor groups worry that CEP audits, which companies pay for, won't require real change in sweatshops." Further, the article concluded with a question and comment: "Can the CEP effort succeed where others have failed? Its standards are similar to those of the International Labor Organization, which governments have failed to enforce for decades. But CEP figures it has a better enforcement mechanism: a market of millions of consumers who will insist on SA 8000–approved products." This conclusion may attribute to ordinary consumers far more power than they are likely to use for the support of humane working conditions.

The CEP believes that:

> The best managers and executives understand the need to be good corporate citizens. They appreciate the value of their corporate and brand name reputations. And they realize the lasting damage that can result from harm to their firm's reputation. . . . Internal codes of conduct are not the solution. Local laws, customs and practices vary widely around the world, creating an unwieldy and unfamiliar patchwork. Factories are taxed by multiple, non-standard audits designed to meet differing requirements and expectations. And even when internal monitoring works, the public and media will lack confidence when it seems like "the fox is guarding the chicken coop."[6]

The success of this initiative to set international ethical standards related to basic workers' needs and rights will depend on the good faith efforts of the companies and the impeccable and unrelenting integrity of the auditors. Public

[5]"Sweatshop Police," *Business Week* (October 20, 1997), 39.
[6]See undated brochure of the Council on Economic Priorities.

accountants with their tradition of independence and objectivity are well qualified to contribute to the implementation of the CEP initiative.

9.5 DEVELOPMENTS TO ENHANCE THE QUALITY OF ETHICAL ENVIRONMENTS

A number of developments underscore attention to ethics. Only three will be identified at this point. They are the appointment of ethics officers in a number of U.S.-based companies, publications of professional accounting associations, and ethics on the agendas of annual shareholders meetings of publicly owned companies.

(a) Ethics Officer Association

To serve this relatively new position of ethics officer in an organization, the Ethics Officer Association (EOA) was established in 1992. Furthermore, professional organizations in accounting provide resources to aid organizations in their development and improvement of ethics programs. The EOA lists the following as its objectives:

- To provide multiple opportunities for wider acquaintance, understanding, and cooperation among ethics officers
- To provide a structure for sharing approaches to specific issues of common concern
- To foster the general advancement of research, learning, sharing, and practice in the field of business ethics

The EOA offers two types of membership: sponsoring partner and individual. As of June 1, 1998, there were more than 500 members. (See Chapter 8 for a discussion of auditor services related to this emerging position.)

Many benefits are provided by the EOA, including the following:

- An annual forum for sponsoring partner representatives, which offers senior-level ethics and compliance professionals an opportunity for open, frank dialogue on ethical and compliance-related issues that face their organizations. The forum provides practical advice on implementing and administering highly effective programs.
- An annual conference that highlights ethics and compliance issues and provides opportunities for the exchange of information about innovations and existing practices in ethics, compliance, and business conduct programs.
- A professional development program provided in conjunction with the Center for Business Ethics at Bentley College, which provides practical knowledge, fundamental theories, and general skills needed by prospective and recently

appointed ethics officers and others who have responsibilities for their organization's ethics, compliance, or business conduct programs.

- Skill enhancement courses provided on topics such as ethics and the law, developing effective and credible communications, ethical reasoning, assessing the ethical environment, and understanding and developing a high-integrity workplace.

- A corporate ethics and compliance library maintained for the use of members.

- A newsletter published four times a year, which informs the membership of current and upcoming conferences and workshops as well as providing articles on various aspects of corporate ethics programs (see Website—http://www.eoa.org).

(b)   Publications from the American Institute of Certified Public Accountants, Institute for Management Accountants, and Institute of Internal Auditors

The American Institute of Certified Public Accountants (AICPA) in early 1998 issued a publication, "Implementing Ethics Strategies within Organizations," which serves as a guide to organizations wanting practical operating principles and information about appropriate approaches for organizing corporate ethics programs.

> More and more, organizations and the public worldwide recognize that business ethics and corporate social responsibility are important concerns. Many individuals and groups—from employees to consumers, from shareholder coalitions to neighborhood associations—are demanding more than profit maximization from business corporations and their leaders, and honesty from not-for-profit organizations. Governments, both through increased attention to corruption and incentive schemes, have encouraged organizations to address ethics specifically. Organizations are being challenged to review their current approaches to ethics and to explore new models and techniques to meet rising stakeholder expectations.[7]

The AICPA has a number of additional publications relevant to the topic of ethics. The Institute for Management Accountants (IMA) and the Institute of Internal Auditors (IIA) give attention to ethics through publishing studies and practical guides, plus providing seminars and conferences on ethical topics.

(c)   Attention to Ethics at Shareholders' Meetings

It is not uncommon for shareholders to raise questions about ethical matters, often discussed in the business press, at shareholders meetings. Public accounting firms provide guidance in preparation for meetings by identifying possible questions.

---

[7]*The CPA Letter/Business & Industry* (April 1998), D2.

Coopers & Lybrand LLP considered the business ethics topic among the "hot topics" for shareholders' meetings, as stated in its 1997 publication:

- Well-publicized ethical lapses have resulted in increased public attention to corporate conduct. Some instances have been specific legal violations such as bribery of government officials, kickbacks, sexual harassment, discrimination, and violations of securities regulations. Others were ethical breaches such as deceptive advertising and sales practices and the lack of timely, effective action in the event of product defects. When businesses violate society's expectations, consumers may take their business elsewhere, key suppliers end relationships, communities protest, and legislators further regulate business. In addition, serious loss in shareowner market value typically accompanies such reputation-impairing events.
- Does the company review its ethics environment and programs on an ongoing basis? What is the company's assessment?
- Does the company have formal values and supporting standards of behavior that are consistent with its corporate mission, strategies, operating policies, and performance objectives?
- How does the company ensure effective oversight of its ethics programs? What board committees, management committees, and compliance areas are there to provide assurance that corporate objectives are met responsibly?
- How does the company communicate with and educate employees on its ethical standards and programs, and how to identify ethical challenges and act responsibility?[8]

Another major public accounting firm, Deloitte & Touche LLP, noted the following in its 1998 publication about shareholder questions:

More and more companies find strategic advantages in developing and maintaining a strong social image while at the same time increasing value to the stockholders. . . . Stockholders will likely pose questions about the company's involvement in local communities, political activities, product and workplace safety, responsible advertising and market themes, and policies on sexual harassment and other gender and racial issues. Stockholders may also be interested in social issues arising internationally, such as the company's compliance with international human rights and child labor laws.

Representative questions that shareholders may ask include the following:

- Have there been any significant employee complaints filed with the Equal Employment Opportunity Commission (EEOC) in the current year? What is the nature of the complaint(s)? Does the company expect a favorable outcome from the EEOC?

[8]Coopers & Lybrand LLP, *Anticipating Questions at Shareholders' Meetings: Hot Topics* (February 1997), 20.

- What steps does the company employ to prevent sexual harassment in its workplace? How does the company address instances of sexual harassment? Does the company have a system in place so that incidents of sexual harassment can be reported in confidence?
- What was the amount contributed to political candidates through political action committees?
- How does the company decide which charitable organizations are eligible to receive contributions?
- Which organizations were the major beneficiaries during 1997?
- How does the company monitor the effectiveness of its contributions?[9]

9.6 POSSIBLE ROLE FOR EDUCATION

As noted in Chapter 6, respondents believed that there is an ethical problem in society because of a lack of ethics. Those respondents were asked to give solutions to the problem. Only a few did so. Responses ranged from "education" to "executive management's commitment to the highest standard of ethics." The responses have inspired a suggestion that an integrated approach can be used to make a difference in the ethical environment. This approach begins at the basic educational level and works its way into the core of business operations in organizations.

The integrated solution that can begin to solve the ethical problems will be to (1) establish business ethics as part of core curriculums in colleges and universities, (2) make business ethics a part of the testing materials in professional certification examinations and in continuing education programs, and (3) make business ethics an important part of every organization's decision-making and operational strategy. Some comments about each action follow.

- *Institute business core curriculum in colleges and universities.* A campaign can be initiated for the integration of business ethics into the curricula of colleges and universities. Proposals or surveys can be sent to business schools to get feedback on what value the teaching of business ethics would add to the business environment. Also, solicitation can be sought on what the contents of such a course should entail, if taught as a separate course, or how the subject can be integrated into business courses. After this feedback is received, a draft syllabus and course description can be developed. The draft can be reviewed by the same individuals surveyed in the initial campaign, as these individuals will be familiar with the subject matter. After acceptable levels of reviews, a process can be started to implement the teaching of business ethics in curriculums across the broad range of programs offered in post-secondary institutions.

[9]Deloitte & Touche LLP, *Questions at Stockholders' Meetings 1998,* 14.

- *Incorporate ethics as part of professional certification and continuing education courses.* Professional organizations such as the AICPA and the IIA, in addition to others, have well-established written codes of ethics. Members (CPAs and certified internal auditors [CIAs]) of these institutes are supposed to adhere to these codes. The question is, are members familiar with the codes and do they follow them? Written codes are good; however, they would be even better if individuals are familiar with the codes and abide by them. The honor system of adhering to codes of ethics appears not to be working, as is evident from the survey results. Consequently, there should be a more pragmatic approach to getting individuals familiar with and adhering to the codes. The same standards that members are asked to uphold can be incorporated into the "common body of knowledge" material used to test members in pursuing a particular professional designation. This process ensures that members have some familiarity with the codes and can apply them in the business surroundings. Further, as members are required to take continuing professional education (CPE) credits in order to maintain their certifications, business ethics should be made part of the CPE process. This process can bring ethical standards to a more serious status in the business community.

- *Reinforcement of ethical standards within business organizations.* Companies can start first by establishing written codes of ethics as a basis for raising employees' awareness level of business ethical standards. This can be supplemented with continuous training and development, internal or external, of employees on the importance of ethical standards within the organization. The importance of ethical standards should be made clear by senior management. For example, a meeting or meetings can be held with all employees where the highest ranking officer (chairperson or president) of the company relays to the employees the importance of ethical standards.

  Also, companies can develop a process for reporting unethical behavior within the company. This process should ensure that employees could report such unethical behavior without fear of reprisal from higher-level employees (managers and supervisors). Companies can even go as far as to establish a position, with enough authority to take action, for employees to report unethical behavior.

  Further, companies should see the value of a written code of ethics and a process for training employees. This condition can be made part of the company's internal control structure. There may be value in a requirement by a monitoring group (such as the SEC) that management attest annually that there is a code of ethics, training of employees, and enforcement efforts in effect in any publicly owned business. An example of a similar measure was instituted by the Federal Reserve Bank to prevent and detect fraud at member banks. The Federal Reserve Bank requires that employees of member banks take a mandatory consecutive two-week vacation if they have three weeks or more of vacation time and a mandatory one-week vacation for those with two weeks or less.

This approach can lead to an overall integration of business ethics in the business environment. The recommended solution is surely not all-inclusive; the approach, however, can begin the process of bringing the importance of ethical standards to the forefront of business operations.

9.7 EROSION OF ETHICAL STANDARDS

There appears to be serious concern about the erosion of ethics in the world society. The public press provides some preliminary awareness of the extent of erosion of ethical standards. Many stories revealed, for example, the extent of fraudulent behavior in relation to the savings and loan crisis of the 1980s in the United States. Small-print listings of individuals and companies that have violated the rules governing securities activities appear regularly in the domestic business press.

Surveys show that employees, to a great extent, believe that ethical conduct is not rewarded and that profits are far more important than doing the right thing. In fact, doing the right thing is difficult because of the pressure. One survey of employees in the financial services industry found that 56 percent of respondents felt pressure to behave unethically, and 48 percent admitted having engaged in an unethical act because of pressure.

There appears to be considerable conflict between values held by individuals or organizations and specific operational objectives. This point was underscored by Jennings, who discussed a survey in which executives, financial officers, middle management, and nonmanagement participated.

> Nine of every ten senior executives in the survey agreed that effective internal controls were critical to effective management. Yet 80 percent of the same group also agreed that even though most companies stress internal control, "when it comes down to compensation, making the numbers is what really matters."[10]

In the same survey, there was a difference in the perception of top management and others regarding "whistle-blowing." While only 11 percent of the CEO's thought that a whistle-blower was taking a real risk, one third of the middle managers and one half of the nonmanagers thought that there was a real risk in being a whistle-blower. Many interesting questions are raised by such findings—among them: Is the difference related to whistle-blowing reflecting the failure of top management to "walk the talk" or are the lower level employees misunderstanding the freedom they have to report ethical violations observed or

---

[10]William C. Jennings, "Viewpoint: A Corporate Culture Must Start at the Top," *The New York Times* (December 29, 1996), 14.

experienced? What kind of effort for enhancing ethical environments would one find in the companies of the respondents?

When there is a look at what is happening globally, the situation related to ethics is not positive. Around the world, scandals have increasingly forced politicians out of office and sent businessmen to jail. Pakistan, Italy, Brazil, and Korea, among others, have been cited as examples where politicians were ousted because of corruption.

The problems of Asian countries and companies are often determined to include extensive corruption. A *Business Week* article referred to the scandal revealed at Nomura Securities Company.[11]

The international status of ethics has led to initiatives by the International Development Fund and the International Chamber of Commerce. The World Bank, the International Monetary Fund, and the 28 democracies in the Organization for Economic Cooperation and Development have begun tackling corruption. The globalization of business intensifies the need to develop ethical guidance to provide confidence to all who wish to be players in the global workplace.

9.8 CHALLENGE TO CPAS IN SUSTAINING TRUST AND PROFITABILITY

There are two dimensions to the challenges to CPAs. One dimension is related to CPAs and their own professional responsibilities; the second, to the opportunities to make a difference in the quality of ethical environments throughout the workplace.

(a) CPAs and Their Professional Responsibilities

There are contemporary challenges to CPAs and the professional standards that have provided the basis for the public respect they have maintained for more than a century. The profession strives to maintain that respect because it is critical to providing quality services. The world has changed; can public accountants maintain their standards in this changed world?

Beginning in the final decades of the 1800s, a few individuals began providing bookkeeping and accounting services to the fast-growing entrepreneurial businesses. By 1887, there was a sufficient number of such individuals to join together in an organization, which later was deemed to be a professional association. The tension between those who believed the services should be considered commercial and those who believed the services should be considered professional persisted for some period of time; in the end, public accounting was deemed professional. There followed a scheme for examinations, certification,

---

[11]"Tokyo's Rigged Markets Need Revolution Not Reform," *Business Week* (March 24, 1997), 54.

and monitoring of members. Early in the 1900s, the leadership in public accounting assumed responsibility for enhancement of the competencies of practitioners
and for the maintenance of the highest level of ethical behavior. As Smith noted,
"The accountant has to a marked degree, become the custodian of the moral standards of the world."[12]

Evidence of the challenge is reflected in two publications: (1) *The Accounting
Profession,* issued by the U.S. General Accounting office; and (2) *Serving the
Public Interest: A New Conceptual Framework for Auditor Independence,* issued
by the AICPA.

The Accounting Profession provides a summary of studies done about the
profession, what the recommendations were, and what followed. In the conclusion was the following statement:

> Response to the major issues raised by the many studies from 1972 through 1994
> shows that the profession has been responsive in making changes to improve finan-
> cial reporting and auditing of public companies. Further, the General Accounting
> Office's analysis of statistical data on the results of peer reviews of accounting firms
> that audit public companies registered with the Securities and Exchange Commis-
> sion shows that most firms now have effective quality control programs to ensure
> adherence with professional standards.[13]

There were some areas, however, in which the General Accounting Office
(GAO) concluded that the actions of the accounting profession have not been
"totally effective in resolving several major issues." The principal findings as
regards issues related to professional behavior in general are the following:

- Progress has been made on the issue of auditor independence, but concerns
  remain.
- An expectation gap still exists for detection of fraud and determining
  effectiveness of internal controls.
- The accounting profession's self-regulation program has improved audit
  quality, but deficiencies persist.

The second publication, *Serving the Public Interest: A New Concept for Auditor Independence,* is a document prepared under the auspices of the AICPA for the
Independence Standards Board (ISB), which was established in May 1997. As
stated in the introduction:

> Auditor independence is of critical importance to the efficient functioning of our
> capital markets, which depend on a continuous flow of reliable financial informa-
> tion. . . . Independence is one of the most deeply ingrained values of the accounting

---

[12]Henry Smith, "Accounting in the Modern State," in W. T. Baxter and Sidney Davidson (eds.), *Studies in Accounting Theory* (Homewood, IL: Richard D. Irwin, 1962), 344.

[13]U.S. Government Accounting Office, *The Accounting Profession* (September 1996), 4.

profession. Indeed, the issue is not whether independence standards and policies should be "strengthened" or "relaxed," but rather what approach best advances the public interest in the highest quality of independent audits of public entities. . . . It is particularly timely that the ISB has been formed now to consider this issue. Dramatic changes in the world economy, in combination with astonishing breakthroughs in information technology, are redefining the audit function, placing new demands on auditors and permanently altering the relationships between accounting firms and their clients. These dynamics suggest a need to replace the existing command and control regulatory system with a more responsive, principle-based model.[14]

It is the position of the paper that there are serious shortcomings of command and control regulation, and the authors point out that such regulation carries "with it a substantial danger that compliance with detailed rules will become a substitute for achievement of the intended policy objective."[15]

This White Paper was issued approximately four years after the Public Oversight Board received a report entitled "Strengthening the Professionalism of the Independent Auditor," from the Advisory Panel on Auditor Independence. The report was prompted by a speech given by the chief accountant of the Securities and Exchange Commission (SEC) on January 11, 1994, to a gathering of accountants in Washington, D.C., in which there was criticism of independent auditors for "supporting their clients' incredible accounting proposals." The chief accountant also stated that accounting firms were cheerleaders on the issue of accounting for stock options issued to employees. The criticism was perceived to be grave and resulted in the Public Oversight Board's appointing an Advisory Panel on Auditor Independence to assess the dimensions of the problem and recommend steps to bolster the professionalism of the independent auditor.

Without revealing the details from interviews with representatives from major public accounting firms, government, private industry, professors of accounting, and representatives of standard-setting groups, the panel, in the report, concluded that there was no need for additional rules, regulations, or legislation dealing with the conflict-of-interest aspect of auditor independence. However, the panel recommended that there were important steps that should be taken in other ways to strengthen the professionalism of independent auditors. The report concludes with the panel's belief that "the SEC and the Public Oversight Board should consider devoting resources to stay informed on a continuing basis about developments in the auditing profession."[16]

The White Paper has received criticism. The ISB has a challenge to reconceptualize independence so that the guidance is unambiguous, realistic, and enforceable. That task is projected to take more than a few months.

---

[14]AICPA, *Serving the Public Interest: A New Concept for Auditor Independence* (October 20, 1997), 1.
[15]Id., 95.
[16](Advisory Panel on Auditor Independence, *Strengthening the Professionalism of the Independent Auditor,* Report to the Public Oversight Board of the SEC Practice Section, AICPA (September 13, 1994), 31.

The ISB must contend with the challenges to expectations that have been accepted for a century. An illustration of the challenge to independence is that posed by Bazerman, Morgan, and Loewenstein when they raised a question about how realistic is it to assume auditors will be objective, and not biased. They turn to psychological research to conclude that "an inescapable conclusion is that impartiality is impossible under current institutional arrangements." They contend that "psychological research would support the position that bias typically enters unconsciously and unintentionally at the stage of making judgments, and such judgments are likely to be unconsciously and powerfully biased as a result of self interest."[17]

The authors fail to deal with the observation that individuals are not alike in relation to the extent that self-interest is an overriding basis for decision making. To what extent does a person who accepts professional standards agreed to by the professionals themselves adhere to those standards? In what circumstances is there variability in adherence to standards? Is there some level of internalization of the requirements for objectivity and integrity that ensures that pressures—and self-interest—will not prevail? Can the process of decision making for a professional be structured in a manner to provide high level assurance that bias was not influential?

There are indeed many questions about CPAs and what qualities of character, experiences, and training are most predictive of behavior. There are many opportunities for extended research in this area for practitioners and those in academic institutions.

(b) CPAs and Their Potential Contributions

Notwithstanding the questions raised in the preceding section, the judgment that today's CPA can continue as a custodian of moral standards is reasonable.

The awareness of the need for high ethical values has extended throughout the globe. All types of individuals, businesses, and government and nonprofit organizations are increasingly reaching the point at which something more needs to be done about the ethical environment. The CPA can be helpful in such efforts.

The evidence of need is convincing. For example, the U.S. Federal Sentencing Guidelines imply that an effective compliance program will be instituted. Organizations have the responsibility to establish a framework and a climate that assures proper ethical conduct. The international interest in the Social Accountability 8000 initiative reinforces the type of workplace environment enlightened leaders seek.

During the final two decades of the twentieth century, many organizations have developed codes of conduct, introduced ethical training, and to some extent have appointed ethics officers. Although such efforts are noteworthy, they are not sufficient to ensure the level of ethical behavior envisioned for the society. Only recently

---

[17]Max H. Bazerman, Kimberly P. Morgan, George F. Loewenstein, "The Impossibility of Auditor Independence," *Sloan Management Review* (Summer 1997), 89–94.

has there been a focus on the question: "Is this organization actually functioning in a manner that implements what it purports is the ethical position it proclaims?"

The answer to this question can, of course, be determined through a careful internal assessment that is designed in an objective manner. However, the most convincing answer is likely to come from an external source—from an individual or firm that has long-standing credibility in the community. What better individual or firm is there than a CPA who is a sole proprietor or is affiliated with a public accounting firm?

Public accountants, both individually and in the firms with which they are affiliated, can bring a unique strategy to standards and their measurement that might be compared with that which CPAs brought to financial information and its measurement during the past century.

Individuals are capable of meeting high ethical standards. An ethical environment can make a difference. It is in the self-interest of every organization to have a high-quality, ethical environment.

Many business leaders are beginning to take a hard look at ethics. They are realizing that there is a serious economic dimension to ethical behavior. Sustainable profitability requires consistent, ethical behavior by both the leadership of the organization and all the employees. As noted in Chapter 3, unethical practices undermine success in the long run. The businesses with which Dennis Levine, Nicholas Leeson, and Joseph Jett were affiliated, as examples, no longer exist as they were at the time serious fraudulent practices were disclosed.

Unethical behavior introduces considerable volatility and uncertainty in an organization. However, the behavior is tolerated, because there are often short-term benefits for superiors and others. Seldom, though, is such behavior a total surprise to some individuals in the company. Those who are not involved often suffer from low morale, because their contributions are not as impressive, often, as the contributions of those who are ruthlessly disregarding the "rules of the game." The return for being exceptionally successful—even if for a short time—is a driver in some environments. Failure to respect high ethical standards is quickly observed by opportunistic individuals, and they soon have a strategy that they believe will lead *only to continued success.* The period over which they are able to operate is often reasonably long. Wise leadership is increasingly not indifferent to the ethical environment provided for all participants in the company—from the board of directors to the newest, most inexperienced first-level employees.

9.9 PROVIDING SERVICES IN A TECHNO-INFORMATION AGE

In *Business Week* magazine, Michael J. Mandel stresses that economic security no longer exists and both risk and rewards are escalating.[18]

---

[18]Michael J. Mandel, "The High Risk Society: Peril and Promise in the New Economy," *Business Week* (October 28, 1996).

Rushworth M. Kidder explains the Chernobyl nuclear power plant accident:

> I learned that, on the night of the accident, two electrical engineers were "playing around" with reactor #4 in what the Soviets later described as an unauthorized experiment. The two engineers wanted to see how long a turbine would freewheel if they took the power off it. That meant shutting down reactor #4. To do so, they had to override six separate alarm systems. . . . These men were not *dumb*. Then what was missing? What they lacked, apparently, was the sense of responsibility, the moral understanding, the sense of conscience, the understanding of ethics—however you want to put it—that somehow would have prevented them from going forward. . . . Shift your thinking forward into the early years of the twenty-first century and ask your self about the kinds of ethical questions that will arise there. . . . The point here is simply that our technology has leveraged our ethics in ways that we never saw in the past.[19]

The basic element of good ethical behavior will serve us in good stead. Integrity, decency, unimpeachable character, and respect for other people are solid foundations upon which to build. No matter how complicated life becomes, the CPA has an ethical code that will always be the basis of sound professional judgment.

What will it take to survive and thrive in the new millennium? For CPAs, consider the following checklist:

- Ability to provide continuous audits
- Continual training and updating of skills
- Ethical leadership
- Ability to hire talented and ethical personnel
- Ability to deal with change ("paradigm shifts")
- Managing the information coming to you

9.10 CPAS ENCOUNTERING THE NEW MILLENNIUM

When asked to recommend what a company should do to prepare itself for the new century, consumer-trends analyst Faith Popcorn stated, "I would try to convince the CEO that the year 2000 will bring a new degree: MBS, which is the 'master of business soul.' MBA was the degree of the eighties and maybe even part of the nineties; MBS will be the degree of the year 2000. The soul of a business involves what we call 'product plus': product plus the ethics of the company."[20]

---

[19]Rushworth M. Kidder, "Ethics: A Matter of Survival," *The Futurist* (March/April 1992), 10.
[20]"Business and the Future," A Roundtable Discussion, *The Futurist* (May–June 1992), 24.

In his book *Heartland Ethics*, Rushworth Kidder referred to his previous book, *An Agenda for the 21st Century,* which discussed six issues including threat of nuclear weapons, environmental problems, and population explosion, among others. He stated, "The sixth [issue] was more surprising: the breakdown in public and private morality. In essence, those who were interviewed were saying, 'If we don't get a handle on ethics in the next century, we'll be as surely doomed as by a nuclear disaster or an environmental catastrophe.' "[21]

The AICPA Vision Project has been trying to define who the CPA will be and how the CPA can best respond to a changing global economy. The profession is fortunate that the public identifies practitioners with integrity, objectivity, and competence, as well as independence. New assurance services will help the CPA respond to the changing marketplace. The CPA WebTrust has already been introduced to "assure" the public that electronic commerce Websites displaying the logo meet standards of consumer information protection, transaction integrity, and sound business practices.

Public accountants are making renewed commitments to stress quality in all that they do. A logical next step is providing services in relation to ethics. The pressure for all types of organizations to actually strive to be as ethical as they proclaim they are has intensified. Wise business leaders will look to CPAs for the kind of assurance they seek to support the words they speak.

[21]Rushworth Kidder, *Heartland Ethics* The Principia (1992), xi.

APPENDIXES

AICPA Code of Professional Conduct

(as amended January 14, 1992)

Bylaws and Implementing Resolutions of Council

(as amended June 17, 1996)

COMPOSITION, APPLICABILITY, AND COMPLIANCE

The Code of Professional Conduct of the American Institute of Certified Public Accountants consists of two sections—(1) the Principles and (2) the Rules. The Principles provide the framework for the Rules, which govern the performance of professional services by members. The Council of the American Institute of Certified Public Accountants is authorized to designate bodies to promulgate technical standards under the Rules, and the bylaws require adherence to those Rules and standards.

The Code of Professional Conduct was adopted by the membership to provide guidance and rules to all members—those in public practice, in industry, in government, and in education—in the performance of their professional responsibilities.

Compliance with the Code of Professional Conduct, as with all standards in an open society, depends primarily on members' understanding and voluntary actions, secondarily on reinforcement by peers and public opinion, and ultimately on disciplinary proceedings, when necessary, against members who fail to comply with the Rules.

OTHER GUIDANCE

The Principles and Rules as set forth herein are further amplified by interpretations and rulings contained in *AICPA Professional Standards* (volume 2).

Interpretations of Rules of Conduct consist of interpretations which have been adopted, after exposure to state societies, state boards, practice units and other interested parties, by the professional ethics division's executive committee to provide guidelines as to the scope and application of the Rules but are not intended to limit such scope or application. A member who departs from such guidelines shall have the burden of justifying such departure in any disciplinary hearing.

Ethics Rulings consist of formal rulings made by the professional ethics division's executive committee after exposure to state societies, state boards, practice units and other interested parties. These rulings summarize the application of Rules of Conduct and interpretations to a particular set of factual circumstances. Members who depart from such rulings in similar circumstances will be requested to justify such departures.

Publication of an interpretation or ethics ruling in the *Journal of Accountancy* constitutes notice to members. Hence, the effective date of the pronouncement is the last day of the month in which the pronouncement is published in the *Journal of Accountancy*. The professional ethics division will take into consideration the time that would have been reasonable for the member to comply with the pronouncement.

A member should also consult, if applicable, the ethical standards of his state CPA society, state board of accountancy, the Securities and Exchange Commission, and any other governmental agency which may regulate his client's business or use his report to evaluate the client's compliance with applicable laws and related regulations.

SECTION 1—PRINCIPLES

Preamble
Membership in the American Institute of Certified Public Accountants is voluntary. By accepting membership, a certified public accountant assumes an obligation of self-discipline above and beyond the requirements of laws and regulations.

These Principles of the Code of Professional Conduct of the American Institute of Certified Public Accountants express the profession's recognition of its responsibilities to the public, to clients, and to colleagues. They guide members in the performance of their professional responsibilities and express the basic tenets of ethical and professional conduct. The Principles call for an unswerving commitment to honorable behavior, even at the sacrifice of personal advantage.

Article I

Responsibilities

In carrying out their responsibilities as professionals, members should exercise sensitive professional and moral judgments in all their activities.

As professionals, certified public accountants perform an essential role in society. Consistent with that role, members of the American Institute of Certified Public Accountants have responsibilities to all those who use their professional services. Members also have a continuing responsibility to cooperate with each other to improve the art of accounting, maintain the public's confidence, and carry out the profession's special responsibilities for self-governance. The collective efforts of all members are required to maintain and enhance the traditions of the profession.

Article II

The Public Interest

Members should accept the obligation to act in a way that will serve the public interest, honor the public trust, and demonstrate commitment to professionalism.

A distinguishing mark of a profession is acceptance of its responsibility to the public. The accounting profession's public consists of clients, credit grantors, governments, employers, investors, the business and financial community, and others who rely on the objectivity and integrity of certified public accountants to maintain the orderly functioning of commerce. This reliance imposes a public interest responsibility on certified public accountants. The public interest is defined as the collective well-being of the community of people and institutions the profession serves.

In discharging their professional responsibilities, members may encounter conflicting pressures from among each of those groups. In resolving those conflicts, members should act with integrity, guided by the precept that when members fulfill their responsibility to the public, clients' and employers' interests are best served.

Those who rely on certified public accountants expect them to discharge their responsibilities with integrity, objectivity, due professional care, and a genuine interest in serving the public. They are expected to provide quality services, enter into fee arrangements, and offer a range of services—all in a manner that demonstrates a level of professionalism consistent with these Principles of the Code of Professional Conduct.

All who accept membership in the American Institute of Certified Public Accountants commit themselves to honor the public trust. In return for the faith that the public reposes in them, members should seek continually to demonstrate their dedication to professional excellence.

Article III

Integrity

To maintain and broaden public confidence, members should perform all professional responsibilities with the highest sense of integrity.

Integrity is an element of character fundamental to professional recognition. It is the quality from which the public trust derives and the benchmark against which a member must ultimately test all decisions.

Integrity requires a member to be, among other things, honest and candid within the constraints of client confidentiality. Service and the public trust should not be subordinated to personal gain and advantage. Integrity can accommodate the inadvertent error and the honest difference of opinion; it cannot accommodate deceit or subordination of principle.

Integrity is measured in terms of what is right and just. In the absence of specific rules, standards, or guidance, or in the face of conflicting opinions, a member should test decisions and deeds by asking: "Am I doing what a person of integrity would do? Have I retained my integrity?" Integrity requires a member to observe both the form and the spirit of technical and ethical standards; circumvention of those standards constitutes subordination of judgment.

Integrity also requires a member to observe the principles of objectivity and independence and of due care.

Article IV

Objectivity and Independence

A member should maintain objectivity and be free of conflicts of interest in discharging professional responsibilities. A member in public practice should be independent in fact and appearance when providing auditing and other attestation services.

Objectivity is a state of mind, a quality that lends value to a member's services. It is a distinguishing feature of the profession. The principle of objectivity imposes the obligation to be impartial, intellectually honest, and free of conflicts of interest. Independence precludes relationships that may appear to impair a member's objectivity in rendering attestation services.

Members often serve multiple interests in many different capacities and must demonstrate their objectivity in varying circumstances. Members in public practice render attest, tax, and management advisory services. Other members prepare financial statements in the employment of others, perform internal auditing services, and serve in financial and management capacities in industry, education, and government. They also educate and train those who aspire to admission into the profession. Regardless of service or capacity, members should protect the integrity of their work, maintain objectivity, and avoid any subordination of their judgment.

For a member in public practice, the maintenance of objectivity and independence requires a continuing assessment of client relationships and public responsibility. Such a member who provides auditing and other attestation services should be independent in fact and appearance. In providing all other services, a member should maintain objectivity and avoid conflicts of interest.

Although members not in public practice cannot maintain the appearance of independence, they nevertheless have the responsibility to maintain objectivity in rendering professional services. Members employed by others to prepare financial statements or to perform auditing, tax, or consulting services are charged with the same responsibility for objectivity as members in public practice and must be scrupulous in their application of generally accepted accounting principles and candid in all their dealings with members in public practice.

Article V

Due Care

A member should observe the profession's technical and ethical standards, strive continually to improve competence and the quality of services, and discharge professional responsibility to the best of the member's ability.

The quest for excellence is the essence of due care. Due care requires a member to discharge professional responsibilities with competence and diligence. It imposes the obligation to perform professional services to the best of a member's ability with concern for the best interest of those for whom the services are performed and consistent with the profession's responsibility to the public.

Competence is derived from a synthesis of education and experience. It begins with a mastery of the common body of knowledge required for designation as a certified public accountant. The maintenance of competence requires a commitment to learning and professional improvement that must continue throughout a member's professional life. It is a member's individual responsibility. In all engagements and in all responsibilities, each member should undertake to achieve a level of competence that will assure that the quality of the member's services meets the high level of professionalism required by these Principles.

Competence represents the attainment and maintenance of a level of understanding and knowledge that enables a member to render services with facility and acumen. It also establishes the limitations of a member's capabilities by dictating that consultation or referral may be required when a professional engagement exceeds the personal competence of a member or a member's firm. Each member is responsible for assessing his or her own competence—of evaluating whether education, experience, and judgment are adequate for the responsibility to be assumed.

Members should be diligent in discharging responsibilities to clients, employers, and the public. Diligence imposes the responsibility to render services promptly and carefully, to be thorough, and to observe applicable technical and ethical standards.

Due care requires a member to plan and supervise adequately any professional activity for which he or she is responsible.

Article VI

Scope and Nature of Services

A member in public practice should observe the Principles of the Code of Professional Conduct in determining the scope and nature of services to be provided.

The public interest aspect of certified public accountants' services requires that such services be consistent with acceptable professional behavior for certified public accountants. Integrity requires that service and the public trust not be subordinated to personal gain and advantage. Objectivity and independence require that members be free from conflicts of interest in discharging professional responsibilities. Due care requires that services be provided with competence and diligence.

Each of these Principles should be considered by members in determining whether or not to provide specific services in individual circumstances. In some instances, they may represent an overall constraint on the nonaudit services that might be offered to a specific client. No hard-and-fast rules can be developed to help members reach these judgments, but they must be satisfied that they are meeting the spirit of the Principles in this regard.

In order to accomplish this, members should

- Practice in firms that have in place internal quality-control procedures to ensure that services are competently delivered and adequately supervised.
- Determine, in their individual judgments, whether the scope and nature of other services provided to an audit client would create a conflict of interest in the performance of the audit function for that client.
- Assess, in their individual judgments, whether an activity is consistent with their role as professionals (for example, Is such activity a reasonable extension or variation of existing services offered by the member or others in the profession?).

SECTION II—RULES

Applicability

The bylaws of the American Institute of Certified Public Accountants require that members adhere to the Rules of the Code of Professional Conduct. Members must be prepared to justify departures from these Rules.

Institute of Management Accountants Standards of Ethical Conduct for Practitioners of Management Accounting and Financial Management

Practitioners of management accounting and financial management have an obligation to the public, their profession, the organization they serve, and themselves, to maintain the highest standards of ethical conduct. In recognition of this obligation, the Institute of Management Accountants has promulgated the following standards of ethical conduct for practitioners of management accounting and financial management. Adherence to these standards, both domestically and internationally, is integral to achieving the Objectives of Management Accounting. Practitioners of management accounting and financial management shall not commit acts contrary to these standards nor shall they condone the commission of such acts by others within their organizations.

Competence. Practitioners of management accounting and financial management have a responsibility to:

- Maintain an appropriate level of professional competence by ongoing development of their knowledge and skills.
- Perform their professional duties in accordance with relevant laws, regulations, and technical standards.
- Prepare complete and clear reports and recommendations after appropriate analysis of relevant and reliable information.

Confidentiality. Practitioners of management accounting and financial management have a responsibility to:

- Refrain from disclosing confidential information acquired in the course of their work except when authorized, unless legally obligated to do so.
- Inform subordinates as appropriate regarding the confidentiality of information acquired in the course of their work and monitor their activities to assure the maintenance of that confidentiality.

- Refrain from using or appearing to use confidential information acquired in the course of their work for unethical or illegal advantage either personally or through third parties.

Integrity. Practitioners of management accounting and financial management have a responsibility to:

- Avoid actual or apparent conflicts of interest and advise all appropriate parties of any potential conflict.
- Refrain from engaging in any activity that would prejudice their ability to carry out their duties ethically.
- Refuse any gift, favor, or hospitality that would influence or would appear to influence their actions.
- Refrain from either actively or passively subverting the attainment of the organization's legitimate and ethical objectives.
- Recognize and communicate professional limitations or other constraints that would preclude responsible judgment or successful performance of an activity.
- Communicate unfavorable as well as favorable information and professional judgments or opinions.
- Refrain from engaging in or supporting any activity that would discredit the profession.

Objectivity. Practitioners of management accounting and financial management have a responsibility to:

- Communicate information fairly and objectively.
- Disclose fully all relevant information that could reasonably be expected to influence an intended user's understanding of the reports, comments, and recommendations presented.

Resolution of Ethical Conflict. In applying the standards of ethical conduct, practitioners of management accounting and financial management may encounter problems in identifying unethical behavior or in resolving an ethical conflict. When faced with significant ethical issues, practitioners of management accounting and financial management should follow the established policies of the organization bearing on the resolution of such conflict. If these policies do not resolve the ethical conflict, such practitioner should consider the following courses of action:

- Discuss such problems with the immediate superior except when it appears that the superior is involved, in which case the problem should be presented initially to the next higher managerial level. If a satisfactory resolution cannot be achieved when the problem is initially presented, submit the issues to the next higher managerial level.

If the immediate superior is the chief executive officer, or equivalent, the acceptable reviewing authority may be a group such as the audit committee, executive committee, board of directors, board of trustees, or owners. Contact with levels above the immediate superior should be initiated only with the superior's knowledge, assuming the superior is not involved. Except where legally prescribed, communication of such problems to authorities or individuals not employed or engaged by the organization is not considered appropriate.

- Clarify relevant ethical issues by confidential discussion with an objective advisor (e.g., IMA Ethics Counseling Service) to obtain a better understanding of possible courses of action.
- Consult your own attorney as to legal obligations and rights concerning the ethical conflict.
- If the ethical conflict still exists after exhausting all levels of internal review, there may be no other recourse on significant matters than to resign from the organization and to submit an informative memorandum to an appropriate representative of the organization. After resignation, depending on the nature of the ethical conflict, it may also be appropriate to notify other parties.

The Institute of Internal Auditors Code of Ethics

Purpose: A distinguishing mark of a profession is acceptance by its members of responsibility to the interests of those it serves. Members of The Institute of Internal Auditors (Members) and Certified Internal Auditors (CIAs) must maintain high standards of conduct in order to effectively discharge this responsibility. The Institute of Internal Auditors (Institute) adopts this *Code of Ethics* for Members and CIAs.

Applicability: This *Code of Ethics* is applicable to all Members and CIAs. Membership in The Institute and acceptance of the "Certified Internal Auditor" designation are voluntary actions. By acceptance, Members and CIAs assume an obligation of self-discipline above and beyond the requirements of laws and regulations.

The standards of conduct set forth in this Code of Ethics provide basic principles in the practice of internal auditing. Members and CIAs should realize that their individual judgment is required in the application of these principles.

CIAs shall use the "Certified Internal Auditor" designation with discretion and in a dignified manner, fully aware of what the designation denotes. The designation shall also be used in a manner consistent with all statutory requirements.

Members who are judged by the Board of Directors of The Institute to be in violation of the standards of conduct of the *Code of Ethics* shall be subject to forfeiture of their membership in The Institute. CIAs who are similarly judged also shall be subject to forfeiture of the "Certified Internal Auditor" designation.

STANDARDS OF CONDUCT

I.   Members and CIAs shall exercise honesty, objectivity, and diligence in the performance of their duties and responsibilities.

II.   Members and CIAs shall exhibit loyalty in all matters pertaining to the affairs of their organization or to whomever they may be rendering a service. However, Members and CIAs shall not knowingly be a party to any illegal or improper activity.

III.   Members and CIAs shall not knowingly engage in acts or activities which are discreditable to the profession of internal auditing or to their organization.

IV. Members and CIAs shall refrain from entering into any activity which may be in conflict with the interest of their organization or which would prejudice their ability to carry out objectively their duties and responsibilities.

V. Members and CIAs shall not accept anything of value from an employee, client, customer, supplier, or business associate of their organization which would impair or be presumed to impair their professional judgment.

VI. Members and CIAs shall undertake only those services which they can reasonably expect to complete with professional competence.

VII. Members and CIAs shall adopt suitable means to comply with the *Standards for the Professional Practice of Internal Auditing.*

VIII. Members and CIAs shall be prudent in the use of information acquired in the course of their duties. They shall not use confidential information for any personal gain nor in any manner which would be contrary to law or detrimental to the welfare of their organization.

IX. Members and CIAs, when reporting on the results of their work, shall reveal all material facts known to them which, if not revealed, could either distort reports of operations under review or conceal unlawful practices.

X. Members and CIAs shall continually strive for improvement in their proficiency, and in the effectiveness and quality of their service.

XI. Members and CIAs, in the practice of their profession, shall be ever mindful of their obligation to maintain the high standards of competence, morality, and dignity promulgated by The Institute. Members shall abide by the *Bylaws* and uphold the objectives of The Institute.

Phillips-Van Heusen
A Shared Commitment

(October 1997—Requirements for Suppliers, Contractors, Business Partners)

A Shared Commitment:

The guidelines you are about to read are of utmost importance to the Phillips-Van Heusen Corporation and to the relationships we form with suppliers, contractors and business partners.

While we place tremendous importance on these relationships, many of which qualify as genuine friendships of long-standing, certain values and standards have always been, and will always remain, paramount. Adherence to these values and standards by the people and companies we do business with is a prerequisite for continuing or establishing relationships with our company.

Indeed, we cannot do business with any company that fails to adhere to these ideals.

We believe that by working together to see these standards enforced, our company and its suppliers, contractors and business partners can help achieve a genuine improvement in the lives of working people around the world.

This mission has been a guiding principle of our company for more than a century, and it shall guide us in the future and take precedence over any economic or business concern.

Bruce J. Klatsky
Chairman, President and Chief Executive Officer

GUIDELINES FOR VENDORS

While respecting cultural differences and economic variances that reflect the particular countries where we and our vendors do business, our goal is to create, and encourage the creation of, model facilities that not only provide good jobs at fair wages, but which also improve conditions in the community at large. Therefore, we actively seek business associations with those who share our concerns.

- *Legal Requirements*

  We expect our vendors to be law abiding citizens and to comply with any and all legal requirement relevant to the conduct of their business. We will seek vendors who respect the legal and moral rights of the employees.

- *Nondiscrimination*

  We will not do business with any vendor who discriminates in employment, including hiring, salary, benefits, advancement, discipline, termination or retirement, on the basis of gender, race, religion, age, disability, sexual orientation, nationality, or social or ethnic origin.

- *Child Labor*

  Employees of our vendors must be over the applicable minimum legal age requirement or be at least 14 years old or older than the age for completing compulsory education in the country of manufacture, whichever is greater. Vendors must observe all legal requirements for the work of authorized minors, particularly those pertaining to hours of work, wages, minimum education and working conditions. We encourage vendors to support night classes and work-study programs, especially for younger workers.

- *Forced Labor*

  We will not be associated with any vendor who uses any form of mental or physical coercion. We will not do business with any vendor who utilizes forced labor whether in the form of prison labor, indentured labor, bonded labor or otherwise.

- *Harassment and Abuse*

  Vendors must treat employees with respect and dignity. No employee shall be subject to any physical, sexual, psychological, or verbal harassment and/or abuse.

- *Health and Safety*

  Employers shall provide a safe and healthy work environment to prevent accident and injury to health. Vendors should make a responsible contribution to the health care needs of their employees.

- *Wages and Benefits*

  We will only do business with vendors who pay employees, as a floor, at least the minimum wage required by local law or the prevailing industry wage—when available, whichever is higher, and who provide all legally mandated benefits. Employees shall be compensated for overtime hours at the rate established by law in the country of manufacture or, in those countries where such laws do not exist, at a rate at least equal to their regular hourly compensation rate.

- *Hours of Work*

  While permitting flexibility in scheduling, we will only do business with vendors who do not exceed prevailing local work hours and who appropriately compensate overtime. No employee should be scheduled for more than sixty hours of work per week and we will favor vendors who utilize work weeks of less than sixty hours. Employees should be allowed at least one day off per seven day week.

- *Freedom of Association*

  Employees should be free to join organizations of their own choice. Vendors shall recognize and respect the right of employees to freedom of association and collective bargaining. Employees should not be subject to intimidation or harassment in the exercise of their right to join or to refrain from joining any organization.

- *Environmental Requirements*

  We are committed to the environment and will favor vendors who share this commitment. We require our vendors to meet all applicable environmental laws in their countries and to nurture a better environment at their facilities and in the communities in which they operate.

- *Commitment to Communities*

  We will favor vendors who share our commitment to contribute to the betterment of the communities in which they operate.

PVH has been committed to the enforcement of these standards and has an ongoing approval and monitoring system. Our goal is to engage our suppliers, contractors and business partners in the implementation of these standards. In the past, we have not established business relationships and we have suspended our association with companies that were found to abuse the rights of the employees. We will continue to do so in the future if any of the standards outlined above are violated.

THE PHILLIPS-VAN HEUSEN COMMITMENT

- To conduct all business in keeping with the highest moral, ethical and legal standards.
- To recruit, train and provide career advancement to all associates without regard to gender, race, religion, age, disability, sexual orientation, nationality, or social or ethnic origin. Diversity in the workplace will be encouraged. Bigotry, racism and sexual harassment will not be tolerated.
- To maintain a workplace environment that encourages frank and open communications.
- To be concerned with the preservation and improvement of our environment.
- To be ever mindful that our dedication to these standards is absolute and will not be compromised.

Kronos®

Code of Conduct and Business Ethics

GENERAL GUIDELINES

A business is usually thought of in economic terms. However, it is also an institution of people. As such, a business has moral standards and ethical responsibilities. Kronos wants to be known as a company that conforms to law, custom, and human values. This document should help guide our conduct as representatives of our Company.

While ethical behavior can often be a matter of law, it is mostly a matter of spirit and intent. Consequently, our ethics guidelines start with these general principles.

- The most important element of ethical behavior is honesty. Honesty is characterized by truthfulness and freedom from deception. These qualities are unchanging, and should vary neither by country nor by culture. They dictate one standard of conduct worldwide. If we are steadfast in this belief, questions of ethical behavior are easily answered in most situations.

- We see no conflict between attention to profit and attention to ethics. In fact, the two should go hand in hand. If we are ethical, we will prosper most in an environment that is fair and open. As we contribute to such an environment, we will also contribute to the good fiscal health of our Company.

- No "code of conduct" can hope to spell out the appropriate moral conduct and ethical behavior for every situation. We must often rely on our own good judgment. Whenever we find ourselves with a hard decision to make, we should seek advice from our management, but most importantly, from our own consciences. Perhaps when confronted with a decision we should be guided with one overriding Principle: Do The Right Thing!

These are the overriding principles which must guide us in the conduct of our business. This document is a start. What counts is how we follow through with actions at every level.

Reprinted with permission from Kronos Incorporated, 400 Fifth Avenue, Waltham, Massachusetts 02154.

185

DIVULGING OR USING CONFIDENTIAL INFORMATION

Financial information about our business is a closely guarded secret. Disclosure of this information could put Kronos at a significant disadvantage with respect to our competition. Therefore, absolutely no disclosure of information relative to our financial operations or standing can be made to anyone outside the Corporation without the prior approval of the Management Committee. This includes, but is not limited to, information concerning the ownership of stock, customer and vendor pricing, salary structures, contract negotiations, methods of financing and corporate plans. Any unauthorized disclosure of such information is a serious violation of the implied agreement of trust and confidence between Kronos and the employee, as well as a violation of the Proprietary Rights and Confidentiality Agreement referred to below.

It is also Company policy that we must not profit from confidential information we obtain during the course of our duties on behalf of the Company. In addition to violating Company policy, it is generally illegal for any employee either personally or on behalf of others, to trade in, or to communicate (tip) such information to others so that they may trade in securities on the basis of material, nonpublic information. All information that an investor might consider important in deciding whether to buy, sell or hold securities is considered material. Information is nonpublic unless it has been effectively disclosed to the public, such as through public filings with the Securities and Exchange Commission or Company press releases. It should be noted that these prohibitions apply not only to trading Kronos securities, but also to securities of *any* company about which an employee obtains material, nonpublic information. Any questions concerning these prohibitions should be directed to the General Counsel.

All employees are required to execute a Proprietary Rights and Confidentiality Agreement as a condition of employment. The Agreement states, among other things, that ideas developed by an employee relating to Kronos or its products are the sole property of Kronos. The principle embodied in that document and the implied trust it requires are expected of each employee.

GIFTS, ENTERTAINMENT AND GRATUITIES

Because we value professional objectivity in our relationships with others, the acceptance of personal gifts or loans to any employee, or any member of his/her immediate family is prohibited unless the criteria below are satisfied. However well meaning the giver, gifts in a business setting often influence the climate of objectivity and thus serve to undermine impartial professional judgment. Employees may accept unsolicited non-monetary gifts when the refusal to do so would be an insult to the giver provided that the gift is of nominal value; or the gift is promotional material clearly marked with company or brand names.

Any offer of a gift of more than nominal value should be reported to your direct supervisor. Any supervisor receiving such a report must report it to a corporate officer.

FINANCIAL INTEGRITY

The improper use of Company funds or accounting for Company transactions is prohibited. In view of this:

- No false or artificial entries shall be made on the books of the Corporation or its subsidiaries for any reason. Many people rely on the accuracy of our published financial information. We stand for the principle that this information should not be misleading in any way and should be prepared according to the highest professional accounting standards.
- No payment on behalf of the Company shall be made with the understanding that it will or might be used for something other than the stated purpose. All payments must be made for clear and valid business purposes and not be in violation of any local or national laws.

RELATIONS WITH SUPPLIERS

A supplier is any business or individual which furnishes goods or services to the Company.

It is the policy of Kronos to select suppliers in a totally impartial manner based upon price, quality, and services offered. Each employee is expected to avoid any action which would imply selection of a supplier on any basis other than in the best interest of Kronos or that would give one supplier an unfair advantage over another.

Employees engaged in the specification and procurement of goods and services, and all members of that employee's immediate family, must not have any interest, either directly or indirectly, in the business of a supplier which would create a conflict of interest. Employees who deal with suppliers have an obligation to avoid even the appearance of beneficial relationship with suppliers. Because of their position and fiduciary responsibility, their actions must conform to the highest standards of ethical conduct.

RELATIONS WITH CUSTOMERS

Kronos will prosper to the degree, and only to the degree, that we continue to serve our customers well. It has always been Kronos' policy to provide the best possible products and services to our customers. We must sell on the merits of our own products and services, not by disparaging competitors or their products and services.

Our competitive appeal must be based on this concept of quality and service and the competence and honesty of our sales presentations. No payments or other inducements should be made to any person, public official, or political party, either domestic or foreign, for the purpose of influencing that person or party to assist Kronos in obtaining or retaining business.

RELATIONS WITH THE PUBLIC AND HOST COMMUNITIES

As a growing multinational company with facilities throughout the world, we have responsibilities to the many countries in which we do business. Those responsibilities involve knowing the different laws and understanding their customs and abiding by them. We recognize that we must become part of the host community. We must behave as citizens rather than as foreigners. We realize that we will be welcome only so long as we make a responsible contribution to the societies in which we operate.

Kronos recognizes that it has no future unless it can operate in a strong and free society. We recognize that we can only exist when people are well educated and free to make their own decisions. We have an obligation to help foster such a culture. The Company conducts its business according to accepted principals of free and open competition and trade. Employees shall not discuss or agree to participate in a boycott of any country's goods or services nor shall an employee enter into any arrangements or agreements with competitors affecting pricing, market conditions, marketing policies, customers, or products.

RESPECT FOR OTHERS

During the typical work day, we inevitably come in contact with fellow employees, job applicants, vendors and others. The men and women we meet may have educational backgrounds, racial characteristics, religious beliefs, political affiliations and other points of view that are different from our own. At Kronos we have worked very hard at creating an environment where such differences are welcomed and are part of our vibrant corporate culture. In fact, we will not tolerate any situation, within a Kronos business setting or while representing Kronos outside the company, where an employee treats others in a discriminatory or hostile manner based upon race, religious belief, sex, age, physical appearance, or other differences. Incidents of such discrimination, sexual or other forms of harassment must be reported to your manager or a corporate officer as soon as discovered. These actions are illegal and patently unethical. Such matters will be aggressively investigated by our Human Resources department and senior management and will be dealt with accordingly.

CONFLICT OF INTEREST POLICY

The term *conflict of interest* describes any situation where an employee is involved in an activity for personal gain which for any reason is in conflict with Kronos' interests or any circumstances that could cast doubt on our ability to act with total objectivity with regard to the Company's interest. We all want to be loyal to Kronos. We also want that loyalty to come easily and free from any conflicting interest. Therefore, our employees and members of the immediate family must not have any financial interest in a competitor, supplier, or any other business that could cause divided loyalty. However, this prohibition on financial interests shall not prevent any employee or member of their immediate family from owning one percent (1%) or less of the equity securities of any publicly traded company. Nor should we have any interest or engage in any activities that could cause speculation or misunderstanding about our loyalty. If you have any doubts or questions about the propriety of your relationship with any outside organization or outside activity, you should discuss it with your manager.

If you intend to perform work for any other company, organization or on your own behalf, you must first consider whether this activity may create a conflict with your obligations to Kronos. If you think there may be a conflict and in every case when the outside work exceeds twenty (20) hours per week, you should notify and obtain approval from your immediate manager. In any event, outside work cannot be performed on Company time. You cannot use the Company's equipment, materials, resources or "inside" information for outside work. Nor should you solicit business or clients or perform outside work on the Company's premises.

We do not object to an employee spending reasonable time on civic responsibilities, professional associations or as a member of a Board of Directors of another company. However, when participation in such activities involves time during the business day or the use of Company facilities or resources, you should first obtain permission from your immediate supervisor. Participation as a member of a Board of Directors of an outside company requires the permission from Kronos' Board of Directors.

This policy is also not intended to prohibit incidental use of such items as the Company fax machines or the telephone system for activities which are permitted pursuant to this Code of Conduct. However, extensive personal use of any Company property is prohibited.

If you have any doubts or questions about the propriety of your relationship with any outside organization or outside activity, you should discuss it with your manager.

Some of the questions we must ask ourselves to determine whether a conflict of interest exists are:

- What is your job at Kronos? For example, could your decisions possibly be affected by your interest in an outside organization?
- What is the extent of your financial interest in this organization?

- When and under what circumstances was the involvement with the outside organization originally made?
- What is the nature and extent of the relationship between Kronos and the outside organization?

EMPLOYEE OBLIGATION TO REPORT POSSIBLE VIOLATIONS

All employees should be alert and sensitive to situations which could result in actions by themselves or others that might violate this policy. If you are uncertain about what is proper conduct in a particular situation, if you are concerned about your own conduct, or if you believe that a fellow employee may have violated the policy, it is your obligation to contact at least one of the following persons or groups:

- Your supervisor
- Your department or function head
- Another function with applicable expertise, such as Human Resources; or
- Any Corporate Officer

Normally, you should discuss the matter first with your immediate supervisor or with your department or function head. Such discussion may provide valuable insight or perspective and result in a resolution of the problem. However, if for any reason you would not be comfortable bringing the matter up with them, you should and are expected to discuss the matter with a higher authority. Violation of this policy will be dealt with in a severe and swift manner.

National Association of State Boards of Accountancy

MODEL CODE OF PROFESSIONAL CONDUCT

Introductory Comments

The Model Code of Professional Conduct set out below has been prepared by the National Association of State Boards of Accountancy as part of its continuing effort to update and promote uniformity in the regulatory systems governing the practice of public accountancy in the various jurisdictions. NASBA first published a Model Code in September 1977. In April 1980, NASBA published a Model Public Accountancy Act, and in May 1981 it published a set of Model Rules, including a revised version of the Model Code, keyed to the Model Act. In November 1984, NASBA published, jointly with the American Institute of Certified Public Accountants (AICPA) a Model Public Accountancy Bill (Model Bill), an improved and updated version of the Model Act, which it also superseded. The present Model Code is in pertinent respects keyed to the Model Bill. Like its predecessor, it could also be included in a comprehensive set of Model Rules, likewise keyed to the Model Bill.

Changes in the Rules of Professional Conduct

In addition to the changes called for by the new statutory framework provided by the Model Bill, this Model Code reflects changes in the legal, ethical and competitive environments in which public accountancy is practiced. Thus, this Model Code would drop entirely the former Rule 105, on incompatible occupations. It would substantially narrow the former prohibition on solicitation, in Rule 404, combining it with similarly narrowed restrictions on advertising (in Rule 403). It would eliminate the explicit restriction on forecasts, in former Rule 205, although there would still be a requirement, in Rules 202 or 203, that licensees conform to authoritative pronouncements establishing professional standards governing forecasts and projections.

The new Model Code would also eliminate the absolute prohibitions on payment and receipt of commissions contained in former Rule 103, and substitute separate, more limited restrictions, one on payment of commissions and two others on receipt of commissions. The restriction on payment of commissions, embodied in this Code in Rule 104, requires only disclosure, in writing, of commissions paid in certain circumstances. The restrictions on receipt of commissions (here termed "other compensation") consist of a prohibition of their receipt in circumstances where they would impair audit independence, which is embodied in Rule 101; and in other circumstances only requirements of disclosure, embodied in Rule 103. The substitution of disclosure requirements for flat prohibitions, as respects both receipt and payment of commissions, rests on the premise that the harm likely to be caused by the payment or receipt of a commission turns on the possibility that the client may be misled, and that this possibility is sufficiently eliminated by written disclosure.

Finally, the prohibition on receipt of contingent fees, formerly in a separate Rule 104, has also been incorporated in Rule 101 on independence, and narrowed to apply only to circumstances where the contingent fees would impair the independence of a practitioner.

In connection with the two changes to the rule on independence just discussed, it will bear emphasis that independence is a veritable keystone of the regulatory system governing the practice of public accountancy of which a code of professional conduct is a part. The public's expectations regarding the reliability of financial information are a principal reason for the regulatory system's existence in the first place, and independence lies at the very heart of the profession's public responsibility.

The fact that this Model Code suggests departures from rules of professional conduct presently in effect in many jurisdictions should not, of course, be understood as necessarily implying a judgment that other rules are invalid, or that only rules following the Model here presented will pass legal muster.

Relationship of a Code to Other Board Rules

The rules comprising a code of professional conduct may be promulgated by a Board of Accountancy either as part of its general rules or separately from its rules dealing with other subjects. The Model Code set out below is presented in a format that principally contemplates separate adoption or publication. Thus, the comments for the most part treat the Code as if it were a freestanding set of rules, and the numbering of the rules that comprise the Code follows its own internal sequence. (See also Discussion of Relationship to State Accountancy Laws below.) If these rules were considered for adoption simply as an integral part of a set of general rules, some of the comments would be inapplicable, and the numbering system might be different.

Certain of the rules suitable to a free-standing code of professional conduct could equally well be dealt with instead by statutory provisions or by Board rules of general application. Because the present version of the Model Code is presented in a format that assumes separate adoption, it includes some provisions of this kind; but the comments following these provisions point out the possibility of the provisions being dealt with by statute (with references to pertinent sections of the Model Bill) or by Model Rule instead. Similarly, the Definitions included in this Code could be applicable to the entirety of a set of Board-promulgated Rules if the Model Code were treated as part of such Rules.

Scope of Professional Practice Covered by the Proposed Model Code

The Model Code is so drawn as to apply to *all* licensees under the state accountancy law administered by the Board, and insofar as appropriately applicable, to all kinds of professional services performed by such licensees, including not merely reports on financial statements but also other services such as tax and management advisory services. The licensees so covered would include, where the applicable accountancy law provided for their licensing, not merely Certified Public Accountants, but also Public Accountants, Registered Public Accountants, Licensed Public Accountants and Accounting Practitioners and the like, and firms of such practitioners. It may be that in some jurisdictions the Board's authority to prescribe rules of conduct does not extend so far: where this is so, appropriate departures from the Model Code will be necessary.

Not all of the Rules of Conduct, of course, have potential application to all aspects of the practice of public accountancy: the rules on independence (Rule 101), on auditing standards (Rule 202) and on accounting principles (Rule 203) are examples of rules principally having application to audit work. The Model Code is, however, intended to be so drafted that the scope of each rule, as respects the kinds of accountancy practice to which it applies, is spelled out in the rule itself, or in the defined terms used in the rule.

Relationship to State Accountancy Laws

As has been mentioned, this Model Code is in various respects designed to mesh with an accountancy law in the form of the Model Bill. Key terms in both are the same; and references to statutory provisions, in particular rules and in accompanying comments in this Model Code, are to specific provisions of the Model Bill. The Model Code also assumes the existence of an accountancy law with provisions corresponding to those of the Model Bill as respects the kinds of persons and professional services to which the rules may properly extend. Adjustments may therefore be required to adapt this Model Code to the accountancy law in effect in a particular jurisdiction, where that law differs from the Model Bill in any of these matters. In some jurisdictions certain of the matters dealt with by the Model Code are covered by statutory provisions: where this is so, the corresponding provision of the Code may have to be eliminated or modified. In addition, in some cases it may be deemed desirable, in order to enhance the enforceability of a particular provision, either to embody the provision itself in the governing statute or to amend the statute so as to avoid any doubt about the Board of Accountancy's authority to adopt such a provision.

Format

The Model Code, if treated as separate from the other rules promulgated by a Board, would be in the three general parts that follow: a Preamble, Definitions, and the Rules of Professional Conduct. If the Model Code were adopted as part of a set of general rules, it might not include a Definitions section, because the pertinent definitions would likely be included in an introductory section of the rules as a whole, rather than as part of a Code of Professional Conduct.

The Preamble is intended to be purely descriptive and explanatory. It contains no substantive prohibitions or requirements: all of these are included instead in the Rules of Conduct.

PREAMBLE

This Code of Professional Conduct is promulgated under the authority granted by [Section 4(h)(4)] of the Public Accountancy Act of _____ , _____ [statutory reference], which delegates to the _____ Board of Accountancy the power and duty to prescribe rules of professional conduct directed to controlling the quality of the practice of public accountancy, and dealing among other things with independence, integrity and objectivity; competence and technical standards; responsibilities to the public; and responsibilities to clients.

The Rules of Professional Conduct set out below rest upon the premises that the reliance of the public in general and of the business community in particular on sound financial reporting, and on the implication of professional competence which is inherent in the authorized use of legally restricted titles relating to the practice of public accountancy, imposes on persons engaged in such practice certain obligations both to their clients and to the public. These obligations, which the Rules of Professional Conduct are intended to enforce where necessary, include the obligation to maintain independence and objectivity of thought and action, to strive continuously to improve one's professional skills, to observe where applicable generally accepted accounting principles and generally accepted auditing standards, to promote sound and informative financial reporting, to hold the affairs of clients in confidence, to uphold the standards of the public accountancy profession, and to maintain high standards of personal conduct in all matters affecting one's fitness to practice public accountancy.

Acceptance of licensure to engage in the practice of public accountancy, or to use titles in offering services to the public which imply a particular competence, involves acceptance by the licensee of such obligations, and accordingly of a duty to abide by the Rules of Professional Conduct.

The Rules of Professional Conduct are intended to have application to all kinds of professional services performed in the practice of public accountancy, including auditing, accounting, review and compilation services, tax services and management advisory services; and to apply as well to all licensees, whether or not engaged in the practice of public accountancy, except where the wording of a Rule clearly indicates that the applicability is more limited.

A licensee who is engaged in the practice of public accountancy outside the United States will not be subject to discipline by the Board for departing, with respect to such foreign practice, from any of the Rules, so long as his conduct is in accordance with the standards of professional conduct applicable to the practice of public accountancy in the country in which he is practicing. However, even in such a case, if a licensee's name is associated with financial statements in such manner as to imply that he is acting as an independent public accountant and under circumstances that would entitle the reader to assume that United States practices are followed, he will be expected to comply with Rules 202, 203, and 204.

In the interpretation and enforcement of the Rules of Professional Conduct, the Board will give consideration, but not necessarily dispositive weight, to relevant interpretations, rulings and opinions issued by the Boards of other jurisdictions.

Comment: The first paragraph of the Preamble should, of course, track the pertinent statutory provisions: in this instance, the language used is from Section 4(h)(4) of the Model Bill. The second and third paragraphs are intended to set forth the conceptual underpinnings of the Rules, and the fourth to describe their general scope. The fifth paragraph is believed to embody the general practice with respect to application of ethics rules to conduct that occurs outside the jurisdiction. It is intended to be framed as a statement of the Board of Accountancy's enforcement policy, rather than as a limitation on the scope of the Rules. The final paragraph is intended to indicate the weight that will be given to interpretations, rulings and opinions issued by entities other than the promulgating Board.

DEFINITIONS

For purposes of these Rules the following terms have the meanings indicated:

(a) *Client* means the person or entity which retains a licensee for the performance of professional services.

Comment: This term is used in Rules 102, 103, 104, 301, and 302. It is of particular significance in Rule 103 (on receipt of other compensation), where it serves to distinguish between persons for whom a licensee performs professional services and persons to whom a licensee sells products or recommends the services or products of others.

(b) *Financial statements* means statements and footnotes related thereto that purport to show actual or anticipated financial position which relates to a point in time, or results of operations, cash flow, or changes in financial position which relate to a period of time, on the basis of generally accepted accounting principles or another comprehensive basis of accounting. The term includes specific elements, accounts or items of such statements, but does not include incidental financial data included in management advisory services reports to support recommendations to a client, nor does it include tax returns and supporting schedules.

Comment: This term is used in Rules 101, 202, and 203, dealing with independence, auditing standards and accounting principles, respectively.

(c) *He, his,* and *him* mean, where applicable, the corresponding feminine and neuter pronouns also.

(d) *Licensee* means the holder of a certificate issued under Section [5] of the Act, or of a permit issued under Sections [6 or 7]; or, in each case, a certificate or permit issued under corresponding provisions of prior law.

Comment: This term is also defined in the Model Bill (Section 3(e)). It may be useful nonetheless to have a separately stated definition in the Code. Alternatively, the Code could, with this term and some others, incorporate the statutory definition by reference.

(e) *Other compensation* means compensation received by a licensee who is engaged in the practice of public accountancy for other than the performance of professional services, including compensation for the sale of products other than work product of the licensee or for referral of products or services of others.

Comment: This term is used in Rules 101 and 103, dealing with independence and receipt of other compensation, respectively.

(f) *Practice of (or practicing) public accountancy* means the offering to perform or the performance by a person holding himself out to the public as a licensee, for a client or potential client, of one or more kinds of services involving the use of accounting or auditing skills, including the issuance of reports on financial statements, or of one or more types of management advisory or consulting services, or the preparation of tax returns or the furnishing of advice on tax matters.

Comment: This duplicates the statutory definition, see Model Bill Section 3(g). See also Comment under "licensee," above. The term is a key to several other defined terms—*other compensation, professional services,* and *quality* *review.* It is also used in Rule 401, on discreditable acts, and Rule 404, on firm names.

(g) *Professional services* means any services performed or offered to be performed by a licensee for a client in the course of the practice of public accountancy.

Comment: This term is used in the definition of two other defined terms: *client* and *other compensation.* It is also used in Rules 102, 201, 301, and 403.

(h) *Quality review* means a study, appraisal, or review of one or more aspects of the professional work of a person or firm in the practice of public accountancy, by a person or persons who hold certificates and who are not affiliated with the person or firm being reviewed.

Comment: This duplicates a statutory definition, see Model Bill Section 3(h). See also Comment under "licensee," above. The term is used in Rule 301, on confidential client communications.

(i) *Report,* when used with reference to financial statements, means an opinion, report, or other form of language that states or implies assurance as to the reliability of any financial statements and that also includes or is accompanied by any statement or implication that the person or firm issuing it has special knowledge or competence in accounting or auditing. Such a statement or implication of special knowledge or competence may arise from use by the issuer of the report of names or titles indicating that he or it is an accountant or auditor, or from the language of the report itself. The term *report* includes any form of language which disclaims an opinion when such form of language is conventionally understood to imply any positive assurance as to the reliability of the financial statements referred to and/or special competence on the part of the person or firm issuing such language; and it includes any other form of language that is conventionally understood to imply such assurance and/or such special knowledge or competence.

Comment: This duplicates a statutory definition, see Model Bill Section 3(i). See also Comment under "licensee," above. The term is used in Rules 101 and 203, on independence and accounting principles, respectively.

RULES OF PROFESSIONAL CONDUCT

Independence, Integrity and Objectivity

Rule 101—*Independence.* A licensee who is performing an engagement in which the licensee will issue a report on financial statements of any client (other than a report in which a lack of independence is disclosed) must be independent with respect to the client in fact and appearance.

(a) Independence will be considered to be impaired if, for example, during the period of his professional engagement, or at the time of issuing his report, the licensee:

    (1) (A) Had or was committed to acquire any direct or material indirect financial interest in the client; or

          (B) Was a trustee of any trust or executor or administrator of any estate if such trust or estate had or was committed to acquire any direct or material indirect financial interest in the client; or

    (2) Had any joint closely held business investment with the client or any officer, director or principal stockholder thereof which was material in relation to the net worth of either the client or the licensee; or

    (3) Had any loan to or from the client or any officer, director or principal stockholder thereof other than loans of the following kinds made by a financial institution under normal lending procedures, terms and requirements:

        (A) Loans obtained by the licensee which are not material in relation to the net worth of the borrower; and

        (B) Home mortgages; and

        (C) Other secured loans, except those secured solely by a guarantee of the licensee.

(b) Independence will also be considered to be impaired if, during the period covered by the financial statements, during the period of the professional engagement or at the time of issuing his report, the licensee:

    (1) Was connected with the client as a promoter, underwriter, voting trustee, director or officer, or in any capacity equivalent to that of a member of management or of an employee; or

    (2) Was a trustee for any pension or profit-sharing trust of the client; or

    (3) Received from a third party, or had a commitment to receive from the client or a third party, with respect to services or products procured or to be procured by the client, other compensation; or

    (4) Had a commitment from the client for a contingent fee. For this purpose, a contingent fee means compensation for the performance of services payment of which, or the amount of which, is contingent upon the findings or results of such services. The examples of impaired independence described in paragraphs (a) and (b) are not intended to be all-inclusive.

Comment: This Rule adds to the requirements with respect to independence that are generally found in existing ethical rules on that subject two prohibitions that have heretofore generally been found in more broadly phrased separate rules: one on receipt of commissions (here called *other compensation,* a term that is defined in paragraph (e) of the Definitions, above), in subparagraph (b)(3); and one on contingent fees, in subparagraph (b)(4). Restricting these prohibitions to circumstances where as a matter of legitimate professional standards independence is required, and where each of the forms of compensation would taint such independence, seems a sensible and entirely defensible way of dealing with attacks that have been mounted on more broadly cast existing rules. As pointed out in the Introductory Comments, the fundamental requirement of audit independence is attended by a substantial public interest—a public interest that is central to the whole system of regulation of the practice of public accountancy. (See also Comment in Appendix.)

It should be noted that the prohibition on contingent fees applies to a fee with respect to other than audit services, so long as the licensee is also performing audit services for the client in question. The exception from the requirement of independence for reports in which a lack of independence is disclosed would allow, among other things, for reports on compilations as to which SSARS 1 requires disclosure of a lack of independence.

Rule 102—*Integrity and objectivity.* A licensee shall not in the performance of professional services knowingly misrepresent facts, nor subordinate his judgment to others. In tax practice, however, a licensee may resolve doubt in favor of his client as long as there is reasonable support for his position.

Rule 103—*Receipt of other compensation.* A licensee who receives or agrees to receive other compensation with respect to services or products recommended, referred or sold by him to another person shall, no later than the making of such recommendation, referral or sale, make the following disclosures to such other person in writing: (a) if the other person is a client, the nature, source and amount of all such other compensation; and (b) if the other person is not a client, the nature and source only of any such other compensation received from a third party. The disclosure required by this Rule shall be made regardless of the amount of the other compensation involved. This Rule does not apply to payments received from the sale of all, or a material part, of an accounting practice, or to retirement payments to persons formerly engaged in the practice of public accountancy.

Comment: The term *other compensation,* used in this Rule, is defined in paragraph (e) of the Definitions, above. The term "client" is also defined in paragraph (a).

This Rule, dealing with a subject often addressed by rules using the term *commissions* instead of *other compensation,* does not, like many such rules, prohibit the receipt of commissions or compensation, but only requires their disclosure in writing in specified circumstances where objectivity may be affected. It should be noted that the possible effect of receipt of other compensation on independence is dealt with in Rule 101(b)(3). This Rule requires two different levels of disclosure, depending upon whether the person with whom the licensee is dealing is a client (meaning a person who retains a licensee for the performance of professional services) or a nonclient. In the first case, the Rule requires disclosure of any other compensation received, whether it is from a third party (as, for example, a commission for a recommendation or referral) or from the client itself; whereas if the other person is not a client, then disclosure is only required with respect to compensation received from third parties. More detailed disclosure is also required where a client is involved. Thus, if a licensee sold some product as principal to someone who had retained the licensee for professional services (that is, a client), the licensee would be required to disclose to the client the profit realized by the licensee on the sale. The reason for applying this requirement in the case of sales to clients but not to nonclients is simply the difference in the degree to which it might be reasonably presumed that the client would be relying upon the licensee for disinterested advice and assistance. This would also avoid the possibility that a licensee could evade the requirement of disclosing commissions received from third parties in dealings with a client by simply purchasing the products in question and then reselling them as principal.

Rule 104—*Payment of commissions.* A licensee shall not pay a commission to a third party to obtain a client unless, prior to being engaged by such client, the licensee discloses to the client in writing the fact and the amount of such commission. This Rule does not apply to payments made by a licensee for the purchase of all, or a material part, of an accounting practice, or to retirement payments to persons formerly engaged in the practice of public accountancy.

Comment: This Rule is more narrowly drawn than some existing rules which altogether prohibit payments of commissions to third parties to obtain a client. While such rules have been attacked as unreasonably restricting competition, the more limited requirement of written disclosure in this Rule provides obvious protection for legitimate interests of the client (or potential client) involved, and should not be vulnerable to such attack. The term *client* is defined in paragraph (a) of the Definitions, above, as one who retains the licensee for performance of professional services.

Competence and Technical Standards

Rule 201—*Competence.* A licensee shall not undertake any engagement for the performance of professional services which he cannot reasonably expect to complete with due professional competence, including compliance, where applicable, with Rules 202, 203 and 204.

Rule 202—*Auditing standards.* A licensee shall not permit his name to be associated with financial statements in such a manner as to imply that he is acting as an independent public accountant with respect to such financial statements unless he has complied with applicable generally accepted auditing standards. Statements on Auditing Standards issued by the American Institute of Certified Public

Accountants, Standards for Audit of Government Organizations, Programs, Activities and Functions issued by the United States General Accounting Office, and other pronouncements having similar generally recognized authority, are considered to be interpretations of generally accepted auditing standards, and departures from such pronouncements, where they are applicable, must be justified by those who do not follow them.

Comment: This version of an important, and virtually universal, ethical rule is intended to give appropriate recognition to pronouncements of what is currently designated as the Auditing Standards Board of the AICPA (whose pronouncements are also given similar recognition by the Securities and Exchange Commission and similar bodies), while also recognizing that there are other sources of generally accepted auditing standards, such as the GAO "Yellow Book." A particular State Board itself might, of course, undertake to issue pronouncements on such matters from time to time, in which case the second sentence of this Rule would require appropriate amendment.

A Rule that, like this Rule and Rules 203 and 204 below, explicitly recognizes the authority of pronouncements made by other bodies than the agency promulgating the Rule, may give rise to questions about whether there is an impermissible delegation of rule-making authority. These three Rules are, however, intended to be so framed as to minimize any doubts on that score. They explicitly recognize what is obvious to anyone familiar with the field: namely, that professional standards governing technical aspects of the practice of public accountancy are, like those of other professional disciplines (such as medicine), for the most part established on a nationwide rather than a local basis, and that they are to a substantial degree formulated by private bodies rather than governmental ones. Recognition of these realities offers the practical advantage of eliminating the need for each State Board separately to promulgate as rules of conduct the substance of all of the various authoritative pronouncements dealing with each area of technical standards.

Nonetheless, these three Rules do not look exclusively or blindly to pronouncements of the bodies to which explicit reference is made for the professional standards that they seek to enforce: rather, they simply acknowledge the general recognition those bodies enjoy, and the consequent authority of their pronouncements, while recognizing also that pronouncements of other bodies may also enjoy such authority. Moreover, they leave latitude for a showing in a specific case that a particular standard, though embodied in a pronouncement of a body like the ASB, does not in fact enjoy general acceptance.

The term *financial statements,* used in this Rule, has been broadened by a new definition, in paragraph (b) of the Definitions, above, to include "anticipated" financial position, results of operations, etc.; and thus to include projections and forecasts. In light of this, and of the fact that there are authoritative pronouncements dealing with such prospective financial statements, which would be incorporated by this Rule, there is no need for a separate rule addressed to forecasts, such as is found in some present codes.

Rule 203—*Accounting principles.* A licensee shall not issue a report asserting that financial statements are presented in conformity with generally accepted accounting principles if such financial statements contain any departure from such accounting principles which has a material effect on the financial statements taken as a whole, unless the licensee can demonstrate that by reason of unusual circumstances the financial statements would otherwise have been misleading. In such a case, the licensee's report must describe the departure, the approximate effects thereof, if practicable, and the reasons why compliance with the principle would result in a misleading statement. For purposes of this Rule generally accepted accounting principles are considered to be defined by pronouncements issued by the Financial Accounting Standards Board and its predecessor entities and similar pronouncements issued by other entities having similar generally recognized authority.

Comment: The terms *report* and *financial statements,* employed in this Rule, are broadly defined in paragraphs (b) and (i) of the Definitions, above.

The Comment following Rule 202 is largely applicable here as well, except that the appropriate reference is to the Financial Accounting Standards Board rather than the AICPA's Auditing Standards Board.

Rule 204—*Other professional standards.* A licensee, in the performance of management advisory services or accounting and review services, shall conform to the professional standards applicable to such services. For purposes of this Rule such professional standards are considered to be defined by Statements on Management Advisory Services and Statements on Standards for Accounting and Review Services, respectively, in each instance issued by the American Institute of Certified Public Accountants, and by similar pronouncements by other entities having similar generally recognized authority.

Comment: This would be a new rule in most jurisdictions, but it would represent a logical extension of the principles underlying Rules 202 and 203. The Comment following Rule 202 is largely applicable here also.

Responsibilities to Clients

Rule 301—*Confidential client communications.* Except by permission of the client, or the heirs, successors, or personal representatives of the client, a licensee or any partner, officer, shareholder or employee of a licensee shall not voluntarily disclose information communicated to him by the client relating to and in connection with professional services rendered to the client by the licensee. Such information shall be deemed confidential, provided, however, that nothing herein shall be construed as prohibiting the disclosure of information required to be disclosed by the standards of the public accounting profession in reporting on the examination of financial statements or as prohibiting disclosures in court proceedings, in investigations or proceedings under Sections [11 or 12] of the Act, in ethical investigations conducted by private professional organizations, or in the course of quality reviews.

Comment: There is a provision in the Model Bill, Section 18, which is in substance identical to this Rule. In a jurisdiction where there was a provision of the accountancy law dealing fully with the substance of this Rule, no corresponding rule would be necessary in the code of professional conduct.

Rule 302—*Clients' records.* A licensee shall furnish to his client or former client, upon request and reasonable notice—

(a) A copy of the licensee's working papers, to the extent that such working papers include records that would ordinarily constitute part of the client's records and are not otherwise available to the client; and

(b) Any accounting or other records belonging to, or obtained from or on behalf of, the client, that the licensee removed from the client's premises or received for the client's account; but the licensee may make and retain copies of such documents of the client when they form the basis for work done by him.

Comment: This subject is dealt with in Section 19(b) of the Model Bill, which is in substance identical to this Rule. As with Rule 301, in any jurisdiction where the accountancy law contained a corresponding provision, no rule of professional conduct on the same subject would be called for; but where there was no such statutory provision, a rule would be appropriate.

Other Responsibilities and Practices

Rule 401—*Discreditable acts.* A licensee shall not commit any act that reflects adversely on his fitness to engage in the practice of public accountancy.

Comment: This is intended as a narrower substitute for the rule commonly found in existing Codes which broadly prohibits acts discreditable to the accounting profession. It would focus on a subject more central to the concerns of State regulatory bodies than the reputation of the accounting profession: namely, the fitness of licensees to engage in those activities for which they have been specifically licensed by the State, or as to which the titles they are licensed to use imply particular fitness.

Rule 402—*Acting through others.* A licensee shall not permit others to carry out on his behalf, either with or without compensation, acts which, if carried out by the licensee, would place him in violation of the Rules of Professional Conduct.

Rule 403—*Advertising and solicitation.* A licensee shall not use or participate in the use of any form of communication, written or oral, having reference to his professional services, which contains a false, fraudulent, misleading, deceptive or unfair statement or claim, nor any form of communication having reference to his professional services which is accomplished or accompanied by coercion, duress, compulsion, intimidation, threats, overreaching, or vexatious or harassing conduct. A false, fraudulent, misleading, deceptive or unfair statement or claim includes but is not limited to a statement or claim which:

(a) Contains a misrepresentation of fact; or

(b) Is likely to mislead or deceive because it fails to make full disclosure of relevant facts; or

(c) Is intended or likely to create false or unjustified expectations of favorable results; or

(d) Implies educational or professional attainments or licensing recognition not supported in fact; or

(e) Represents that professional services can or will be competently performed for a stated fee when this is not the case, or makes representations with respect to fees for professional services that do not disclose all variables that may reasonably be expected to affect the fees that will in fact be charged; or

(f) Contains other representations or implications that in reasonable probability will cause a person of ordinary prudence to misunderstand or be deceived.

Comment: This Rule is intended to reflect the current state of the law as to constitutionally permissible restrictions on both advertising and in-person solicitation. Unlike some extant ethical rules on these subjects, this Rule treats advertising and solicitation together in a single rule, since the principal harm potentially presented by both types of activities—namely, misleading potential clients—is the same. Additionally, the Rule contains no general prohibition on solicitation of non-clients because of doubt that any such broad prohibition would survive legal attack. Finally, the Rule has no general prohibition on use of testimonials or laudatory statements, or on representations as to specialties, since such prohibitions are also unlikely to survive legal attack to the extent that they reach beyond misleading representations.

Rule 404—*Firm names.* No licensee shall engage in the practice of public accountancy using a professional or firm name or designation that is misleading about the legal form of the firm, or about the persons who are partners, officers, or shareholders of the firm, or about any other matter, provided, however, that names of one or more former partners or shareholders may be included in the name of a firm or its successor.

Comment: This Rule is substantively identical to Section 14(k) of the Model Bill. In a jurisdiction where the accountancy law has a provision corresponding to Section 14(k), there would be no need to deal with the subject by a rule of professional conduct. In jurisdictions where there is no such statutory provision, however, a rule of professional conduct on the subject would be appropriate. It should be noted that the Model Bill provision has been drafted so as to emphasize the harm which is sought to be prevented: namely, misleading the public. It does not include any flat prohibition on use of fictitious names, although these are frequently found in existing codes, along with the other restrictions on firm names, because there does not seem to be a significant difference between fictitious names which are not themselves misleading, and the use of names of deceased partners.

Rule 405—*Communications*. A licensee shall respond in writing to any communication from the Board requesting a response, within thirty days of the mailing of such communication by registered or certified mail, to the last address furnished to the Board by the licensee.

Comment: A rule such as this could be included in a code of professional conduct, but it could also (and probably more appropriately) be included among rules of general application.

APPENDIX

COMMENT REGARDING THE MODEL RULES ON OTHER COMPENSATION AND CONTINGENT FEES

The purpose of this paper is to summarize the deliberations and rationale of the NASBA Task Force on Ethics and Unauthorized Practice (Task Force) in revising NASBA's Model Code of Professional Conduct (Model Code), with particular reference to the rules concerning contingent fees and commissions, or "other compensation."

In 1984, the Task Force was assigned the task of revising the Model Code following the publication of the Model Public Accountancy Bill (Model Bill) that had been promulgated jointly by NASBA and the AICPA. The guiding principles for the Task Force's efforts were (i) to adapt NASBA's previous Model Code for use in conjunction with the Model Bill, and (ii) to consider possible changes in particular model rules of professional conduct in light of changes in the real-life practice environment and in the legal and constitutional framework governing state board regulation of the practice of public accountancy.

The Task Force pursued its task in depth. It spent considerable time interviewing accounting profession regulators and holding discussions with NASBA counsel, various state boards' counsel, and practitioners. During the course of the Task Force's work, the substance of its deliberations and its tentative views were exposed to NASBA members, state boards, the AICPA, practitioners and federal regulatory authorities on numerous occasions, including, NASBA Annual Meetings (1985–1988), NASBA regional meetings (1986–1988) and visits by Task Force members with various state boards during 1986. A draft of a proposed revised

Model Code was sent to all NASBA members in May, 1987. Comments received as a result of this exposure led to several changes in the draft of the Model Code. The revised Model Code was adopted by the Board of Directors of NASBA on September 24, 1988, subject to certain minor editorial revisions and clarifications.

Among the changes reflected in the revised Model Code were significant revisions in the treatment of contingent fees and of commissions. The virtually total prohibition on receipt of contingent fees, which was previously in a separate rule, was incorporated in the rule on independence (Rule 101), and narrowed to apply only to cases where the contingent fee was material in amount. The former similarly broad prohibition on receipt of commissions (termed in the new Model Rules *other compensation*) was also narrowed to a prohibition on their receipt only in circumstances where they would impair audit independence, and then only when material in amount (Rule 101). In cases where there is no requirement of independence, there is no prohibition on receipt of commissions but only a requirement of disclosure (Rule 103). The former prohibition on payment of commissions was similarly narrowed to require only disclosure (Rule 104).

In December, 1988, NASBA's Board of Directors directed the Task Force to consider again whether the restrictions on receipt of other compensation and contingent fees in the context of the rule on audit independence should be limited to such compensation or fees only when material in amount; or whether in the context of audit independence such compensation or fees might appropriately be prohibited altogether. The Task Force reconsidered this question and the NASBA Board of Directors, at its April 1989 meeting, amended the Model Code by eliminating the materiality limitations in the rule on independence. The rules requiring disclosure of the payment of commissions, and of the receipt of other compensation in circumstances where independence is not in question, remain unchanged.

It should be pointed out that, subject to limitations imposed by varying state statutory frameworks, as well as certain federal statutory and constitutional restraints, state boards of accountancy have a latitude of choice regarding the rules of professional conduct that they promulgate, which is by no means limited to the particular recommendations set out in NASBA's Model Code. The Task Force formulated its recommended rules with a view toward achieving a reasonable basis of enforcement in today's legal environment. The effort should not be viewed as favoring or opposing contingent fees or other compensation. Rather, the revised model rules provide for the retention of limited prohibitions on other compensation and contingent fees. Such prohibitions have been narrowed because the legal advice provided to NASBA suggested such an approach was necessary to achieve enforcement of rules in this area. If a state desired to impose broader prohibitions, e.g. a complete prohibition against the acceptance of other compensation (commissions), it would likely have to impose such prohibitions by legislation rather than by rules and regulations.

As has been pointed out, the Model Code assumes the existence of an accountancy law with provisions corresponding to those of the Model Bill. Adjustments may therefore be required to conform the Model Code to the accountancy law in effect in a particular state if the law differs from the Model Bill.

The current Model Bill does not contain any provision concerning other compensation (commissions) or contingent fees. As such, the Task Force has neither adopted nor formally considered a position that either recommends or opposes such a legislative provision.

Submitted by:
*NASBA Committee on Behavioral Standards
(formerly known as NASBA Task Force on Ethics and Unauthorized Practice)
April 29, 1989

*Dennis Spackman, Chairman of the Ethics Committee of NASBA, indicated the following:

The NASBA *Model Code of Conduct,* April 1989, was developed with the objective of promoting uniformity in the regulation of the practice of accountancy in the 54 licensing jurisdictions. Its provisions were, like the joint AICPA/NASBA Model Act, designed to accommodate the changing environment of the accounting profession. The prominence of major issues of the day however, overshadowed efforts of its promotion.

The need for uniformity has continued to grow. In response, NASBA has established an Ethics Committee which has adopted as one of its primary objectives the formulation of a "Proposed Model Code of Conduct" that could be adopted by a majority of both the membership of the AICPA and the state boards of accountancy.

Considerable progress has been made in the *development* of the model code. If adopted it is hoped the Proposed Model Code of Conduct will, while preserving the confidence and respect the public has given the profession:

- Serve as the primary guide to professional behavior and decision making relative to the conduct of CPAs in all avenues of professional endeavor
- Be principles-based so it is easily understood and followed by members of the profession
- Facilitate self-regulation and discipline within and among members of the profession
- Inspire members of the profession to cultivate high ideals of self discipline, moral judgment, and the exercise of ethical behavior in the best interests of the public
- Assure an equitable balance is maintained between the interests of the public and the need for a healthy, viable profession
- Address the needs and concerns of the evolving profession well into the next century

1997 Federal Sentencing Guidelines

Chapter One—Introduction and General Application Principles

PART A—INTRODUCTION

1. Authority

The United States Sentencing Commission ("Commission") is an independent agency in the judicial branch composed of seven voting and two nonvoting, *ex officio* members. Its principal purpose is to establish sentencing policies and practices for the federal criminal justice system that will assure the ends of justice by promulgating detailed guidelines prescribing the appropriate sentences for offenders convicted of federal crimes.

The guidelines and policy statements promulgated by the Commission are issued pursuant to Section 994(a) of Title 28, United States Code.

2. The Statutory Mission

The Sentencing Reform Act of 1984 (Title II of the Comprehensive Crime Control Act of 1984) provides for the development of guidelines that will further the basic purposes of criminal punishment: deterrence, incapacitation, just punishment, and rehabilitation. The Act delegates broad authority to the Commission to review and rationalize the federal sentencing process.

The Act contains detailed instructions as to how this determination should be made, the most important of which directs the Commission to create categories of offense behavior and offender characteristics. An offense behavior category might consist, for example, of "bank robbery/committed with a gun/$2500 taken." An offender characteristic category might be "offender with one prior

conviction not resulting in imprisonment." The Commission is required to prescribe guideline ranges that specify an appropriate sentence for each class of convicted persons determined by coordinating the offense behavior categories with
the offender characteristic categories. Where the guidelines call for imprisonment, the range must be narrow: The maximum of the range cannot exceed the
minimum by more than the greater of 25 percent or six months [28 U.S.C.
§ 994(b)(2)].

Pursuant to the Act, the sentencing court must select a sentence from within
the guideline range. If, however, a particular case presents atypical features, the
Act allows the court to depart from the guidelines and sentence outside the prescribed range. In that case, the court must specify reasons for departure
[18 U.S.C. § 3553(b)]. If the court sentences within the guideline range, an
appellate court may review the sentence to determine whether the guidelines
were correctly applied. If the court departs from the guideline range, an appellate court may review the reasonableness of the departure [18 U.S.C. § 3742].
The Act also abolishes parole, and substantially reduces and restructures good
behavior adjustments.

The Commission's initial guidelines were submitted to Congress on April 13,
1987. After the prescribed period of Congressional review, the guidelines took
effect on November 1, 1987, and apply to all offenses committed on or after that
date. The Commission has the authority to submit guideline amendments each
year to Congress between the beginning of a regular Congressional session and
May 1. Such amendments automatically take effect 180 days after submission
unless a law is enacted to the contrary [28 U.S.C. § 994(p)].

The initial sentencing guidelines and policy statements were developed after
extensive hearings, deliberation, and consideration of substantial public comment. The Commission emphasizes, however, that it views the guideline-writing
process as evolutionary. It expects, and the governing statute anticipates, that continuing research, experience, and analysis will result in modifications and revisions to the guidelines through submission of amendments to Congress. To this
end, the Commission is established as a permanent agency to monitor sentencing
practices in the federal courts.

3. The Basic Approach (Policy Statement)

To understand the guidelines and their underlying rationale, it is important to
focus on the three objectives that Congress sought to achieve in enacting the
Sentencing Reform Act of 1984. The Act's basic objective was to enhance the
ability of the criminal justice system to combat crime through an effective, fair
sentencing system. To achieve this end, Congress first sought honesty in sentencing. It sought to avoid the confusion and implicit deception that arose out of
the pre-guidelines sentencing system which required the court to impose an
indeterminate sentence of imprisonment and empowered the parole commission

to determine how much of the sentence an offender actually would serve in prison. This practice usually resulted in a substantial reduction in the effective length of the sentence imposed, with defendants often serving only about one-third of the sentence imposed by the court.

Second, Congress sought reasonable uniformity in sentencing by narrowing the wide disparity in sentences imposed for similar criminal offenses committed by similar offenders. Third, Congress sought proportionality in sentencing through a system that imposes appropriately different sentences for criminal conduct of differing severity.

Honesty is easy to achieve: The abolition of parole makes the sentence imposed by the court the sentence the offender will serve, less approximately 15 percent for good behavior. There is a tension, however, between the mandate of uniformity and the mandate of proportionality. Simple uniformity—sentencing every offender to five years—destroys proportionality. Having only a few simple categories of crimes would make the guidelines uniform and easy to administer, but might lump together offenses that are different in important respects. For example, a single category for robbery that included armed and unarmed robberies, robberies with and without injuries, robberies of a few dollars and robberies of millions, would be far too broad.

A sentencing system tailored to fit every conceivable wrinkle of each case would quickly become unworkable and seriously compromise the certainty of punishment and its deterrent effect. For example, a bank robber with (or without) a gun, which the robber kept hidden (or brandished), might have frightened (or merely warned), injured seriously (or less seriously), tied up (or simply pushed) a guard, teller, or customer, at night (or at noon), in an effort to obtain money for other crimes (or for other purposes), in the company of a few (or many) other robbers, for the first (or fourth) time.

The list of potentially relevant features of criminal behavior is long; the fact that they can occur in multiple combinations means that the list of possible permutations of factors is virtually endless. The appropriate relationships among these different factors are exceedingly difficult to establish, for they are often context specific. Sentencing courts do not treat the occurrence of a simple bruise identically in all cases, irrespective of whether that bruise occurred in the context of a bank robbery or in the context of a breach of peace. This is so, in part, because the risk that such a harm will occur differs depending on the underlying offense with which it is connected; and also because, in part, the relationship between punishment and multiple harms is not simply additive. The relation varies depending on how much other harm has occurred. Thus, it would not be proper to assign points for each kind of harm and simply add them up, irrespective of context and total amounts.

The larger the number of subcategories of offense and offender characteristics included in the guidelines, the greater the complexity and the less workable the system. Moreover, complex combinations of offense and offender characteristics would apply and interact in unforeseen ways to unforeseen situations, thus failing to cure the unfairness of a simple, broad category system. Finally, and perhaps most importantly, probation officers and courts, in applying a complex system having numerous subcategories, would be required to make a host of decisions regarding whether the underlying facts were sufficient to bring the case within a particular subcategory. The greater the number of decisions required and the greater their complexity, the greater the risk that different courts would apply the guidelines differently to situations that, in fact, are similar, thereby re-introducing the very disparity that the guidelines were designed to reduce.

In view of the arguments, it would have been tempting to retreat to the simple, broad category approach and to grant courts the discretion to select the proper point along a broad sentencing range. Granting such broad discretion, however, would have risked correspondingly broad disparity in sentencing, for different courts may exercise their discretionary powers in different ways. Such an approach would have risked a return to the wide disparity that Congress established the Commission to reduce and would have been contrary to the Commission's mandate set forth in the Sentencing Reform Act of 1984.

In the end, there was no completely satisfying solution to this problem. The Commission had to balance the comparative virtues and vices of broad, simple categorization and detailed, complex subcategorization, and within the constraints established by that balance, minimize the discretionary powers of the sentencing court. Any system will, to a degree, enjoy the benefits and suffer from the drawbacks of each approach.

A philosophical problem arose when the Commission attempted to reconcile the differing perceptions of the purposes of criminal punishment. Most observers of the criminal law agree that the ultimate aim of the law itself, and of punishment in particular, is the control of crime. Beyond this point, however, the consensus seems to break down. Some argue that appropriate punishment should be defined primarily on the basis of the principle of "just desserts." Under this principle, punishment should be scaled to the offender's culpability and the resulting harms. Others argue that punishment should be imposed primarily on the basis of practical "crime control" considerations. This theory calls for sentences that most effectively lessen the likelihood of future crime, either by deterring others or incapacitating the defendant.

Adherents of each of these points of view urged the Commission to choose between them and accord one primacy over the other. As a practical matter, however, this choice was unnecessary because in most sentencing decisions the application of either philosophy will produce the same or similar results.

In its initial set of guidelines, the Commission sought to solve both the practical and philosophical problems of developing a coherent sentencing system by taking an empirical approach that used as a starting point data estimating pre-guidelines sentencing practice. It analyzed data drawn from 10,000 presentence investigations, the differing elements of various crimes as distinguished in substantive criminal statutes, the U.S. Parole Commission's guidelines and statistics, and data from other relevant sources in order to determine which distinctions were important in pre-guidelines practice. After consideration, the Commission accepted, modified, or rationalized these distinctions.

This empirical approach helped the Commission resolve its practical problem by defining a list of relevant distinctions that, although of considerable length, was short enough to create a manageable set of guidelines. Existing categories are relatively broad and omit distinctions that some may believe important, yet they include most of the major distinctions that statutes and data suggest made a significant difference in sentencing decisions. Relevant distinctions not reflected in the guidelines probably will occur rarely and sentencing courts may take such unusual cases into account by departing from the guidelines.

The Commission's empirical approach also helped resolve its philosophical dilemma. Those who adhere to a just desserts philosophy may concede that the lack of consensus might make it difficult to say exactly what punishment is deserved for a particular crime. Likewise, those who subscribe to a philosophy of crime control may acknowledge that the lack of sufficient data might make it difficult to determine exactly the punishment that will best prevent that crime. Both groups might therefore recognize the wisdom of looking to those distinctions that judges and legislators have, in fact, made over the course of time. These established distinctions are ones that the community believes, or has found over time, to be important from either a just desserts or crime control perspective.

The Commission did not simply copy estimates of pre-guidelines practice as revealed by the data, even though establishing offense values on this basis would help eliminate disparity because the data represent averages. Rather, it departed from the data at different points for various important reasons. Congressional statutes, for example, suggested or required departure, as in the case of the Anti–Drug Abuse Act of 1986 that imposed increased and mandatory minimum sentences. In addition, the data revealed inconsistencies in treatment, such as punishing economic crime less severely than other apparently equivalent behavior.

Despite these policy-oriented departures from pre-guidelines practice, the guidelines represent an approach that begins with, and builds upon, empirical data. The guidelines will not please those who wish the Commission to adopt a single philosophical theory and then work deductively to establish a simple and perfect set of categorizations and distinctions. The guidelines may prove acceptable, however, to those who seek more modest, incremental improvements in the status quo, who believe the best is often the enemy of the good, and who recognize that these guidelines are, as the Act contemplates, the first step in an evolutionary process. After spending considerable time and resources exploring alternative approaches, the Commission developed these guidelines as a practical effort toward the achievement of a more honest, uniform, equitable, proportional, and therefore effective sentencing system.

Chapter Eight—
Sentencing of Organizations

Introductory Commentary The guidelines and policy statements in this chapter apply when the convicted defendant is an organization. Organizations can act only through agents and, under federal criminal law, generally are vicariously liable for offenses committed by their agents. At the same time, individual agents are responsible for their own criminal conduct. Federal prosecutions of organizations therefore frequently involve individual and organizational co-defendants. Convicted individual agents of organizations are sentenced in accordance with the guidelines and policy statements in the preceding chapters. This chapter is designed so that the sanctions imposed upon organizations and their agents, taken together, will provide just punishment, adequate deterrence, and incentives for organizations to maintain internal mechanisms for preventing, detecting, and reporting criminal conduct.

This chapter reflects the following general principles: First, the court must, whenever practicable, order the organization to remedy any harm caused by the offense. The resources expended to remedy the harm should not be viewed as punishment, but rather as a means of making victims whole for the harm caused. Second, if the organization operated primarily for a criminal purpose or primarily by criminal means, the fine should be set sufficiently high to divest the organization of all its assets. Third, the fine range for any other organization should be based on the seriousness of the offense and the culpability of the organization. The seriousness of the offense generally will be reflected by the highest of the pecuniary gain, the pecuniary loss, or the amount in a guideline offense level fine table. Culpability generally will be determined by the steps taken by the organization prior to the offense to prevent and detect criminal conduct, the level and extent of involvement in or tolerance of the offense by certain personnel, and the organization's actions after an offense has been committed. Fourth, probation is an appropriate sentence for an organizational defendant when needed to ensure that another sanction will be fully implemented, or to ensure that steps will be taken within the organization to reduce the likelihood of future criminal conduct.[1]

PART A—GENERAL APPLICATION PRINCIPLES

§ 8A1.1. Applicability of Chapter Eight

This chapter applies to the sentencing of all organizations for felony and Class A misdemeanor offenses.

[1]*Historical Note:* Effective November 1, 1991.

Commentary
Application Notes:

1. *Organization* means "a person other than an individual." 18 U.S.C. § 18. The term includes corporations, partnerships, associations, joint-stock companies, unions, trusts, pension funds, unincorporated organizations, governments and political subdivisions thereof, and non-profit organizations.

2. The fine guidelines in §§ 8C2.2 through 8C2.9 apply only to specified types of offenses. The other provisions of this chapter apply to the sentencing of all organizations for all felony and Class A misdemeanor offenses. For example, the restitution and probation provisions in Parts B and D of this chapter apply to the sentencing of an organization, even if the fine guidelines in §§ 8C2.2 through 8C2.9 do not apply.[2]

§ 8A1.2. Application Instructions—Organizations

(a) Determine from Part B (Remedying Harm from Criminal Conduct) the sentencing requirements and options relating to restitution, remedial orders, community service, and notice to victims.

(b) Determine from Part C (Fines) the sentencing requirements and options relating to fines:

    (1) If the organization operated primarily for a criminal purpose or primarily by criminal means, apply § 8C1.1 (Determining the Fine—Criminal Purpose Organizations).

    (2) Otherwise, apply § 8C2.1 (Applicability of Fine Guidelines) to identify the counts for which the provisions of §§ 8C2.2 through 8C2.9 apply. For such counts:

        (A) Refer to § 8C2.2 (Preliminary Determination of Inability to Pay Fine) to determine whether an abbreviated determination of the guideline fine range may be warranted.

        (B) Apply § 8C2.3 (Offense Level) to determine the offense level from Chapter Two (Offense Conduct) and Chapter Three, Part D (Multiple Counts).

        (C) Apply § 8C2.4 (Base Fine) to determine the base fine.

        (D) Apply § 8C2.5 (Culpability Score) to determine the culpability score.

        (E) Apply § 8C2.6 (Minimum and Maximum Multipliers) to determine the minimum and maximum multipliers corresponding to the culpability score.

        (F) Apply § 8C2.7 (Guideline Fine Range—Organizations) to determine the minimum and maximum of the guideline fine range.

---

[2]*Historical Note:* Effective November 1, 1991.

(G) Refer to § 8C2.8 (Determining the Fine Within the Range) to determine the amount of the fine within the applicable guideline range.

(H) Apply § 8C2.9 (Disgorgement) to determine whether an increase to
the fine is required.

For any count or counts not covered under § 8C2.1 (Applicability of
Fine Guidelines), apply § 8C2.10 (Determining the Fine for Other
Counts).

(3) Apply the provisions relating to the implementation of the sentence of a
fine in Part C, Subpart 3 (Implementing the Sentence of a Fine).

(4) For grounds for departure from the applicable guideline fine range, refer
to Part C, Subpart 4 (Departures from the Guideline Fine Range).

(c) Determine from Part D (Organizational Probation) the sentencing requirements and options relating to probation.

(d) Determine from Part E (Special Assessments, Forfeitures, and Costs) the sentencing requirements relating to special assessments, forfeitures, and costs.

Commentary
Application Notes:

1. Determinations under this chapter are to be based upon the facts and information specified in the applicable guideline. Determinations that reference
other chapters are to be made under the standards applicable to determinations under those chapters.

2. The definitions in the Commentary to § 1B1.1 (Application Instructions) and
the guidelines and commentary in §§ 1B1.2 through 1B1.8 apply to determinations under this chapter unless otherwise specified. The adjustments in
Chapter Three, Parts A (Victim-Related Adjustments), B (Role in the
Offense), C (Obstruction), and E (Acceptance of Responsibility) do not
apply. The provisions of Chapter Six (Sentencing Procedures and Plea
Agreements) apply to proceedings in which the defendant is an organization.
Guidelines and policy statements not referenced in this chapter, directly or
indirectly, do not apply when the defendant is an organization; e.g., the pol-
icy statements in Chapter Seven (Violations of Probation and Supervised
Release) do not apply to organizations.

3. The following are definitions of terms used frequently in this chapter:

   (a) *Offense* means the offense of conviction and all relevant conduct under
   § 1B1.3 (Relevant Conduct) unless a different meaning is specified or is
   otherwise clear from the context. The term *instant* is used in connection
   with "offense," "federal offense," or "offense of conviction," as the case
   may be, to distinguish the violation for which the defendant is being sentenced from a prior or subsequent offense, or from an offense before
   another court (e.g., an offense before a state court involving the same
   underlying conduct).

(b) *High-level personnel of the organization* means individuals who have substantial control over the organization or who have a substantial role in the making of policy within the organization. The term includes: a director; an executive officer; an individual in charge of a major business or functional unit of the organization, such as sales, administration, or finance; and an individual with a substantial ownership interest. *High-level personnel of a unit of the organization* is defined in the Commentary to § 8C2.5 (Culpability Score).

(c) *Substantial authority personnel* means individuals who within the scope of their authority exercise a substantial measure of discretion in acting on behalf of an organization. The term includes high-level personnel, individuals who exercise substantial supervisory authority (e.g., a plant manager, a sales manager), and any other individuals who, although not a part of an organization's management, nevertheless exercise substantial discretion when acting within the scope of their authority (e.g., an individual with authority in an organization to negotiate or set price levels or an individual authorized to negotiate or approve significant contracts). Whether an individual falls within this category must be determined on a case-by-case basis.

(d) *Agent* means any individual, including a director, an officer, an employee, or an independent contractor, authorized to act on behalf of the organization.

(e) An individual *condoned* an offense if the individual knew of the offense and did not take reasonable steps to prevent or terminate the offense.

(f) *Similar misconduct* means prior conduct that is similar in nature to the conduct underlying the instant offense, without regard to whether or not such conduct violated the same statutory provision. For example, prior Medicare fraud would be misconduct similar to an instant offense involving another type of fraud.

(g) *Prior criminal adjudication* means conviction by trial, plea of guilty (including an *Alford* plea), or plea of *nolo contendere.*

(h) Pecuniary gain is derived from 18 U.S.C. § 3571(d) and means the additional before-tax profit to the defendant resulting from the relevant conduct of the offense. Gain can result from either additional revenue or cost savings. For example, an offense involving odometer tampering can produce additional revenue. In such a case, the pecuniary gain is the additional revenue received because the automobiles appeared to have less mileage, i.e., the difference between the price received or expected for the automobiles with the apparent mileage and the fair market value of the automobiles with the actual mileage. An offense involving defense procurement fraud related to defective product testing can produce pecuniary gain resulting from cost savings. In such a case, the pecuniary gain is the amount saved because the product was not tested in the required manner.

(i) *Pecuniary loss* is derived from 18 U.S.C. § 3571(d) and is equivalent to the term *loss* as used in Chapter Two (Offense Conduct). *See* Commentary to §§ 2B1.1 (Larceny, Embezzlement, and Other Forms of Theft), 2F1.1 (Fraud and Deceit), and definitions of "tax loss" in Chapter Two, Part T (Offenses Involving Taxation).

(j) An individual was *willfully ignorant of the offense* if the individual did not investigate the possible occurrence of unlawful conduct despite knowledge of circumstances that would lead a reasonable person to investigate whether unlawful conduct had occurred.

(k) An *effective program to prevent and detect violations of law* means a program that has been reasonably designed, implemented, and enforced so that it generally will be effective in preventing and detecting criminal conduct. Failure to prevent or detect the instant offense, by itself, does not mean that the program was not effective. The hallmark of an effective program to prevent and detect violations of law is that the organization exercised due diligence in seeking to prevent and detect criminal conduct by its employees and other agents. Due diligence requires at a minimum that the organization must have taken the following types of steps:

(1) The organization must have established compliance standards and procedures to be followed by its employees and other agents that are reasonably capable of reducing the prospect of criminal conduct.

(2) Specific individual(s) within high-level personnel of the organization must have been assigned overall responsibility to oversee compliance with such standards and procedures.

(3) The organization must have used due care not to delegate substantial discretionary authority to individuals whom the organization knew, or should have known through the exercise of due diligence, had a propensity to engage in illegal activities.

(4) The organization must have taken steps to communicate effectively its standards and procedures to all employees and other agents, e.g., by requiring participation in training programs or by disseminating publications that explain in a practical manner what is required.

(5) The organization must have taken reasonable steps to achieve compliance with its standards, e.g., by utilizing monitoring and auditing systems reasonably designed to detect criminal conduct by its employees and other agents and by having in place and publicizing a reporting system whereby employees and other agents could report criminal conduct by others within the organization without fear of retribution.

(6) The standards must have been consistently enforced through appropriate disciplinary mechanisms, including, as appropriate, discipline of individuals responsible for the failure to detect an offense. Adequate discipline of individuals responsible for an offense is a necessary component of enforcement; however, the form of discipline that will be appropriate will be case specific.

(7) After an offense has been detected, the organization must have taken all reasonable steps to respond appropriately to the offense and to prevent further similar offenses—including any necessary modifications to its program to prevent and detect violations of law.

The precise actions necessary for an effective program to prevent and detect violations of law will depend upon a number of factors. Among the relevant factors are:

(i) Size of the organization—The requisite degree of formality of a program to prevent and detect violations of law will vary with the size of the organization: the larger the organization, the more formal the program typically should be. A larger organization generally should have established written policies defining the standards and procedures to be followed by its employees and other agents.

(ii) Likelihood that certain offenses may occur because of the nature of its business—If because of the nature of an organization's business there is a substantial risk that certain types of offenses may occur, management must have taken steps to prevent and detect those types of offenses. For example, if an organization handles toxic substances, it must have established standards and procedures designed to ensure that those substances are properly handled at all times. If an organization employs sales personnel who have flexibility in setting prices, it must have established standards and procedures designed to prevent and detect price-fixing. If an organization employs sales personnel who have flexibility to represent the material characteristics of a product, it must have established standards and procedures designed to prevent fraud.

(iii) Prior history of the organization—An organization's prior history may indicate types of offenses that it should have taken actions to prevent. Recurrence of misconduct similar to that which an organization has previously committed casts doubt on whether it took all reasonable steps to prevent such misconduct.

An organization's failure to incorporate and follow applicable industry practice or the standards called for by any applicable governmental regulation weighs against a finding of an effective program to prevent and detect violations of law.[3]

---

[3] *Historical Note:* Effective November 1, 1991; November 1, 1997.

PART B—REMEDYING HARM FROM CRIMINAL CONDUCT

Introductory Commentary

As a general principle, the court should require that the organization take all appropriate steps to provide compensation to victims and otherwise remedy the harm caused or threatened by the offense. A restitution order or an order of probation requiring restitution can be used to compensate identifiable victims of the offense. A remedial order or an order of probation requiring community service can be used to reduce or eliminate the harm threatened, or to repair the harm caused by the offense, when that harm or threatened harm would otherwise not be remedied. An order of notice to victims can be used to notify unidentified victims of the offense.[4]

§ 8B1.1. Restitution—Organizations

(a) In the case of an identifiable victim, the court shall—

    (1) enter a restitution order for the full amount of the victim's loss, if such order is authorized under 18 U.S.C. § 2248, § 2259, § 2264, § 2327, § 3663, or § 3663A; or

    (2) impose a term of probation or supervised release with a condition requiring restitution for the full amount of the victim's loss, if the offense is not an offense for which restitution is authorized under 18 U.S.C. § 3663(a)(1) but otherwise meets the criteria for an order of restitution under that section.

(b) *Provided,* that the provisions of subsection (a) do not apply—

    (1) when full restitution has been made; or

    (2) in the case of a restitution order under § 3663; a restitution order under 18 U.S.C. § 3663A that pertains to an offense against property described in 18 U.S.C. § 3663A(c)(1)(A)(ii); or a condition of restitution imposed pursuant to subsection (a)(2) above, to the extent the court finds, from facts on the record, that (A) the number of identifiable victims is so large as to make restitution impracticable; or (B) determining complex issues of fact related to the cause or amount of the victim's losses would complicate or prolong the sentencing process to a degree that the need to provide restitution to any victim is outweighed by the burden on the sentencing process.

(c) If a defendant is ordered to make restitution to an identifiable victim and to pay a fine, the court shall order that any money paid by the defendant shall first be applied to satisfy the order of restitution.

(d) A restitution order may direct the defendant to make a single, lump sum payment, partial payments at specified intervals, in-kind payments, or a combi-

---

[4]*Historical Note:* Effective November 1, 1991.

nation of payments at specified intervals and in-kind payments. *See* 18 U.S.C. § 3664(f)(3)(A). An in-kind payment may be in the form of (1) return of property; (2) replacement of property; or (3) if the victim agrees, services rendered to the victim or to a person or organization other than the victim. *See* 18 U.S.C. § 3664(f)(4).

(e) A restitution order may direct the defendant to make nominal periodic payments if the court finds from facts on the record that the economic circumstances of the defendant do not allow the payment of any amount of a restitution order, and do not allow for the payment of the full amount of a restitution order in the foreseeable future under any reasonable schedule of payments.

(f) *Special Instruction*

   (1) This guideline applies only to a defendant convicted of an offense committed on or after November 1, 1997. Notwithstanding the provisions of § 1B1.11 (Use of Guidelines Manual in Effect on Date of Sentencing), use the former § 8B1.1 (set forth in Appendix C, amendment 571) in lieu of this guideline in any other case.

Commentary

Background: Section 3553(a)(7) of Title 18, United States Code, requires the court, "in determining the particular sentence to be imposed," to consider "the need to provide restitution to any victims of the offense." Orders of restitution are authorized under 18 U.S.C. §§ 2248, 2259, 2264, 2327, 3663, and 3663A. For offenses for which an order of restitution is not authorized, restitution may be imposed as a condition of probation.[5]

§ 8B1.2. Remedial Orders—Organizations (Policy Statement)

(a) To the extent not addressed under § 8B1.1 (Restitution—Organizations), a remedial order imposed as a condition of probation may require the organization to remedy the harm caused by the offense and to eliminate or reduce the risk that the instant offense will cause future harm.

(b) If the magnitude of expected future harm can be reasonably estimated, the court may require the organization to create a trust fund sufficient to address that expected harm.

Commentary

Background: The purposes of a remedial order are to remedy harm that has already occurred and to prevent future harm. A remedial order requiring corrective action by the organization may be necessary to prevent future injury from the instant offense, e.g., a product recall for a food and drug violation or a clean-up order for an environmental violation. In some cases in which a remedial order potentially may be

---

[5]*Historical Note:* Effective November 1, 1991; November 1, 1997.

appropriate, a governmental regulatory agency, e.g., the Environmental Protection Agency or the Food and Drug Administration, may have authority to order remedial measures. In such cases, a remedial order by the court may not be necessary. If a remedial order is entered, it should be coordinated with any administrative or civil actions taken by the appropriate governmental regulatory agency.[6]

§ 8B1.3.   Community Service—Organizations (Policy Statement)

Community service may be ordered as a condition of probation where such community service is reasonably designed to repair the harm caused by the offense.

Commentary

Background: An organization can perform community service only by employing its resources or paying its employees or others to do so. Consequently, an order that an organization perform community service is essentially an indirect monetary sanction, and therefore generally less desirable than a direct monetary sanction. However, where the convicted organization possesses knowledge, facilities, or skills that uniquely qualify it to repair damage caused by the offense, community service directed at repairing damage may provide an efficient means of remedying harm caused.

In the past, some forms of community service imposed on organizations have not been related to the purposes of sentencing. Requiring a defendant to endow a chair at a university or to contribute to a local charity would not be consistent with this section unless such community service provided a means for preventive or corrective action directly related to the offense and therefore served one of the purposes of sentencing set forth in 18 U.S.C. § 3553(a).[7]

§ 8B1.4   Order of Notice to Victims—Organizations

Apply § 5F1.4 (Order of Notice to Victims).[8]

PART C—FINES

1.   DETERMINING THE FINE—CRIMINAL PURPOSE ORGANIZATIONS

§ 8C1.1   Determining the Fine—Criminal Purpose Organizations

If, upon consideration of the nature and circumstances of the offense and the history and characteristics of the organization, the court determines that the organization operated primarily for a criminal purpose or primarily by criminal means,

---

[6]*Historical Note:* Effective November 1, 1991.
[7]Id.
[8]Id.

the fine shall be set at an amount (subject to the statutory maximum) sufficient to divest the organization of all its net assets. When this section applies, Subpart 2 (Determining the Fine—Other Organizations) and § 8C3.4 (Fines Paid by Owners of Closely Held Organizations) do not apply.

Commentary
Application Note:
1. *Net assets,* as used in this section, means the assets remaining after payment of all legitimate claims against assets by known innocent bona fide creditors.

Background: This guideline addresses the case in which the court, based upon an examination of the nature and circumstances of the offense and the history and characteristics of the organization, determines that the organization was operated primarily for a criminal purpose (e.g., a front for a scheme that was designed to commit fraud; an organization established to participate in the illegal manufacture, importation, or distribution of a controlled substance) or operated primarily by criminal means (e.g., a hazardous waste disposal business that had no legitimate means of disposing of hazardous waste). In such a case, the fine shall be set at an amount sufficient to remove all of the organization's net assets. If the extent of the assets of the organization is unknown, the maximum fine authorized by statute should be imposed, absent innocent bona fide creditors.[9]

2. DETERMINING THE FINE—OTHER ORGANIZATIONS

§ 8C2.1. Applicability of Fine Guidelines

The provisions of §§ 8C2.2 through 8C2.9 apply to each count for which the applicable guideline offense level is determined under:

(a) §§ 2B1.1, 2B1.3, 2B2.3, 2B4.1, 2B5.3, 2B6.1;
     §§ 2C1.1, 2C1.2, 2C1.4, 2C1.6, 2C1.7;
     §§ 2D1.7, 2D3.1, 2D3.2;
     §§ 2E3.1, 2E4.1, 2E5.1, 2E5.3;
     §§ 2F1.1, 2F1.2;
     § 2G3.1;
     §§ 2K1.1, 2K2.1;
     § 2L1.1;
     § 2N3.1;
     § 2R1.1;

---

[9]*Historical Note:* Effective November 1, 1991.

§§ 2S1.1, 2S1.2, 2S1.3;

§§ 2T1.1, 2T1.4, 2T1.6, 2T1.7, 2T1.8, 2T1.9, 2T2.1, 2T2.2, 2T3.1; or

(b) §§ 2E1.1, 2X1.1, 2X2.1, 2X3.1, 2X4.1, with respect to cases in which the offense level for the underlying offense is determined under one of the guideline sections listed in subsection (a) above.

Commentary
Application Notes:

1. If the Chapter Two offense guideline for a count is listed in subsection (a) or (b) above, and the applicable guideline results in the determination of the offense level by use of one of the listed guidelines, apply the provisions of §§ 8C2.2 through 8C2.9 to that count. For example, §§ 8C2.2 through 8C2.9 apply to an offense under § 2K2.1 (an offense guideline listed in subsection (a)), unless the cross reference in that guideline requires the offense level to be determined under an offense guideline section not listed in subsection (a).

2. If the Chapter Two offense guideline for a count is not listed in subsection (a) or (b) above, but the applicable guideline results in the determination of the offense level by use of a listed guideline, apply the provisions of §§ 8C2.2 through 8C2.9 to that count. For example, where the conduct set forth in a count of conviction ordinarily referenced to § 2N2.1 (an offense guideline not listed in subsection (a)) establishes § 2F1.1 (Fraud and Deceit) as the applicable offense guideline (an offense guideline listed in subsection (a)), §§ 8C2.2 through 8C2.9 would apply because the actual offense level is determined under § 2F1.1 (Fraud and Deceit).

Background: The fine guidelines of this subpart apply only to offenses covered by the guideline sections set forth in subsection (a) above. For example, the provisions of §§ 8C2.2 through 8C2.9 do not apply to counts for which the applicable guideline offense level is determined under Chapter Two, Part Q (Offenses Involving the Environment). For such cases, § 8C2.10 (Determining the Fine for Other Counts) is applicable.[10]

§ 8C2.2. Preliminary Determination of Inability to Pay Fine

(a) Where it is readily ascertainable that the organization cannot and is not likely to become able (even on an installment schedule) to pay restitution required under § 8B1.1 (Restitution—Organizations), a determination of the guideline fine range is unnecessary because, pursuant to § 8C3.3(a), no fine would be imposed.

---

[10]*Historical Note:* Effective November 1, 1991. Amended effective November 1, 1992; November 1, 1993.

(b) Where it is readily ascertainable through a preliminary determination of the minimum of the guideline fine range (*see* §§ 8C2.3 through 8C2.7) that the organization cannot and is not likely to become able (even on an installment schedule) to pay such minimum guideline fine, a further determination of the guideline fine range is unnecessary. Instead, the court may use the preliminary determination and impose the fine that would result from the application of § 8C3.3 (Reduction of Fine Based on Inability to Pay).

Commentary
Application Notes:
1. In a case of a determination under subsection (a), a statement that "the guideline fine range was not determined because it is readily ascertainable that the defendant cannot and is not likely to become able to pay restitution" is recommended.

2. In a case of a determination under subsection (b), a statement that "no precise determination of the guideline fine range is required because it is readily ascertainable that the defendant cannot and is not likely to become able to pay the minimum of the guideline fine range" is recommended.

Background: Many organizational defendants lack the ability to pay restitution. In addition, many organizational defendants who may be able to pay restitution lack the ability to pay the minimum fine called for by § 8C2.7(a). In such cases, a complete determination of the guideline fine range may be a needless exercise. This section provides for an abbreviated determination of the guideline fine range that can be applied where it is readily ascertainable that the fine within the guideline fine range determined under § 8C2.7 (Guideline Fine Range—Organizations) would be reduced under § 8C3.3 (Reduction of Fine Based on Inability to Pay).[11]

§ 8C2.3.   Offense Level

(a) For each count covered by § 8C2.1 (Applicability of Fine Guidelines), use the applicable Chapter Two guideline to determine the base offense level and apply, in the order listed, any appropriate adjustments contained in that guideline.

(b) Where there is more than one such count, apply Chapter Three, Part D (Multiple Counts) to determine the combined offense level.

Commentary
Application Notes:
1. In determining the offense level under this section, *defendant,* as used in Chapter Two, includes any agent of the organization for whose conduct the organization is criminally responsible.

[11]*Historical Note:* Effective November 1, 1991.

2. In determining the offense level under this section, apply the provisions of §§ 1B1.2 through 1B1.8. Do not apply the adjustments in Chapter Three, Parts A (Victim-Related Adjustments), B (Role in the Offense), C (Obstruction), and E (Acceptance of Responsibility).[12]

§ 8C2.4. Base Fine

(a) The base fine is the greatest of:
    (1) the amount from the table in subsection (d) below corresponding to the offense level determined under § 8C2.3 (Offense Level); or
    (2) the pecuniary gain to the organization from the offense; or
    (3) the pecuniary loss from the offense caused by the organization, to the extent the loss was caused intentionally, knowingly, or recklessly.

(b) *Provided,* that if the applicable offense guideline in Chapter Two includes a special instruction for organizational fines, that special instruction shall be applied, as appropriate.

(c) *Provided, further,* that to the extent the calculation of either pecuniary gain or pecuniary loss would unduly complicate or prolong the sentencing process, that amount, i.e., gain or loss as appropriate, shall not be used for the determination of the base fine.

(d) **Offense Level Fine Table**

Offense Level	Amount	Offense Level	Amount
6 or less	$5,000	23	$1,600,000
7	$7,500	24	$2,100,000
8	$10,000	25	$2,800,000
9	$15,000	26	$3,700,000
10	$20,000	27	$4,800,000
11	$30,000	28	$6,300,000
12	$40,000	29	$8,100,000
13	$60,000	30	$10,500,000
14	$85,000	31	$13,500,000
15	$125,000	32	$17,500,000
16	$175,000	33	$22,000,000
17	$250,000	34	$28,500,000
18	$350,000	35	$36,000,000
19	$500,000	36	$45,500,000
20	$650,000	37	$57,500,000
21	$910,000	38 or more	$72,500,000
22	$1,200,000		

---

[12]*Historical Note:* Effective November 1, 1991.

Commentary
Application Notes:

1. *Pecuniary gain, pecuniary loss,* and *offense* are defined in the Commentary to § 8A1.2 (Application Instructions—Organizations). Note that subsections (a)(2) and (a)(3) contain certain limitations as to the use of pecuniary gain and pecuniary loss in determining the base fine. Under subsection (a)(2), the pecuniary gain used to determine the base fine is the pecuniary gain to the organization from the offense. Under subsection (a)(3), the pecuniary loss used to determine the base fine is the pecuniary loss from the offense caused by the organization, to the extent that such loss was caused intentionally, knowingly, or recklessly.

2. Under 18 U.S.C. § 3571(d), the court is not required to calculate pecuniary loss or pecuniary gain to the extent that determination of loss or gain would unduly complicate or prolong the sentencing process. Nevertheless, the court may need to approximate loss in order to calculate offense levels under Chapter Two. See Commentary to § 2B1.1 (Larceny, Embezzlement, and Other Forms of Theft). If loss is approximated for purposes of determining the applicable offense level, the court should use that approximation as the starting point for calculating pecuniary loss under this section.

3. In a case of an attempted offense or a conspiracy to commit an offense, pecuniary loss and pecuniary gain are to be determined in accordance with the principles stated in § 2X1.1 (Attempt, Solicitation, or Conspiracy).

4. In a case involving multiple participants (i.e., multiple organizations, or the organization and individual(s) unassociated with the organization), the applicable offense level is to be determined without regard to apportionment of the gain from or loss caused by the offense. See § 1B1.3 (Relevant Conduct). However, if the base fine is determined under subsections (a)(2) or (a)(3), the court may, as appropriate, apportion gain or loss considering the defendant's relative culpability and other pertinent factors. Note also that under § 2R1.1(d)(1), the volume of commerce, which is used in determining a proxy for loss under § 8C2.4(a)(3), is limited to the volume of commerce attributable to the defendant.

5. Special instructions regarding the determination of the base fine are contained in §§ 2B4.1 (Bribery in Procurement of Bank Loan and Other Commercial Bribery); 2C1.1 (Offering, Giving, Soliciting, or Receiving a Bribe; Extortion Under Color of Official Right); 2C1.2 (Offering, Giving, Soliciting, or Receiving a Gratuity); 2E5.1 (Offering, Accepting, or Soliciting a Bribe or Gratuity Affecting the Operation of an Employee Welfare or Pension Benefit Plan; Prohibited Payments or Lending of Money by Employer or Agent to Employees, Representatives, or Labor Organizations); 2R1.1 (Bid-Rigging, Price-Fixing or Market-Allocation Agreements Among Competitors); 2S1.1 (Laundering of Monetary Instruments); and 2S1.2 (Engaging in Monetary Transactions in Property Derived from Specified Unlawful Activity).

Background: Under this section, the base fine is determined in one of three ways: (1) by the amount, based on the offense level, from the table in subsection (d); (2) by the pecuniary gain to the organization from the offense; and (3) by the pecuniary loss caused by the organization, to the extent that such loss was caused intentionally, knowingly, or recklessly. In certain cases, special instructions for determining the loss or offense level amount apply. As a general rule, the base fine measures the seriousness of the offense. The determinants of the base fine are selected so that, in conjunction with the multipliers derived from the culpability score in § 8C2.5 (Culpability Score), they will result in guideline fine ranges appropriate to deter organizational criminal conduct and to provide incentives for organizations to maintain internal mechanisms for preventing, detecting, and reporting criminal conduct. In order to deter organizations from seeking to obtain financial reward through criminal conduct, this section provides that, when greatest, pecuniary gain to the organization is used to determine the base fine. In order to ensure that organizations will seek to prevent losses intentionally, knowingly, or recklessly caused by their agents, this section provides that, when greatest, pecuniary loss is used to determine the base fine in such circumstances. Chapter Two provides special instructions for fines that include specific rules for determining the base fine in connection with certain types of offenses in which the calculation of loss or gain is difficult, e.g., price-fixing and money laundering. For these offenses, the special instructions tailor the base fine to circumstances that occur in connection with such offenses and that generally relate to the magnitude of loss or gain resulting from such offenses.[13]

§ 8C2.5. Culpability Score

(a) Start with 5 points and apply subsections (b) through (g) below.

(b) Involvement in or Tolerance of Criminal Activity
     If more than one applies, use the greatest:
     (1) If—
          (A) the organization had 5,000 or more employees and
               (i)   an individual within high-level personnel of the organization participated in, condoned, or was willfully ignorant of the offense; or
               (ii) tolerance of the offense by substantial authority personnel was pervasive throughout the organization; or
          (B) the unit of the organization within which the offense was committed had 5,000 or more employees and
               (i)   an individual within high-level personnel of the unit participated in, condoned, or was willfully ignorant of the offense; or

---

[13]*Historical Note:* Effective November 1, 1991. Amended effective November 1, 1993; November 1, 1995.

      (ii) tolerance of the offense by substantial authority personnel was pervasive throughout such unit,

    add **5** points; or

  (2) If—

    (A) the organization had 1,000 or more employees and

      (i) an individual within high-level personnel of the organization participated in, condoned, or was willfully ignorant of the offense; or

      (ii) tolerance of the offense by substantial authority personnel was pervasive throughout the organization; or

    (B) the unit of the organization within which the offense was committed had 1,000 or more employees and

      (i) an individual within high-level personnel of the unit participated in, condoned, or was willfully ignorant of the offense; or

      (ii) tolerance of the offense by substantial authority personnel was pervasive throughout such unit,

    add **4** points; or

  (3) If—

    (A) the organization had 200 or more employees and

      (i) an individual within high-level personnel of the organization participated in, condoned, or was willfully ignorant of the offense; or

      (ii) tolerance of the offense by substantial authority personnel was pervasive throughout the organization; or

    (B) the unit of the organization within which the offense was committed had 200 or more employees and

      (i) an individual within high-level personnel of the unit participated in, condoned, or was willfully ignorant of the offense; or

      (ii) tolerance of the offense by substantial authority personnel was pervasive throughout such unit,

    add **3** points; or

  (4) If the organization had 50 or more employees and an individual within substantial authority personnel participated in, condoned, or was willfully ignorant of the offense, add **2** points; or

  (5) If the organization had 10 or more employees and an individual within substantial authority personnel participated in, condoned, or was willfully ignorant of the offense, add **1** point.

(c) Prior History

  If more than one applies, use the greater:

  (1) If the organization (or separately managed line of business) committed any part of the instant offense less than 10 years after (A) a criminal adjudication based on similar misconduct; or (B) civil or administrative

adjudication(s) based on two or more separate instances of similar misconduct, add **1** point; or

(2) If the organization (or separately managed line of business) committed any part of the instant offense less than 5 years after (A) a criminal adjudication based on similar misconduct; or (B) civil or administrative adjudication(s) based on two or more separate instances of similar misconduct, add **2** points.

(d) Violation of an Order

If more than one applies, use the greater:

(1) (A) If the commission of the instant offense violated a judicial order or injunction, other than a violation of a condition of probation; or (B) if the organization (or separately managed line of business) violated a condition of probation by engaging in similar misconduct, *i.e.,* misconduct similar to that for which it was placed on probation, add **2** points; or

(2) If the commission of the instant offense violated a condition of probation, add **1** point.

(e) Obstruction of Justice

If the organization willfully obstructed or impeded, attempted to obstruct or impede, or aided, abetted, or encouraged obstruction of justice during the investigation, prosecution, or sentencing of the instant offense, or, with knowledge thereof, failed to take reasonable steps to prevent such obstruction or impedance or attempted obstruction or impedance, add **3** points.

(f) Effective Program to Prevent and Detect Violations of Law

If the offense occurred despite an effective program to prevent and detect violations of law, subtract **3** points.

Provided, that this subsection does not apply if an individual within high-level personnel of the organization, a person within high-level personnel of the unit of the organization within which the offense was committed where the unit had 200 or more employees, or an individual responsible for the administration or enforcement of a program to prevent and detect violations of law participated in, condoned, or was willfully ignorant of the offense. Participation of an individual within substantial authority personnel in an offense results in a rebuttable presumption that the organization did not have an effective program to prevent and detect violations of law.

Provided, further, that this subsection does not apply if, after becoming aware of an offense, the organization unreasonably delayed reporting the offense to appropriate governmental authorities.

(g) Self-Reporting, Cooperation, and Acceptance of Responsibility

If more than one applies, use the greatest:

(1) If the organization (A) prior to an imminent threat of disclosure or government investigation; and (B) within a reasonably prompt time after

becoming aware of the offense, reported the offense to appropriate governmental authorities, fully cooperated in the investigation, and clearly demonstrated recognition and affirmative acceptance of responsibility for its criminal conduct, subtract **5** points; or

(2) If the organization fully cooperated in the investigation and clearly demonstrated recognition and affirmative acceptance of responsibility for its criminal conduct, subtract **2** points; or

(3) If the organization clearly demonstrated recognition and affirmative acceptance of responsibility for its criminal conduct, subtract **1** point.

Commentary
Application Notes:

1. *Substantial authority personnel, condoned, willfully ignorant of the offense, similar misconduct, prior criminal adjudication,* and *effective program to prevent and detect violations of law* are defined in the Commentary to § 8A1.2 (Application Instructions—Organizations).

2. For purposes of subsection (b), *unit of the organization* means any reasonably distinct operational component of the organization. For example, a large organization may have several large units such as divisions or subsidiaries, as well as many smaller units such as specialized manufacturing, marketing, or accounting operations within these larger units. For purposes of this definition, all of these types of units are encompassed within the term *unit of the organization.*

3. *High-level personnel of the organization* is defined in the Commentary to § 8A1.2 (Application Instructions—Organizations). With respect to a unit with 200 or more employees, *high-level personnel of a unit of the organization* means agents within the unit who set the policy for or control that unit. For example, if the managing agent of a unit with 200 employees participated in an offense, three points would be added under subsection (b)(3); if that organization had 1,000 employees and the managing agent of the unit with 200 employees were also within high-level personnel of the entire organization, four points (rather than three) would be added under subsection (b)(2).

4. Pervasiveness under subsection (b) will be case specific and depend on the number, and degree of responsibility, of individuals within substantial authority personnel who participated in, condoned, or were willfully ignorant of the offense. Fewer individuals need to be involved for a finding of pervasiveness if those individuals exercised a relatively high degree of authority. Pervasiveness can occur either within an organization as a whole or within a unit of an organization. For example, if an offense were committed in an organization with 1,000 employees but the tolerance of the offense was pervasive only within a unit of the organization with 200 employees (and no high-level personnel of the organization participated in, condoned, or was willfully ignorant of the offense), three points would be added under subsec-

tion (b)(3). If, in the same organization, tolerance of the offense was pervasive throughout the organization as a whole, or an individual within high-level personnel of the organization participated in the offense, four points (rather than three) would be added under subsection (b)(2).

5. A *separately managed line of business,* as used in subsections (c) and (d), is a subpart of a for-profit organization that has its own management, has a high degree of autonomy from higher managerial authority, and maintains its own separate books of account. Corporate subsidiaries and divisions frequently are separately managed lines of business. Under subsection (c), in determining the prior history of an organization with separately managed lines of business, only the prior conduct or criminal record of the separately managed line of business involved in the instant offense is to be used. Under subsection (d), in the context of an organization with separately managed lines of business, in making the determination whether a violation of a condition of probation involved engaging in similar misconduct, only the prior misconduct of the separately managed line of business involved in the instant offense is to be considered.

6. Under subsection (c), in determining the prior history of an organization or separately managed line of business, the conduct of the underlying economic entity shall be considered without regard to its legal structure or ownership. For example, if two companies merged and became separate divisions and separately managed lines of business within the merged company, each division would retain the prior history of its predecessor company. If a company reorganized and became a new legal entity, the new company would retain the prior history of the predecessor company. In contrast, if one company purchased the physical assets but not the ongoing business of another company, the prior history of the company selling the physical assets would not be transferred to the company purchasing the assets. However, if an organization is acquired by another organization in response to solicitations by appropriate federal government officials, the prior history of the acquired organization shall not be attributed to the acquiring organization.

7. Under subsections (c)(1)(B) and (c)(2)(B), the civil or administrative adjudication(s) must have occurred within the specified period (ten or five years) of the instant offense.

8. Adjust the culpability score for the factors listed in subsection (e) whether or not the offense guideline incorporates that factor, or that factor is inherent in the offense.

9. Subsection (e) applies where the obstruction is committed on behalf of the organization; it does not apply where an individual or individuals have attempted to conceal their misconduct from the organization. The Commentary to § 3C1.1 (Obstructing or Impeding the Administration of Justice) provides guidance regarding the types of conduct that constitute obstruction.

10. The second proviso in subsection (f) contemplates that the organization will be allowed a reasonable period of time to conduct an internal investigation. In addition, no reporting is required by this proviso if the organization reasonably concluded, based on the information then available, that no offense had been committed.

11. *Appropriate governmental authorities,* as used in subsections (f) and (g)(1), means the federal or state law enforcement, regulatory, or program officials having jurisdiction over such matter. To qualify for a reduction under subsection (g)(1), the report to appropriate governmental authorities must be made under the direction of the organization.

12. To qualify for a reduction under subsection (g)(1) or (g)(2), cooperation must be both timely and thorough. To be timely, the cooperation must begin essentially at the same time as the organization is officially notified of a criminal investigation. To be thorough, the cooperation should include the disclosure of all pertinent information known by the organization. A prime test of whether the organization has disclosed all pertinent information is whether the information is sufficient for law enforcement personnel to identify the nature and extent of the offense and the individual(s) responsible for the criminal conduct. However, the cooperation to be measured is the cooperation of the organization itself, not the cooperation of individuals within the organization. If, because of the lack of cooperation of particular individual(s), neither the organization nor law enforcement personnel are able to identify the culpable individual(s) within the organization despite the organization's efforts to cooperate fully, the organization may still be given credit for full cooperation.

13. Entry of a plea of guilty prior to the commencement of trial combined with truthful admission of involvement in the offense and related conduct ordinarily will constitute significant evidence of affirmative acceptance of responsibility under subsection (g), unless outweighed by conduct of the organization that is inconsistent with such acceptance of responsibility. This adjustment is not intended to apply to an organization that puts the government to its burden of proof at trial by denying the essential factual elements of guilt, is convicted, and only then admits guilt and expresses remorse. Conviction by trial, however, does not automatically preclude an organization from consideration for such a reduction. In rare situations, an organization may clearly demonstrate an acceptance of responsibility for its criminal conduct even though it exercises its constitutional right to a trial. This may occur, for example, where an organization goes to trial to assert and preserve issues that do not relate to factual guilt (e.g., to make a constitutional challenge to a statute or a challenge to the applicability of a statute to its conduct). In each such instance, however, a determination that an organization has accepted responsibility will be based primarily upon pretrial statements and conduct.

14. In making a determination with respect to subsection (g), the court may determine that the chief executive officer or highest ranking employee of an organization should appear at sentencing in order to signify that the organization has clearly demonstrated recognition and affirmative acceptance of responsibility.

Background: The increased culpability scores under subsection (b) are based on three interrelated principles. First, an organization is more culpable when individuals who manage the organization or who have substantial discretion in acting for the organization participate in, condone, or are willfully ignorant of criminal conduct. Second, as organizations become larger and their managements become more professional, participation in, condonation of, or willful ignorance of criminal conduct by such management is increasingly a breach of trust or abuse of position. Third, as organizations increase in size, the risk of criminal conduct beyond that reflected in the instant offense also increases whenever management's tolerance of that offense is pervasive. Because of the continuum of sizes of organizations and professionalization of management, subsection (b) gradually increases the culpability score based upon the size of the organization and the level and extent of the substantial authority personnel involvement.[14]

§ 8C2.6   Minimum and Maximum Multipliers

Using the culpability score from § 8C2.5 (Culpability Score) and applying any applicable special instruction for fines in Chapter Two, determine the applicable minimum and maximum fine multipliers from the table below.

Culpability Score	Minimum Multiplier	Maximum Multiplier
10 or more	2.00	4.00
9	1.80	3.60
8	1.60	3.20
7	1.40	2.80
6	1.20	2.40
5	1.00	2.00
4	0.80	1.60
3	0.60	1.20
2	0.40	0.80
1	0.20	0.40
0 or less	0.05	0.20

[14]*Historical Note:* Effective November 1, 1991.

Commentary
Application Note:
1. A special instruction for fines in § 2R1.1 (Bid-Rigging, Price-Fixing, or Market-Allocation Agreements Among Competitors) sets a floor for minimum and maximum multipliers in cases covered by that guideline.[15]

§ 8C2.7.   Guideline Fine Range—Organizations

(a) The minimum of the guideline fine range is determined by multiplying the base fine determined under § 8C2.4 (Base Fine) by the applicable minimum multiplier determined under § 8C2.6 (Minimum and Maximum Multipliers).
(b) The maximum of the guideline fine range is determined by multiplying the base fine determined under § 8C2.4 (Base Fine) by the applicable maximum multiplier determined under § 8C2.6 (Minimum and Maximum Multipliers).[16]

§ 8C2.8.   Determining the Fine Within the Range (Policy Statement)

(a) In determining the amount of the fine within the applicable guideline range, the court should consider:
   (1) the need for the sentence to reflect the seriousness of the offense, promote respect for the law, provide just punishment, afford adequate deterrence, and protect the public from further crimes of the organization;
   (2) the organization's role in the offense;
   (3) any collateral consequences of conviction, including civil obligations arising from the organization's conduct;
   (4) any nonpecuniary loss caused or threatened by the offense;
   (5) whether the offense involved a vulnerable victim;
   (6) any prior criminal record of an individual within high-level personnel of the organization or high-level personnel of a unit of the organization who participated in, condoned, or was willfully ignorant of the criminal conduct;
   (7) any prior civil or criminal misconduct by the organization other than that counted under § 8C2.5(c);
   (8) any culpability score under § 8C2.5 (Culpability Score) higher than 10 or lower than 0;
   (9) partial but incomplete satisfaction of the conditions for one or more of the mitigating or aggravating factors set forth in § 8C2.5 (Culpability Score); and
   (10) any factor listed in 18 U.S.C. § 3572(a).

[15]*Historical Note:* Effective November 1, 1991.
[16]Id.

(b) In addition, the court may consider the relative importance of any factor used to determine the range, including the pecuniary loss caused by the offense, the pecuniary gain from the offense, any specific offense characteristic used to determine the offense level, and any aggravating or mitigating factor used to determine the culpability score.

Commentary
Application Notes:

1. Subsection (a)(2) provides that the court, in setting the fine within the guideline fine range, should consider the organization's role in the offense. This consideration is particularly appropriate if the guideline fine range does not take the organization's role in the offense into account. For example, the guideline fine range in an antitrust case does not take into consideration whether the organization was an organizer or leader of the conspiracy. A higher fine within the guideline fine range ordinarily will be appropriate for an organization that takes a leading role in such an offense.

2. Subsection (a)(3) provides that the court, in setting the fine within the guideline fine range, should consider any collateral consequences of conviction, including civil obligations arising from the organization's conduct. As a general rule, collateral consequences that merely make victims whole provide no basis for reducing the fine within the guideline range. If criminal and civil sanctions are unlikely to make victims whole, this may provide a basis for a higher fine within the guideline fine range. If punitive collateral sanctions have been or will be imposed on the organization, this may provide a basis for a lower fine within the guideline fine range.

3. Subsection (a)(4) provides that the court, in setting the fine within the guideline fine range, should consider any nonpecuniary loss caused or threatened by the offense. To the extent that nonpecuniary loss caused or threatened (e.g., loss of or threat to human life; psychological injury; threat to national security) by the offense is not adequately considered in setting the guideline fine range, this factor provides a basis for a higher fine within the range. This factor is more likely to be applicable where the guideline fine range is determined by pecuniary loss or gain, rather than by offense level, because the Chapter Two offense levels frequently take actual or threatened nonpecuniary loss into account.

4. Subsection (a)(6) provides that the court, in setting the fine within the guideline fine range, should consider any prior criminal record of an individual within high-level personnel of the organization or a unit of the organization. Since an individual within high-level personnel either exercises substantial control over the organization or a unit of the organization or has a substantial role in the making of policy within the organization or a unit of the organization, any prior criminal misconduct of such an individual may be relevant to the determination of the appropriate fine for the organization.

5. Subsection (a)(7) provides that the court, in setting the fine within the guideline fine range, should consider any prior civil or criminal misconduct by the organization other than that counted under § 8C2.5(c). The civil and criminal misconduct counted under § 8C2.5(c) increases the guideline fine range. Civil or criminal misconduct other than that counted under § 8C2.5(c) may provide a basis for a higher fine within the range. In a case involving a pattern of illegality, an upward departure may be warranted.

6. Subsection (a)(8) provides that the court, in setting the fine within the guideline fine range, should consider any culpability score higher than ten or lower than zero. As the culpability score increases above ten, this may provide a basis for a higher fine within the range. Similarly, as the culpability score decreases below zero, this may provide a basis for a lower fine within the range.

7. Under subsection (b), the court, in determining the fine within the range, may consider any factor that it considered in determining the range. This allows for courts to differentiate between cases that have the same offense level but differ in seriousness (e.g., two fraud cases at offense level 12, one resulting in a loss of $21,000, the other $40,000). Similarly, this allows for courts to differentiate between two cases that have the same aggravating factors, but in which those factors vary in their intensity (e.g., two cases with upward adjustments to the culpability score under § 8C2.5(c)(2) (prior criminal adjudications within 5 years of the commencement of the instant offense, one involving a single conviction, the other involving two or more convictions).

Background: Subsection (a) includes factors that the court is required to consider under 18 U.S.C. §§ 3553(a) and 3572(a) as well as additional factors that the Commission has determined may be relevant in a particular case. A number of factors required for consideration under 18 U.S.C. § 3572(a) (e.g., pecuniary loss, the size of the organization) are used under the fine guidelines in this subpart to determine the fine range, and therefore are not specifically set out again in subsection (a) of this guideline. In unusual cases, factors listed in this section may provide a basis for departure.[17]

§ 8C2.9. Disgorgement

The court shall add to the fine determined under § 8C2.8 (Determining the Fine Within the Range) any gain to the organization from the offense that has not and will not be paid as restitution or by way of other remedial measures.

---

[17]*Historical Note:* Effective November 1, 1991.

Commentary
Application Note:

1. This section is designed to ensure that the amount of any gain that has not and will not be taken from the organization for remedial purposes will be added to the fine. This section typically will apply in cases in which the organization has received gain from an offense but restitution or remedial efforts will not be required because the offense did not result in harm to identifiable victims, e.g., money laundering, obscenity, and regulatory reporting offenses. Money spent or to be spent to remedy the adverse effects of the offense, e.g., the cost to retrofit defective products, should be considered as disgorged gain. If the cost of remedial efforts made or to be made by the organization equals or exceeds the gain from the offense, this section will not apply.[18]

§ 8C2.10. Determining the Fine for Other Counts

For any count or counts not covered under § 8C2.1 (Applicability of Fine Guidelines), the court should determine an appropriate fine by applying the provisions of 18 U.S.C. § 3553 and 3572. The court should determine the appropriate fine amount, if any, to be imposed in addition to any fine determined under § 8C2.8 (Determining the Fine Within the Range) and § 8C2.9 (Disgorgement).

Commentary
Background: The Commission has not promulgated guidelines governing the setting of fines for counts not covered by § 8C2.1 (Applicability of Fine Guidelines). For such counts, the court should determine the appropriate fine based on the general statutory provisions governing sentencing. In cases that have a count or counts not covered by the guidelines in addition to a count or counts covered by the guidelines, the court shall apply the fine guidelines for the count(s) covered by the guidelines, and add any additional amount to the fine, as appropriate, for the count(s) not covered by the guidelines.[19]

3. IMPLEMENTING THE SENTENCE OF A FINE

§ 8C3.1. Imposing a Fine

(a) Except to the extent restricted by the maximum fine authorized by statute or any minimum fine required by statute, the fine or fine range shall be that determined under § 8C1.1 (Determining the Fine—Criminal Purpose Organizations); § 8C2.7 (Guideline Fine Range—Organizations) and § 8C2.9 (Disgorgement); or § 8C2.10 (Determining the Fine for Other Counts), as appropriate.

---

[18]*Historical Note:* Effective November 1, 1991.
[19]Id.

(b) Where the minimum guideline fine is greater than the maximum fine authorized by statute, the maximum fine authorized by statute shall be the guideline fine.

(c) Where the maximum guideline fine is less than a minimum fine required by statute, the minimum fine required by statute shall be the guideline fine.

Commentary

Background: This section sets forth the interaction of the fines or fine ranges determined under this chapter with the maximum fine authorized by statute and any minimum fine required by statute for the count or counts of conviction. The general statutory provisions governing a sentence of a fine are set forth in 18 U.S.C. § 3571.

When the organization is convicted of multiple counts, the maximum fine authorized by statute may increase. For example, in the case of an organization convicted of three felony counts related to a $200,000 fraud, the maximum fine authorized by statute will be $500,000 on each count, for an aggregate maximum authorized fine of $1,500,000.[20]

§ 8C3.2.   Payment of the Fine—Organizations

(a) If the defendant operated primarily for a criminal purpose or primarily by criminal means, immediate payment of the fine shall be required.

(b) In any other case, immediate payment of the fine shall be required unless the court finds that the organization is financially unable to make immediate payment or that such payment would pose an undue burden on the organization. If the court permits other than immediate payment, it shall require full payment at the earliest possible date, either by requiring payment on a date certain or by establishing an installment schedule.

Commentary
Application Note:

1.   When the court permits other than immediate payment, the period provided for payment shall in no event exceed five years. 18 U.S.C. § 3572(d).[21]

§ 8C3.3.   Reduction of Fine Based on Inability to Pay

(a) The court shall reduce the fine below that otherwise required by § 8C1.1 (Determining the Fine—Criminal Purpose Organizations), or § 8C2.7 (Guideline Fine Range—Organizations) and § 8C2.9 (Disgorgement), to the extent that imposition of such fine would impair its ability to make restitution to victims.

---

[20]*Historical Note:* Effective November 1, 1991.
[21]Id.

(b) The court may impose a fine below that otherwise required by § 8C2.7 (Guideline Fine Range—Organizations) and § 8C2.9 (Disgorgement) if the court finds that the organization is not able and, even with the use of a reasonable installment schedule, is not likely to become able to pay the minimum fine required by § 8C2.7 (Guideline Fine Range—Organizations) and § 8C2.9 (Disgorgement).

Provided, that the reduction under this subsection shall not be more than necessary to avoid substantially jeopardizing the continued viability of the organization.

Commentary
Application Note:
1. For purposes of this section, an organization is not able to pay the minimum fine if, even with an installment schedule under § 8C3.2 (Payment of the Fine—Organizations), the payment of that fine would substantially jeopardize the continued existence of the organization.

Background:
Subsection (a) carries out the requirement in 18 U.S.C. § 3572(b) that the court impose a fine or other monetary penalty only to the extent that such fine or penalty will not impair the ability of the organization to make restitution for the offense; however, this section does not authorize a criminal purpose organization to remain in business in order to pay restitution.[22]

§ 8C3.4. Fines Paid by Owners of Closely Held Organizations

The court may offset the fine imposed upon a closely held organization when one or more individuals, each of whom owns at least a 5 percent interest in the organization, has been fined in a federal criminal proceeding for the same offense conduct for which the organization is being sentenced. The amount of such offset shall not exceed the amount resulting from multiplying the total fines imposed on those individuals by those individuals' total percentage interest in the organization.

Commentary
Application Notes:
1. For purposes of this section, an organization is closely held, regardless of its size, when relatively few individuals own it. In order for an organization to be closely held, ownership and management need not completely overlap.
2. This section does not apply to a fine imposed upon an individual that arises out of offense conduct different from that for which the organization is being sentenced.

---

[22]*Historical Note:* Effective November 1, 1991.

Background: For practical purposes, most closely held organizations are the alter egos of their owner-managers. In the case of criminal conduct by a closely held corporation, the organization and the culpable individual(s) both may be convicted. As a general rule in such cases, appropriate punishment may be achieved by offsetting the fine imposed upon the organization by an amount that reflects the percentage ownership interest of the sentenced individuals and the magnitude of the fines imposed upon those individuals. For example, an organization is owned by five individuals, each of whom has a twenty percent interest; three of the individuals are convicted; and the combined fines imposed on those three equals $100,000. In this example, the fine imposed upon the organization may be offset by up to 60 percent of their combined fine amounts, i.e., by $60,000.[23]

4. DEPARTURES FROM THE GUIDELINE FINE RANGE

Introductory Commentary The statutory provisions governing departures are set forth in 18 U.S.C. § 3553(b). Departure may be warranted if the court finds "that there exists an aggravating or mitigating circumstance of a kind, or to a degree, not adequately taken into consideration by the Sentencing Commission in formulating the guidelines that should result in a sentence different from that described." This subpart sets forth certain factors that, in connection with certain offenses, may not have been adequately taken into consideration by the guidelines. In deciding whether departure is warranted, the court should consider the extent to which that factor is adequately taken into consideration by the guidelines and the relative importance or substantiality of that factor in the particular case.

To the extent that any policy statement from Chapter Five, Part K (Departures) is relevant to the organization, a departure from the applicable guideline fine range may be warranted. Some factors listed in Chapter Five, Part K that are particularly applicable to organizations are listed in this subpart. Other factors listed in Chapter Five, Part K may be applicable in particular cases. While this subpart lists factors that the Commission believes may constitute grounds for departure, the list is not exhaustive.[24]

§ 8C4.1.   Substantial Assistance to Authorities— Organizations (Policy Statement)

(a) Upon motion of the government stating that the defendant has provided substantial assistance in the investigation or prosecution of another organization

---

[23]*Historical Note:* Effective November 1, 1991.
[24]Id.

that has committed an offense, or in the investigation or prosecution of an individual not directly affiliated with the defendant who has committed an offense, the court may depart from the guidelines.

(b) The appropriate reduction shall be determined by the court for reasons stated on the record that may include, but are not limited to, consideration of the following:

(1) the court's evaluation of the significance and usefulness of the organization's assistance, taking into consideration the government's evaluation of the assistance rendered;

(2) the nature and extent of the organization's assistance; and

(3) the timeliness of the organization's assistance.

Commentary
Application Note:

1. Departure under this section is intended for cases in which substantial assistance is provided in the investigation or prosecution of crimes committed by individuals not directly affiliated with the organization or by other organizations. It is not intended for assistance in the investigation or prosecution of the agents of the organization responsible for the offense for which the organization is being sentenced.[25]

§ 8C4.2.   Risk of Death or Bodily Injury (Policy Statement)

If the offense resulted in death or bodily injury, or involved a foreseeable risk of death or bodily injury, an upward departure may be warranted. The extent of any such departure should depend, among other factors, on the nature of the harm and the extent to which the harm was intended or knowingly risked, and the extent to which such harm or risk is taken into account within the applicable guideline fine range.[26]

§ 8C4.3.   Threat to National Security (Policy Statement)

If the offense constituted a threat to national security, an upward departure may be warranted.[27]

§ 8C4.4.   Threat to the Environment (Policy Statement)

If the offense presented a threat to the environment, an upward departure may be warranted.[28]

---

[25]*Historical Note:* Effective November 1, 1991.
[26]Id.
[27]Id.
[28]Id.

§ 8C4.5.   Threat to a Market (Policy Statement)

If the offense presented a risk to the integrity or continued existence of a market, an upward departure may be warranted. This section is applicable to both private markets (e.g., a financial market, a commodities market, or a market for consumer goods) and public markets (e.g., government contracting).[29]

§ 8C4.6.   Official Corruption (Policy Statement)

If the organization, in connection with the offense, bribed or unlawfully gave a gratuity to a public official, or attempted or conspired to bribe or unlawfully give a gratuity to a public official, an upward departure may be warranted.[30]

§ 8C4.7.   Public Entity (Policy Statement)

If the organization is a public entity, a downward departure may be warranted.[31]

§ 8C4.8.   Members or Beneficiaries of the Organization as Victims (Policy Statement)

If the members or beneficiaries, other than shareholders, of the organization are direct victims of the offense, a downward departure may be warranted. If the members or beneficiaries of an organization are direct victims of the offense, imposing a fine upon the organization may increase the burden upon the victims of the offense without achieving a deterrent effect. In such cases, a fine may not be appropriate. For example, departure may be appropriate if a labor union is convicted of embezzlement of pension funds.[32]

§ 8C4.9.   Remedial Costs that Greatly Exceed Gain (Policy Statement)

If the organization has paid or has agreed to pay remedial costs arising from the offense that greatly exceed the gain that the organization received from the offense, a downward departure may be warranted. In such a case, a substantial fine may not be necessary in order to achieve adequate punishment and deterrence. In deciding whether departure is appropriate, the court should consider the level and extent of substantial authority personnel involvement in the offense and

---

[29]*Historical Note:* Effective November 1, 1991.
[30]Id.
[31]Id.
[32]Id.

the degree to which the loss exceeds the gain. If an individual within high-level personnel was involved in the offense, a departure would not be appropriate under this section. The lower the level and the more limited the extent of substantial authority personnel involvement in the offense, and the greater the degree to which remedial costs exceeded or will exceed gain, the less will be the need for a substantial fine to achieve adequate punishment and deterrence.[33]

§ 8C4.10. Mandatory Programs to Prevent and Detect Violations of Law (Policy Statement)

If the organization's culpability score is reduced under § 8C2.5(f) (Effective Program to Prevent and Detect Violations of Law) and the organization had implemented its program in response to a court order or administrative order specifically directed at the organization, an upward departure may be warranted to offset, in part or in whole, such reduction.[34]

§ 8C4.11. Exceptional Organizational Culpability (Policy Statement)

If the organization's culpability score is greater than 10, an upward departure may be appropriate.

If no individual within substantial authority personnel participated in, condoned, or was willfully ignorant of the offense; the organization at the time of the offense had an effective program to prevent and detect violations of law; and the base fine is determined under § 8C2.4(a)(1), § 8C2.4(a)(3), or a special instruction for fines in Chapter Two (Offense Conduct), a downward departure may be warranted. In a case meeting these criteria, the court may find that the organization had exceptionally low culpability and therefore a fine based on loss, offense level, or a special Chapter Two instruction results in a guideline fine range higher than necessary to achieve the purposes of sentencing. Nevertheless, such fine should not be lower than if determined under § 8C2.4(a)(2).[35]

PART D—ORGANIZATIONAL PROBATION

Introductory Commentary   Section 8D1.1 sets forth the circumstances under which a sentence to a term of probation is required. Sections 8D1.2 through 8D1.5 address the length of the probation term, conditions of probation, and violations of probation conditions.[36]

---

[33]Id.
[34]Id.
[35]Id.
[36]Id.

§ 8D1.1. Imposition of Probation—Organizations

(a) The court shall order a term of probation:

   (1) if such sentence is necessary to secure payment of restitution (§ 8B1.1),
        enforce a remedial order (§ 8B1.2), or ensure completion of community
        service (§ 8B1.3);

   (2) if the organization is sentenced to pay a monetary penalty (e.g., restitu-
        tion, fine, or special assessment), the penalty is not paid in full at the
        time of sentencing, and restrictions are necessary to safeguard the orga-
        nization's ability to make payments;

   (3) if, at the time of sentencing, an organization having 50 or more employ-
        ees does not have an effective program to prevent and detect violations
        of law;

   (4) if the organization within five years prior to sentencing engaged in sim-
        ilar misconduct, as determined by a prior criminal adjudication, and any
        part of the misconduct underlying the instant offense occurred after that
        adjudication;

   (5) if an individual within high-level personnel of the organization or the unit
        of the organization within which the instant offense was committed partic-
        ipated in the misconduct underlying the instant offense and that individual
        within five years prior to sentencing engaged in similar misconduct, as
        determined by a prior criminal adjudication, and any part of the miscon-
        duct underlying the instant offense occurred after that adjudication;

   (6) if such sentence is necessary to ensure that changes are made within the
        organization to reduce the likelihood of future criminal conduct;

   (7) if the sentence imposed upon the organization does not include a fine; or

   (8) if necessary to accomplish one or more of the purposes of sentencing set
        forth in 18 U.S.C. § 3553(a)(2).

Commentary

Background: Under 18 U.S.C. § 3561(a), an organization may be sentenced to
a term of probation. Under 18 U.S.C. § 3551(c), imposition of a term of probation
is required if the sentence imposed upon the organization does not include a fine.[37]

§ 8D1.2. Term of Probation—Organizations

(a) When a sentence of probation is imposed—

   (1) In the case of a felony, the term of probation shall be at least one year but
        not more than five years.

   (2) In any other case, the term of probation shall be not more than five years.

---

[37]Id.

Commentary
Application Note:

1. Within the limits set by the guidelines, the term of probation should be sufficient, but not more than necessary, to accomplish the court's specific objectives in imposing the term of probation. The terms of probation set forth in this section are those provided in 18 U.S.C. § 3561(b).[38]

§ 8D1.3. Conditions of Probation—Organizations

(a) Pursuant to 18 U.S.C. § 3563(a)(1), any sentence of probation shall include the condition that the organization not commit another federal, state, or local crime during the term of probation.

(b) Pursuant to 18 U.S.C. § 3563(a)(2), if a sentence of probation is imposed for a felony, the court shall impose as a condition of probation at least one of the following: (1) restitution, (2) notice to victims of the offense pursuant to 18 U.S.C. § 3555, or (3) an order requiring the organization to reside, or refrain from residing, in a specified place or area, unless the court finds on the record that extraordinary circumstances exist that would make such condition plainly unreasonable, in which event the court shall impose one or more other conditions set forth in 18 U.S.C. § 3563(b).

Note: Section 3563(a)(2) of Title 18, United States Code, provides that, absent unusual circumstances, a defendant convicted of a felony shall abide by at least one of the conditions set forth in 18 U.S.C. § 3563(b)(2), (b)(3), and (b)(13). Before the enactment of the Antiterrorism and Effective Death Penalty Act of 1996, those conditions were a fine [(b)(2)], an order of restitution [(b)(3)], and community service [(b)(13)]. Whether or not the change was intended, the Act deleted the fine condition and renumbered the restitution and community service conditions in 18 U.S.C. § 3563(b), but failed to make a corresponding change in the referenced paragraphs under 18 U.S.C. § 3563(a)(2). Accordingly, the conditions now referenced are restitution [(b)(2)], notice to victims pursuant to 18 U.S.C. § 3555 [(b)(3)], and an order that the defendant reside, or refrain from residing, in a specified place or area [(b)(13)].

(c) The court may impose other conditions that (1) are reasonably related to the nature and circumstances of the offense or the history and characteristics of the organization; and (2) involve only such deprivations of liberty or property as are necessary to effect the purposes of sentencing.[39]

---

[38]Id.

[39]*Historical Note:* Effective November 1, 1991. Amended effective November 1, 1997.

§ 8D1.4. Recommended Conditions of Probation—Organizations (Policy Statement)

(a) The court may order the organization, at its expense and in the format and media specified by the court, to publicize the nature of the offense committed, the fact of conviction, the nature of the punishment imposed, and the steps that will be taken to prevent the recurrence of similar offenses.

(b) If probation is imposed under § 8D1.1(a)(2), the following conditions may be appropriate to the extent they appear necessary to safeguard the organization's ability to pay any deferred portion of an order of restitution, fine, or assessment:

   (1) The organization shall make periodic submissions to the court or probation officer, at intervals specified by the court, reporting on the organization's financial condition and results of business operations, and accounting for the disposition of all funds received.

   (2) The organization shall submit to: (A) a reasonable number of regular or unannounced examinations of its books and records at appropriate business premises by the probation officer or experts engaged by the court; and (B) interrogation of knowledgeable individuals within the organization. Compensation to and costs of any experts engaged by the court shall be paid by the organization.

   (3) The organization shall be required to notify the court or probation officer immediately upon learning of (A) any material adverse change in its business or financial condition or prospects, or (B) the commencement of any bankruptcy proceeding, major civil litigation, criminal prosecution, or administrative proceeding against the organization, or any investigation or formal inquiry by governmental authorities regarding the organization.

   (4) The organization shall be required to make periodic payments, as specified by the court, in the following priority: (1) restitution; (2) fine; and (3) any other monetary sanction.

(c) If probation is ordered under § 8D1.1(a)(3), (4), (5), or (6), the following conditions may be appropriate:

   (1) The organization shall develop and submit to the court a program to prevent and detect violations of law, including a schedule for implementation.

   (2) Upon approval by the court of a program to prevent and detect violations of law, the organization shall notify its employees and shareholders of its criminal behavior and its program to prevent and detect violations of law. Such notice shall be in a form prescribed by the court.

   (3) The organization shall make periodic reports to the court or probation officer, at intervals and in a form specified by the court, regarding the

organization's progress in implementing the program to prevent and detect violations of law. Among other things, such reports shall disclose any criminal prosecution, civil litigation, or administrative proceeding commenced against the organization, or any investigation or formal inquiry by governmental authorities of which the organization learned since its last report.

(4) In order to monitor whether the organization is following the program to prevent and detect violations of law, the organization shall submit to: (A) a reasonable number of regular or unannounced examinations of its books and records at appropriate business premises by the probation officer or experts engaged by the court; and (B) interrogation of knowledgeable individuals within the organization. Compensation to and costs of any experts engaged by the court shall be paid by the organization.

Commentary
Application Notes:

1. In determining the conditions to be imposed when probation is ordered under § 8D1.1(a)(3) through (6), the court should consider the views of any governmental regulatory body that oversees conduct of the organization relating to the instant offense. To assess the efficacy of a program to prevent and detect violations of law submitted by the organization, the court may employ appropriate experts who shall be afforded access to all material possessed by the organization that is necessary for a comprehensive assessment of the proposed program. The court should approve any program that appears reasonably calculated to prevent and detect violations of law, provided it is consistent with any applicable statutory or regulatory requirement.

   Periodic reports submitted in accordance with subsection (c)(3) should be provided to any governmental regulatory body that oversees conduct of the organization relating to the instant offense.[40]

§ 8D1.5.   Violations of Conditions of Probation—Organizations (Policy Statement)

Upon a finding of a violation of a condition of probation, the court may extend the term of probation, impose more restrictive conditions of probation, or revoke probation and resentence the organization.

---

[40]*Historical Note:* Effective November 1, 1991.

Commentary
Application Note:
1. In the event of repeated, serious violations of conditions of probation, the appointment of a master or trustee may be appropriate to ensure compliance with court orders.[41]

PART E—SPECIAL ASSESSMENTS, FORFEITURES, AND COSTS

§ 8E1.1. Special Assessments—Organizations

A special assessment must be imposed on an organization in the amount prescribed by statute.

Commentary
Application Notes:
1. This guideline applies if the defendant is an organization. It does not apply if the defendant is an individual. *See* § 5E1.3 for special assessments applicable to individuals.
2. The following special assessments are provided by statute (*see* 18 U.S.C. § 3013):

    For Offenses Committed By Organizations On Or After April 24, 1996:

    (A) $400, if convicted of a felony;

    (B) $125, if convicted of a Class A misdemeanor;

    (C) $50, if convicted of a Class B misdemeanor; or

    (D) $25, if convicted of a Class C misdemeanor or an infraction.

    For Offenses Committed By Organizations On Or After November 18, 1988 But Prior To April 24, 1996:

    (E) $200, if convicted of a felony;

    (F) $125, if convicted of a Class A misdemeanor;

    (G) $50, if convicted of a Class B misdemeanor; or

    (H) $25, if convicted of a Class C misdemeanor or an infraction.

    For Offenses Committed By Organizations Prior To November 18, 1988:

    (I) $200, if convicted of a felony;

    (J) $100, if convicted of a misdemeanor.
3. A special assessment is required by statute for each count of conviction.

[41]Id.

Background: Section 3013 of Title 18, United States Code, added by The Victims of Crimes Act of 1984, Pub. L. No. 98-473, Title II, Chap. XIV, requires courts to impose special assessments on convicted defendants for the purpose of funding the Crime Victims Fund established by the same legislation.[42]

§ 8E1.2.   Forfeiture—Organizations

Apply § 5E1.4 (Forfeiture).[43]

§ 8E1.3.   Assessment of Costs—Organizations

As provided in 28 U.S.C. § 1918, the court may order the organization to pay the costs of prosecution. In addition, specific statutory provisions mandate assessment of costs.[44]

---

[42]*Historical Note:* Effective November 1, 1991; November 1, 1997.
[43]*Historical Note:* Effective November 1, 1991.
[44]Id.

Index